CELLULOID MIRRORS

Hollywood and American Society Since 1945

BOOKS BY RONALD L. DAVIS

The Social and Cultural Life of the 1920s
■
A History of Music in American Life
■
Hollywood Anecdotes
■
Hollywood Beauty:
Linda Darnell and the American Dream
■
The Glamour Factory:
Inside Hollywood's Big Studio System
■
John Ford: Hollywood's Old Master

CELLULOID MIRRORS
Hollywood and American Society Since 1945

Ronald L. Davis
Southern Methodist University

WADSWORTH
CENGAGE Learning™

Australia • Brazil • Japan • Korea • Mexico • Singapore • Spain
United Kingdom • United States

WADSWORTH
CENGAGE Learning

Celluloid Mirrors:
Hollywood and American
Society Since 1945
Ronald L. Davis

Publisher:
Christopher P. Klein

Senior Acquisitions Editor:
David C. Tatom

Developmental Editor:
Kristie Kelly

Project Editor: Tashia Stone

Senior Production Manager:
Kathleen Ferguson

Art Director: Garry Harman

Digital Composition:
Paul G. Zinn

Cover Image: Orson Welles
and Rita Hayworth in *The
Lady From Shanghai*, photo
courtesy of Columbia
Pictures

Copyright acknowledgments
begin on page 243, which
constitutes a continuation of
this copyright page.

Library of Congress Catalog Card Number: 95-82105

ISBN-13: 978-0-15-501568-5
ISBN-10: 0-15-501568-0

Wadsworth Cengage Learning
20 Davis Drive
Belmont, CA 94002-3098, USA

Cengage Learning is a leading provider of customized
learning solutions with office locations around the
globe, including Singapore, the United Kingdom,
Australia, Mexico, Brazil, and Japan. Locate your local
office at **www.cengage.com/global**

Cengage Learning products are represented in Canada
by Nelson Education, Ltd.

To learn more about Wadsworth, visit
www.cengage.com/wadsworth

Purchase any of our products at your local college store
or at our preferred online store **www.cengagebrain.com**

Printed in the United States of America
2 3 4 5 6   16 15 14 13 12

For Gideon,
student, friend, travel companion,
from Byesville to Tasmania,
with thanks

CONTENTS

PREFACE

Hollywood changed drastically in the years after World War II. Beginning in 1947 the motion picture industry entered a recession that lasted for more than a decade. Although the end of the Golden Age of movies has been attributed to television, that explanation is too simplistic. The baby boom, the migration to the suburbs, and shifts in consumer spending to new housing, automobiles, and home appliances contributed to Hollywood's postwar recession. By the late 1950s the motion picture studios were adjusting to new conditions, but their structures were permanently altered. The major film companies not only diversified into television production, but eventually entered related leisure-time fields as well. Hollywood became more than a center for moviemaking; it was also a town that produced television shows seen around the world and headquartered other forms of entertainment.

Beginning in the 1960s this diversification led to conglomerates taking over the Hollywood studios, in part for their prestige and publicity, in part to meet the needs of a new era in entertainment. Modern marketing techniques were employed, centering on the enormous exposure offered by television. By 1990 theater attendance accounted for only 30 percent of a movie's revenue; television and the video market accounted for the other 70 percent. Still, theaters continued to determine motion picture hits, usually during the opening week of a film's release.

The demise of the old moguls and the acquisition of Hollywood's studios by giant parent corporations resulted in an instability of leadership. With the decline of the old studio system, independent production became the dominant pattern in the motion picture industry, while the studios themselves loaned money and rented equipment and space to the companies working on their lots. With the abolition of long-term contracts for studio workers, agents and lawyers emerged as powerful forces in negotiating deals and putting production packages together.

Amid the tumult of rapid change, Hollywood's movies lost some of their glamour but grew in maturity. The elimination of the old Production Code would result in such previous abominations as profanity, nudity, explicit sex, drugs, excessive violence, and homosexuality becoming commonplace in American films after the late 1960s. The antihero replaced the Golden Age heroes with their derring-do, and psychological depths were explored with a frankness previously unknown in Hollywood's output.

During the decades since World War II, the entertainment industry has reflected shifting American values and changing business practices. As it did during the Golden Age, Hollywood has both mirrored and influenced attitudes and behavior, stamping American images on world culture. By 1992 the foreign market for American movies and television shows had reached a peak of $7 billion, as the demand for cable television programming and videocassettes continued to grow. Meanwhile, the mystique of Hollywood, with all of its fantasies and seductiveness, remained intact, thrilling new generations with dreams of riches and grandeur.

Celluloid Mirrors is a look at the relationship between Hollywood and American society since 1945, as seen by a historian who discovered movies during the last months of World War II. In the intervening years I have watched contemporary history find its way into American films in various interpretations. As director of the Southern Methodist University Oral History Program between 1973 and 1995, I taped interviews with some 500 Hollywood workers—actors, directors, producers, and craftspeople—and over the course of those years had my childhood fantasy world brought to terms with reality. Those interviews collectively remain the apex of my career in history.

As every writer on film knows, our work is made immeasurably easier by the efficient staffs of the Margaret Herrick Library of the Academy of Motion Picture Arts and Sciences, the Mayer Library at the American Film Institute, and the Doheny Library at the University of Southern California. My own research has also been aided by the Hamon Arts Library on the Southern Methodist University campus and the special collections housed in SMU's DeGolyer Library.

Special thanks must be extended to my assistant, Claudia Erdmann, and to my initial sounding boards, Jane Elder and Eleanor Solon. R. Hal Williams, Paul Boller, and Kathryn Lang read the manuscript in an early draft and made valuable suggestions from their years of teaching, writing, and editing. Walter Seltzer offered the expertise of a long-time Hollywood professional, while Floyd Betts gave me the layman's reaction. Richard Etulain and Gerald Nash at the University of New Mexico have been helpful in shaping this project, and Drake Bush and Kristie Kelly of Harcourt Brace have been ideal editors—prompt, specific, and consistently insightful. I welcome this opportunity to thank them all.

Daniel Orlovsky and my colleagues in the History Department at SMU continue to amaze me with their vitality and encouragement. With uncommon interest, James Jones, dean of SMU's Dedman College, provided funds for photographs and research. Finally, I convey my deep appreciation to Gideon Ong, who made trips to Los Angeles and New York a pleasure, and to my Hollywood support system: Carol Bruce, Lizabeth Scott, Walter and Mickey Seltzer, Gene and Marjorie Fowler, Mary Anita Loos and Carl von Saltza, Catherine McLeod and Don Keefer, Trudi Dieterle, Undeen Darnell Hunter, Elaine Larson, and Vince Monteleone. They are my kind of people.

Ronald L. Davis
Dallas, Texas

Marilyn Monroe, Hollywood's most publicized sex symbol of the 1950s, on the set of The Seven Year Itch.

Chapter 1

THE DECLINE OF
THE BIG STUDIOS

Cowboy star Gene Autry was entertaining troops on Iwo Jima in August 1945 when news came that the Japanese were negotiating a surrender. "I never saw a bunch of men quite so crazy," Autry reported. "They had reason to be. Most of them were Marines who were getting ready for the next invasion, and that news meant that a lot of them would not have to die." Back home the movie industry prepared to launch a Victory Loan Campaign, continuing the patriotic policy its leaders had adopted even before the United States entered World War II.

Jack Warner, head of production at Warner Bros., embraced as his credo "to provide the kind of screen entertainment that would best serve the interest of our nation at war." His policy was reflected in the studio's output of films, ranging from wartime adventure and propaganda pictures to the Academy Award–winning classic *Casablanca* (1942). With gasoline rationed during the war and sports crippled by the draft, movies held a near monopoly on the country's entertainment outside the home. At neighborhood theaters, where bills changed three times a week, families could see up to six different movies every seven days. The hazards of war created a need for entertainment, an escape from daily headlines of distant battles and worry over the safety of friends and loved ones.

Once the war was over, Hollywood's influence around the globe seemed greater than before. Like the United States itself, the Hollywood studios stood at the summit of their power. The old moguls—Louis B. Mayer, Darryl Zanuck, Harry Cohn, Jack Warner, and Sam Goldwyn, in particular—ran their empires with absolute authority. Their methods were primitive and crude, and they ruled their dominions with knowledge and the strength of mastodons. The star system was at its zenith; millions of moviegoers worshiped the incandescent personalities who lit the silver screen, devouring the myths concocted by publicists for gossip columns and fan magazines. For the studios, stars were valuable properties, and they groomed the actors and actresses they had under contract, developed them, protected them, and built careers that lasted.

Hollywood specialized in lavish, escapist entertainment with plenty of action, romance, and sentiment. The old moguls considered themselves the purveyors of family amusement, and their product mirrored the values they considered quintessentially American: movement, pace, material success, optimism, progress, the triumph of right over wrong. In movie palaces across the country, true love endured a lifetime, and the uncommitted were expected to live in emotional suspension until the ideal partner came along. While audiences basked in Hollywood's kitsch, dissidents complained that its output was glossy and fake.

Nevertheless, in 1946 American movies attained their highest level of popular appeal, grossing $1.7 billion, the most profitable year in film's half-century of existence. Average weekly attendance at movie theaters soared to 90 million. Roughly ninety cents of every entertainment dollar in America went for the movies, and motion picture stocks reached unprecedented heights. The structure of the industry remained monolithic. Each studio was a feudal society of contract personnel supervised by an established hierarchy, responsible to the mogul in charge. In New York, banks such as Chase Manhattan, allied with the movie industry since the Great Depression, supplied massive sums of money to finance films on the basis of Hollywood's magic names.

But there were signs of change. The same month the war ended, former child star Shirley Temple, the darling of the Depression years, married Sergeant John Agar. Hollywood was growing up. Two months later, furnishings from "Falcon Lair," the former estate of silent star Rudolph Valentino, were sold at auction. Old Hollywood soon would vanish.

Actor Glenn Ford returned from the Marine Corps to be told by his studio head that there were no longer jobs for him in movies, that in his absence the business had been taken over by other people. William Holden, a rising star before the war, was told the same thing. Both survived the crisis and went on to major careers in films, but it was evident that Hollywood suffered from postwar anxieties that permeated most of the nation.

In 1946 Samuel Goldwyn released *The Best Years of Our Lives*, an intelligent, humane screenplay by Robert Sherwood that looked at the problems of readjustment facing American veterans as they returned to civilian life. The film was a realistic effort to portray the tensions and confusions of the immediate postwar period, when traditional values were on the brink of irreversible change. Directed by the masterful William Wyler, *The Best Years of Our Lives* won the Academy Award for best picture and remains among the finest films Hollywood ever produced, rich in entertainment yet an honest record of its moment in history.

Although the United States and its allies had won the war, the country had lost an essential part of its self-image—the freedom to lead an isolated, unentangled existence. All of the significant events of the Cold War confirmed the need for America's permanent involvement in world affairs. The introduction of nuclear weapons merely supplied an exclamation point to that necessity. The age of simplicity was over. Even more dramatically than in Hollywood, the United States found maturity thrust upon it.

Movie studios tried to respond to the new era, turning from war-oriented themes to contemporary social issues and adult material. *Gentleman's Agreement* and *Crossfire* (both 1947) attacked anti-Semitism; *Intruder in the Dust* (1948) and *Home of the Brave* (1949) made strong pleas for tolerance and understanding of blacks. *Boomerang* (1947) was an exposé of legal corruption; *The Snake Pit* (1948) dealt with mental illness and the pitiable conditions in American mental institutions; *All the King's Men* (1949) focused on demagoguery in politics. But these were exceptions to Hollywood's mainstream of romance and escapism. By then the studios had begun to face real problems, which they were ill-prepared to handle.

THE 1945–1946 STRIKES

In March 1945, the Conference of Studio Unions called a strike of Hollywood's painters, carpenters, electricians, office workers, story analysts, and members of other craft unions. The following October, with the war effort no longer a restriction, the striking unions put into effect a bold strategy. Rather than picket all the studios equally, they would concentrate maximum pressure on one at a time, beginning with Warner Bros. Before 6:00 a.m. on Friday, October 5, 1945, more than 1,000 pickets amassed in front of the main gate at Warner Bros. Within a few minutes the first three cars attempting to drive onto the lot were overturned. Police throughout Los Angeles county were alerted to a full-scale labor war, and Warner Bros. was forced to halt production for two days.

Calls went out for camera operators, sound technicians, teamsters, and other nonstrikers to report to the studio in Burbank the following Monday, so that Warner Bros. could resume operations with a skeletal staff. When nonstrikers crashed the picket lines on Monday morning, more than fifty people were injured. Police and local fire departments attacked the picketers with fire hoses and tear gas, but the strikers held their ground. That night hundreds of workers slept inside the studio rather than risk similar clashes the next morning. Meanwhile, 10,000 sympathetic union members at the nearby Lockheed aircraft plant, as well as students from the University of Southern California and the University of California at Los Angeles, threatened to join the picket lines outside Warner Bros. The State Guard was alerted to stand ready to move in if violence got out of hand.

The strike, led by Herbert Sorrell of the Painters Union, lasted nearly eight months. Conservatives voiced a growing belief that organized labor had been infiltrated by foreign agitators. Senator Jack B. Tenney, chairman of the California State Committee on Un-American Activities, sent the following telegram to Governor Earl Warren on October 9: "This jurisdictional strike is spearhead of long-range Communist strategy to control motion picture industry as potent medium of propaganda." The prolonged labor confrontation polarized the film industry that had seemingly been united throughout the war. From a studio rooftop, an angry Jack Warner watched the turmoil in the streets below and vowed to fight the Communists he believed were behind the disturbance. "A lot of us supported the strike and marched in picket lines and incurred Jack Warner's disfavor," said screenwriter Ring Lardner, Jr., later one of the Hollywood Ten accused of Communist sympathies.

Liberals within the Screen Actors Guild found themselves outnumbered and outmaneuvered by the guild's president Ronald Reagan when actors voted overwhelmingly to cross the picket lines and continue working. Character actress Rosemary DeCamp

Caucus Room of the House Office Building during the opening of the House Un-American Activities Committee's investigation into alleged Communist infiltration of the movie industry.

remembered being escorted to work at Warner Bros. by an armed guard and seeing squads with blackjacks and rifles from her car window. Thousands of people fought in the middle of Barham Boulevard with clubs, knives, brass knuckles, chains, and battery cables. Suddenly Tinseltown was reminiscent of Detroit, Oakland, or Chicago, where labor violence had occurred during the 1930s.

Soon Universal was shut down, then RKO. Actor Kirk Douglas was making *The Strange Love of Martha Ivers* when strikers gathered outside Paramount—yelling, waving clubs, and pounding on the sides of limousines as they neared the studio gate. "We continued to shoot," Douglas said, "but it meant that we were locked in at the studio; if we went out, we couldn't get back in."

On October 24, 1945, the executive council of the American Federation of Labor ordered the strike stopped. Soon the National Labor Relations Board ruled against studio producers, in favor of the unions, but antagonism against liberals and left-wingers had hardened during the strife.

Between August 1945 and August 1946, 4,600 strikes, involving 5 million workers, occurred in industries across the nation. A second, more violent strike broke out in Hollywood during September 1946, when studio employees demanded a 25-percent pay increase. The wage hike was granted, costing the studios an estimated $16.5 million annually, yet the strike resulted in the disappearance of the Conference of Studio Unions and a purge of leftist labor leaders.

The aftermath of these nationwide strikes, Winston Churchill's speech about the Iron Curtain at Fulton, Missouri, the initiation of the Truman Doctrine in Greece and Turkey, and the congressional elections of 1946, which resulted in a Republican victory, indicated a general turn to the political right across the United States and the start of the Cold War. For Hollywood the strikes tore open a wound that had been festering since the formation of the craft unions during the 1930s.

HUAC INVESTIGATIONS AND THE BLACKLIST

In the spring of 1947, with the liberalism of the Roosevelt years under siege, a decisive battle began in Hollywood. J. Parnell Thomas, the new chairman of the House Un-American Activities Committee (HUAC), arrived in Los Angeles on May 9 and established himself at the Biltmore Hotel. On taking charge of the House Committee, Thomas had vowed to "expose and ferret out" Communists and Communist sympathizers in Hollywood. In 1938 the Committee, then headed by Representative Martin Dies of Texas, had determined to flush out subversives within the movie capital, and Dies spent a year collecting data on what he deemed Communist activity in the film business, winning banner headlines for himself.

Parnell Thomas, a former insurance broker from New Jersey, who had been a member of the Dies Committee, proved an aggressive leader. Capitalizing on the Cold War atmosphere, he began interviewing cooperative witnesses in Hollywood behind closed doors, seeking evidence of Communist propaganda in wartime and postwar scripts. All of those who testified were sympathetic to the House Committee's aims, and most were members of the reactionary Motion Picture Alliance for the Preservation of American Ideals, which welcomed the Committee's intervention. Sensational tidbits from the investigations were leaked to the press, such as Lela Rogers's contention that her daughter, actress Ginger Rogers, had been forced to speak subversive lines in *Tender Comrade* (1943), namely "Share and share alike—that's democracy." Actor Robert

Taylor told of his reluctance to accept the leading role in *Song of Russia* (1944), while conservative novelist Ayn Rand objected to "a suspicious number of smiling children" in the movie, as well as questionable scenes in *Mission to Moscow* (1943), even though both pictures had been made at the request of Washington officials to strengthen the U.S.–Soviet alliance during the war.

On the basis of his preliminary findings, Thomas on September 21, 1947, issued subpoenas to forty-three members of the film industry, summoning them to appear in Washington, D.C., as witnesses before the HUAC's public hearings in October. The majority of those summoned were members of the conservative Motion Picture Alliance, but nineteen were suspected Communists or former Communists. HUAC agents meanwhile visited executive offices throughout Hollywood and issued warnings about "unpleasant consequences" should studio leaders fail to cooperate with the Committee's investigations.

Thomas and his associates welcomed a chance to bask in the glamour of Hollywood's celebrities; questioning the famous assured them national attention from the media. Newsreel cameras whirred and flashbulbs popped on Monday, October 20, 1947, when the Committee began its hearings on alleged Communist infiltration of the movie industry in the crowded caucus room of the old House Office Building. For forty-eight hours the atmosphere seemed friendly. Thomas repeatedly pointed out the importance of the movie industry in shaping public opinion. He prepared his ground carefully, aware that members of the Motion Picture Alliance were eager to testify against their liberal colleagues.

On the third day Hollywood began devouring its own. The leftist Nineteen were aware of the political change in the country, but the vehemence of conservative witnesses shocked them. When German playwright Bertolt Brecht was called to testify, he answered the Committee's questions, denied that he was a Communist, and within hours returned to Europe. Another ten of the left-wing group were called to the stand: screenwriters John Howard Lawson, Dalton Trumbo, Ring Lardner, Jr., Alvah Bessie, Lester Cole, Samuel Ornitz, and Albert Maltz; producer Adrian Scott; and directors Edward Dmytryk and Herbert Biberman. They comprised the famous Hollywood Ten.

The Ten arrived in Washington to find their hotel rooms bugged, and after prolonged consultation made the decision to stand on the First Amendment's guarantee of freedom of speech rather than the

Fifth Amendment's protection against self-incrimination. They would remain unanimous and refuse to answer questions regarding their Communist affiliations, turning the hearings into a forum to discredit the Committee itself. "I am not on trial here, Mr. Chairman," John Howard Lawson told Thomas. "This committee is on trial before the American people."

To lend support to these "unfriendly" witnesses and protest the procedures of the House Committee, liberals in Hollywood formed the Committee for the First Amendment. "We were principally concerned with the assault on civil liberties," said screenwriter Philip Dunne, one of the organizers of the group, "what to us looked like persecution of the so-called unfriendly witnesses, and the reputations of hundreds of others whose names were being slandered."

A plane was chartered to take representatives of the Committee for the First Amendment to Washington, and a mass meeting was held at Shrine Auditorium in Los Angeles the night before they left. On board the plane were Humphrey Bogart, Lauren Bacall, Gene Kelly, John Huston, Jane Wyatt, Marsha Hunt, John Garfield, Philip Dunne, and others. "We were so angry that headline-hunting Congressmen would use Hollywood and motion pictures as a step to their own glorification," said actress Marsha Hunt. In Washington the Committee for the First Amendment called a press conference and members appeared on network radio broadcasts. "We all sat there in the hearing room of the House," Marsha Hunt recalled, "as concerned citizens and filmmakers."

The Hollywood Ten were an individualistic, opinionated, often contentious group who had reached adulthood during the 1930s, when Marxism was fashionable among intellectuals. All of them had been members of the Communist Party, but most only for a short while. From their standpoint the issues at stake were constitutional rights and freedom of thought. When called before the House Committee, they took an evasive stance. Asked, not for the first time, whether he was or ever had been a Communist, Ring Lardner, Jr., replied, "It depends on the circumstances. I could answer, but if I did, I would hate myself in the morning." Dalton Trumbo was equally vague. "Very many questions can be answered 'yes' or 'no' only by a moron or a slave," he told the Committee.

By October 30, when the hearings ended, "unfriendly" witnesses had been dragged from the stand, sometimes shouting invectives. On November 24, Congress voted to cite the Hollywood Ten for contempt.

Each returned to California aware that arrest and imprisonment would be imminent unless the Supreme Court intervened.

Terrified that charges of Communism could wreck the industry, fifty studio executives and producers met at the Waldorf-Astoria Hotel in New York on November 24 to decide a course of action. Two days later they issued a statement that they would not knowingly "employ a Communist or a member of any party or group which advocates the overthrow of the Government by force or by any illegal or unconstitutional means." As a result of this Waldorf-Astoria decree, loyalty oaths became compulsory, and the Hollywood blacklist began.

Bound by the Waldorf agreement, Dore Schary, the liberal vice president of RKO, was forced to dismiss Edward Dmytryk and Adrian Scott, director and producer of *Crossfire*. Earlier Schary had promised that studio employees suspected of Communist membership would not be punished. Several members of the Committee for the First Amendment also found themselves unemployable in Hollywood. An article entitled "I'm No Communist" appeared in *Photoplay* magazine in March 1948 under Humphrey Bogart's byline, revealing the pressure brought to bear on the stars who had flown to Washington to support the Hollywood Ten.

Jewish immigrants for the most part, the moguls feared being branded un-American. But they also feared that bad press might cause the American public to forsake Hollywood's films unless the industry acted to clean out subversives. Since the banks favored a blacklist, studio heads felt they had no choice in the matter.

The Communist scare put an end to producers' forays into postwar social comment. *Boomerang*, *The Best Years of Our Lives*, even *The Grapes of Wrath* (1940) had been called into question by the Motion Picture Alliance and offered to J. Parnell Thomas for scrutiny during his preliminary investigations. Afraid of further interrogation, the studios returned almost exclusively to pure entertainment, except for a series of anti-Communist pictures exhibited as a public relations ploy.

Twentieth Century-Fox rushed *The Iron Curtain* (1948) into production, a ludicrous exposition of a Russian spy case in Canada. MGM responded with *The Red Danube* (1949), the story of a ballerina hounded by Russian agents. In *My Son John* (1952), Broadway actress Helen Hayes played an American mother stricken by the discovery that her son is a subversive.

By 1950 the Hollywood Ten had lost their appeals, and by September all were in prison. On June 8, Dalton Trumbo and John Howard Lawson, who had served as test cases for the Ten, were handcuffed together and driven to the jail in the District of Columbia by U.S. marshals. Edward Dmytryk and Albert Maltz were sent to the prison camp at Mill Point, West Virginia. Ring Lardner, Jr., and Lester Cole were imprisoned at Danbury, Connecticut, where they were joined by J. Parnell Thomas, convicted of payroll padding.

In accord with the Waldorf-Astoria decree, the Screen Actors Guild, under the leadership of Ronald Reagan and George Murphy, pledged its support of the anti-Communist crusade. Meanwhile, the Motion Picture Alliance for the Preservation of American Ideals, angry and aggressively antilabor, became more militant, railing that Communism was rampant throughout the movie colony. Prominent among the Alliance's members were such staunch right-wingers as actors Adolphe Menjou and John Wayne, director Cecil B. DeMille, gossip columnist Hedda Hopper, and producer Walt Disney.

In July 1950, with guild president Joseph L. Mankiewicz in Europe, DeMille mobilized the board of the Screen Directors Guild and succeeded in getting a mandatory loyalty oath passed. At a membership meeting on October 22, DeMille tried to unseat the liberal Mankiewicz and singled out twenty-five of his fellow directors as subversives; many of them were foreign-born. Mankiewicz, present to chair the meeting, stated that he opposed the mandatory oath, as well as the blacklist, and favored a secret ballot when votes were taken on the issues at hand. After much haranguing on both sides, guild members gave Mankiewicz an overwhelming vote of confidence, but not until DeMille had shouted, "This is war!"

The blacklist lengthened during the early 1950s with the appearance of *Red Channels*, a booklet listing 151 people in the entertainment business who had supposedly been associated with "Communist causes." The names cited, according to the ex-FBI agents who compiled them, were gathered from government reports, files of radical newspapers, programs of rallies, letterheads of leftist organizations, and other official and unofficial documents. Many of those listed had signed petitions supporting the Hollywood Ten or criticized the procedures of the House Un-American Activities Committee. Suddenly *Red Channels* was on every producer's desk; agents were told not to present a client for employment if his or her name was on any of the subversive lists.

Early in 1951, with the Hollywood Ten still in prison, HUAC opened a second round of hearings, with Representative John S.

Wood of Georgia in command. The Committee's tactics were ferocious, all the more damning since the later hearings were televised. A summons from the Committee now meant either the kiss of death professionally or a license to inform on friends and colleagues. Actor Larry Parks, on the brink of superstardom with two screen portrayals of singer Al Jolson to his credit, was the first to name names before the Committee. Unlike the Hollywood Ten, Parks freely admitted that he had joined the Communist Party in 1941, when he was twenty-five years old, and broke with it four years later. He had compunctions, however, about naming people who had been in the Party with him. "Do not make me crawl through the mud like an informer," Parks pleaded near tears, while the Committee hammered away at him. It was a degrading experience from which the actor never recovered. His studio, Columbia, negated his contract; he made only three more movies before his death, playing a supporting role in each one. Parks's wife, actress Betty Garrett, who had never been a Communist, was dropped from the Metro-Goldwyn-Mayer roster at the height of her fame, as a result of her husband's testimony.

The proliferating blacklist ruined hundreds of careers in films, including those of actors John Garfield and Lee J. Cobb, actresses Gale Sondergaard and Anne Revere (who had recently won an Academy Award), and screenwriter Carl Foreman. Actress Kim Hunter, who won an Oscar for *A Streetcar Named Desire* in 1951, was blacklisted because of petitions she had signed. "I couldn't have been more apolitical," said Hunter, "but I did feel strongly about human rights, civil rights, injustices of all kinds. At that time it was dangerous to express such feelings openly."

Some of those blacklisted turned to alcohol, a few committed suicide, others went to Europe. Families were wrecked, and workers of the same persuasion sometimes quit speaking to one another. It was a time when friends became afraid of friends, clients distrusted agents, informers loathed themselves for their lack of courage, and intellectual content all but disappeared from Hollywood's movies.

HUAC's hold on public opinion increased after the rise of Senator Joseph McCarthy (whose name became synonymous with red-baiting), the trial of Ethel and Julius Rosenberg (found guilty of treason), the fall of China to the Communists, the outbreak of the Korean War, and the Soviet Union's first successful atomic explosion. In the hysteria of McCarthyism, membership in the Communist Party became linked with espionage; anyone who had ever been a Communist was treated as a potential spy for the Soviet Union. The witch-hunt threatened higher education, the publishing world, even the ministry.

HUAC's interrogation of Hollywood weakened the movie industry at the very time when box office receipts were starting to decline. Producers became timid and turned out bland and sanctimonious films that soon proved an embarrassment. Disillusionment swept over the industry, and its sense of fraternity shattered. As a town centered around the picture business, Hollywood had defined itself in part by its social life. As community life died, so did much of the Tinseltown gaiety.

In April 1951, after serving his jail sentence, Edward Dmytryk escaped further reprisals by recanting his former political beliefs and making a second appearance before the House Committee. This time he answered all of the Committee's questions and named twenty-six people whom he knew to have had Communist affiliations, six of them colleagues in the Screen Directors Guild. The following year Dmytryk signed a four-picture contract with producer Stanley Kramer, and the director worked steadily in Hollywood until his retirement.

During HUAC's second set of hearings, former Communists followed a more expedient strategy than the Hollywood Ten had. By answering the Committee's questions and supplying names, they could expect to continue working. Those who refused to testify and stood on the Fifth Amendment ran no risk of imprisonment, but they would assuredly be blacklisted. Some three dozen witnesses took the first alternative, more than two hundred chose the latter.

The times were troubled and dangerous; survival in the face of harassment and uncertainty outweighed honor and personal integrity in many cases. Director Michael Gordon, whom Dymtryk had named as a fellow Communist, remembered sleeping in a motel room the night before he left Los Angeles rather than implicate friends who offered him hospitality. Joseph Losey, another director, moved to England; his final memory of life in the United States was of hiding in a darkened house to avoid being served with a subpoena.

The blacklist was a panicked industry's sacrifice to power politics. While Hollywood's glamour continued on the surface, its creative core showed symptoms of decay as the industry's leaders grew increasingly frightened. Although the HUAC investigations failed to produce proof of Communist propaganda in American films, they left a legacy of anger and hurt that persisted for decades.

THE DIVORCEMENT DECREES

If the hearings of the House Committee on Un-American Activities and their aftermath divided Hollywood, the federal government's divorcement of the studios from their theaters destroyed the industry's basic structure. The five major Hollywood studios (Paramount, Metro-Goldwyn-Mayer, Warner Bros., Twentieth Century-Fox, and RKO) owned or controlled chains of theaters and therefore dominated all three phases of the motion picture business—production, distribution, and exhibition. Columbia and Universal were smaller companies that operated in symbiotic relationship with the Big Five; both had their own studios and distribution facilities that proved useful to the majors in supplying additional product for program changes and double features. United Artists functioned as a distributor for independent producers, yet still worked in conjunction with the five majors. In the *Paramount* decision of May 1948, the Supreme Court declared that this cooperative arrangement constituted a vertically integrated monopoly, in violation of antitrust laws, and ordered the Big Five to divorce themselves from their theaters.

The big studio system depended on block booking; theaters agreed to take a package of the studio's films, bad pictures along with the good, even before they were made. Each of the major companies aimed to turn out between fifty and sixty movies a year, one for each week's bill in their theaters. To furnish sufficient product, the Hollywood studios became factories, producing as many pictures of quality as possible, but supplementing them with budget movies their theaters were obligated to show. The cheaper films kept contract personnel working and filled the company's screens with formula entertainment that sold on the strength of stars and imaginative advertising.

The Department of Justice's antitrust division had filed suit against Hollywood's five major and three minor companies in July 1938, accusing them of monopolistic practices in restraint of trade. After hearing complaints from independent exhibitors that block booking still existed, the suit was reopened in 1944. After thousands of pages of testimony, lower-court decisions, and appeals, the issue was settled in the landmark *Paramount* case. The Supreme Court decided unanimously that the Big Five must dispose of their chains of movie houses. Subsequent decrees by the court ended such trade practices as block booking and unfair clearances that prolonged the time before independent theaters could exhibit new films.

The *Paramount* decision signaled a halt to the consolidated empires Hollywood moguls had built over the two previous decades. Companies now were to be split, with film production and distribution separated from exhibition in the theaters. Without block booking the studios were stripped of their guaranteed market. Each film had to be sold theater by theater on a picture-by-picture basis.

Divestiture was painful and slow, taking the companies more than ten years to complete. Paramount and RKO were the first to comply with the divorcement decrees, but MGM and its parent company, Loew's, dragged their feet until 1959. Exhibitors no longer had the resources to promote pictures with the extensive publicity campaigns that movies had received under the big studio system, when millions of dollars were spent on advertising Hollywood's current product. The result was that movie palaces, built under the old regime, suffered a further decline in attendance.

THE MOVE TO SUBURBIA

Other factors in the postwar lifestyles of Americans contributed to the loss of audiences. With the war over, people whose lives had been disrupted by the Great Depression and World War II wanted to buy homes and start families. During 1946 the birth rate in the United States increased to an unprecedented high, and the middle-class began moving to the suburbs in record numbers, away from downtown movie houses and the old neighborhood theaters. With increases in the cost of living, young adults, previously ardent movie fans, preferred to concentrate on raising children and buying cars, refrigerators, and automatic washing machines. They entertained more at home, gardened, took courses at local colleges, played records on high-fidelity equipment, and listened to the radio. With bills to pay and baby-sitters expensive and difficult to find, middle-class Americans grew more selective in their movie attendance. The average film no longer could be counted on to return its cost.

The rapid shift in population and the sweeping changes in national mood caught Hollywood by surprise. First-run theaters concentrated in the downtown areas of the larger cities previously accounted for around 75 percent of a movie's box office receipts, but as freeways led Americans to less expensive housing developments farther from the inner city, the old movie palaces became isolated. Neighborhood theaters in dying sections of town soon looked run-down, and many closed their doors. Few theaters existed in the suburbs, and the chains that had the most capital for investment in new ones were prevented from building theaters by the divorcement decrees. Years before the television boom, movies began losing their mass audience. Contrary to popular opinion, people in higher income brackets attended motion pictures more regularly than people at lower economic levels, and the more education a person had, the more likely he or she was to frequent the movies.

THE ADVENT OF TELEVISION

The crowning blow to the studios came with the introduction of commercial television into American homes. Television had been a technical reality since the late 1930s. During the 1939 World's Fair in New York, NBC had made its television debut, and both NBC and CBS had inaugurated commercial broadcasting in Manhattan two years later. By the end of 1941 six commercial television stations were in operation and 10,000 sets had been sold, mainly in the New York area. Early in 1942, however, the government suspended television manufacturing and most programming until after the war. In 1946, when restrictions were lifted, television sets began to be made in substantial numbers. A million receivers had been sold by 1949; two years later, with 1,000 new sets purchased every twenty-four hours, the sales reached ten million. By 1955 television sets had become a status symbol in the minds of middle-class and suburban Americans; more than half of all households in the United States had sets.

Watching television quickly became an obsession. During prime-time viewing, streets were deserted as families gathered around the living room to watch Milton Berle, Lucille Ball, Ed Sullivan, Sid Caesar, and Imogene Coca go through their weekly paces. Video programming fit more conveniently into daily schedules of busy Americans than a night at the movies. There was no need for baby-sitters, no problem with parking, and best of all, the entertainment was free. Most of the programming was live, and local stations supplied news, weather information, and shows of regional interest.

The major motion picture companies tried to add a television wing shortly after the war, but the Federal Communications Commission's antitrust policy prevented their doing so. Earlier it had been thought that the old moguls turned a deaf ear to television and were so blinded by their success before and during the war that they failed to recognize the challenge from the networks. Recent scholarship has pointed out that they were more astute. "The failure of the studios to establish themselves as forces in television broadcasting was a result of FCC policy, not Hollywood incompetence," film historian Timothy R. White wrote.

Samuel Goldwyn, one of the pioneers in the picture business, predicted as early as 1949 that within a few years a coaxial cable would provide a television network linking the entire country:

> The future of motion pictures, conditioned as it will be by the competition of television, is going to have no room for the deadwood of the present or the faded glories of the past. . . . It will take brains instead of just money to make pictures. . . . I am convinced that television will cause Hollywood to achieve new heights.

MEETING THE CHALLENGE

Goldwyn's brave words were in part defensive. Hollywood was scared. Unless producers came up with innovations fast, the studios risked losing their hold on mass entertainment. Yet with political hysteria rampant, the innovations would need to be in technology more than content.

Hollywood first retaliated by offering movie audiences what they could not see on television—a wide screen. Cinerama, a process using three cameras mounted one beside the other to photograph panoramic vistas closely approximating human vision, was introduced at the Broadway Theater in New York on September 30, 1952, with multitrack stereophonic sound. *This Is Cinerama*, the first film in the new process, opened with a Coney Island roller coaster ride, which put spectators in the front car, took them to La Scala in Milan, and ended with an air tour of Bryce and Zion Canyons, Yosemite, and the Grand Canyon. Audiences and critics alike were overwhelmed, and the picture became a major attraction, playing for 122 weeks in New York alone. By December 1953, *This Is Cinerama* had grossed more than $10 million.

Conversion of a single theater to the huge curved screen and enhanced sound system cost fifty to a hundred thousand dollars, so cinerama was limited to twenty cities in the United States and eight in foreign countries. Jiggling lines between the three panels on the screen and uneven color matches proved distracting, but *This Is*

Cinerama eventually grossed more than $32 million. Although *Cinerama Holiday* (1955), another travelogue, also did well, the public's interest in the process diminished with *Seven Wonders of the World* (1957).

Less than two months after the premiere of the first cinerama picture, *Bwana Devil* opened simultaneously at two theaters in Los Angeles. Arch Oboler, an independent filmmaker who had earned a reputation as a radio writer, wrote and directed this simple adventure yarn of game hunters in Africa, investing $10,000 of his own money and raising the rest for what studio heads dismissed as a capricious gamble. What made *Bwana Devil* noteworthy was that it was the first feature released in 3-D. Oboler simply bolted two cameras together, and when the film was seen through polaroid glasses, its double image created a three-dimensional effect. The ineptly made picture, shot in the brown hills north of Los Angeles, starred Robert Stack and Barbara Britton and was distributed by United Artists after an initial showing in Los Angeles. Critics roasted the film, but audiences shrieked with delight as African natives appeared to throw spears at them from the screen and lions threatened to leap into their laps. *Bwana Devil* earned $154,000 within the first week, as audiences stood in lines stretching around the block. By March 1953 it had grossed more than $5 million.

For a brief time 3-D was hailed as the revolution that would save Hollywood. Warner Bros. rushed a remake of *The Mystery of the Wax Museum* (1933) into production, calling it *The House of Wax* (1953), the first 3-D picture from a major studio. Within three weeks after its release, the film had grossed more than $1 million. Audiences thrilled as tongues of fire leapt from the screen and the smell of smoke wafted through air-conditioning systems at premier theaters.

Warner Bros. followed its first 3-D offering with *The Charge at Feather River* (1953), an inexpensive western. That same year Paramount scrapped *Sangaree* after twelve days of shooting and began again in 3-D, adding $400,000 to the film's budget. Universal released two cheaply-made exploitation movies in 3-D, *It Came from Outer Space* (1953) and *The Creature from the Black Lagoon* (1954), while Columbia made *Man in the Dark* (1953). But audiences soon tired of the novelty.

The 3-D craze lasted barely twelve months. *Kiss Me, Kate* (1953), a lavish MGM musical, opened at Radio City Music Hall in 3-D to tepid business, then was exhibited throughout most of the country with success in a flat version. So was Alfred Hitchcock's *Dial M for Murder* (1954), which had also been made in a 3-D version.

Meanwhile, executives at Twentieth Century-Fox based their future on a more economical version of the wide screen called CinemaScope. Early in 1953 Darryl F. Zanuck, the studio's production head, announced that Fox was converting its entire output to the CinemaScope process. Zanuck had already done away with his studio's cheaper films, since they most closely approximated what viewers could see night after night on television.

The bulky CinemaScope cameras utilized regular 35-millimeter film but were difficult to move when shooting action sequences on location. The CinemaScope image, projected on a curved screen, was two and one-half times as wide as it was high and eliminated the distracting lines that had bothered Cinerama audiences. Most directors and cinematographers hated the new process, objecting to its distortions and finding its extended vision inappropriate for intimate scenes. "CinemaScope is fine," director George Stevens said, "if you want a system that shows a boa constrictor to better advantage than a man." But the process caused a tremendous response from the public and proved the one novelty, besides stereophonic sound, to make a lasting impact on the movie business. "CinemaScope may have ruined the art of motion pictures for a decade," cameraman Leon Shamroy said. "It also saved the industry."

Twentieth Century-Fox executives chose *The Robe*, their costliest picture of 1953, to launch the CinemaScope experiment, and its success was impressive. Based on Lloyd C. Douglas's best-selling novel, *The Robe* netted $16 million within its first four months in the theaters. By then 1,500 CinemaScope screens had been installed throughout the United States and Canada. The studio rushed twelve more CinemaScope pictures into production, including *How to Marry a Millionaire* and *King of the Khyber Rifles*. Each film opened with a short concert by the Twentieth Century-Fox orchestra, an attempt to lend elegance to the theater-going experience. The initial CinemaScope pictures generated record earnings that stabilized the studio's financial condition, while economists began talking about a "CinemaScope rebound."

Zanuck made contracts with Metro-Goldwyn-Mayer, Warner Bros., Columbia, and Universal, allowing them to use the new wide-screen process. Meanwhile, Paramount announced its own technique called VistaVision, which utilized a camera and projector through which the film traveled horizontally rather than vertically and resulted in a sharper image. Paramount premiered VistaVision in April 1954 at Radio City Music Hall with *White Christmas*, which became a perennial holiday musical starring Bing Crosby. Increased profits from wide-screen pictures, however, depended on extensive promotion campaigns and long runs in theaters at higher admission prices.

The major studios decided to concentrate on fewer and more expensive movies. The Todd-AO process, which used 70-millimeter film to achieve dimensions nearly as large as Cinerama, but without the distracting lines, was successfully introduced in the summer of 1955 with *Oklahoma!*, the film version of Rodgers and Hammerstein's record-breaking Broadway musical. The picture cost $4 million and was initially shown in specially equipped theaters on a reserved-seat basis. Michael Todd's *Around the World in Eighty Days* followed in 1956, winning the Academy Award that year for best picture and establishing Todd-AO as a hallmark of special-event features. Still, by 1958 the downward trend in box office receipts returned, despite Hollywood's boast that "Movies Are Better Than Ever."

The appearance of Smell-O-Vision and AromaRama during the decade's final year suggested the extent of the industry's desperation. AromaRama, a gimmick devised by Walter Reade, Jr., spewed out seventy-two different smells during the showing of *Behind the Great Wall* (1959). Michael Todd, Jr.'s *Scent of Mystery* (1960) employed the Smell-O-Vision process, which involved an apparatus under each seat to release odors that corresponded with scenes on the screen, ranging from baked bread and salty ocean breezes to the villain's pipe tobacco and the scent of port wine. A fan wafted away each smell before the next one was released. Humorist Henny Youngman saw the movie and remarked: "I didn't understand the picture. I had a cold."

CHANGES AT HOME AND ABROAD

Movie executives not only underestimated the rapidity of television's growth, they also were slow to grasp other fundamental changes affecting the industry. With World War II over, film distributors attempted to recover their overseas markets, which had earlier added millions of dollars to Hollywood's gross. Steady production during the war had built up an immense backlog of films that had not been exhibited in countries controlled by the Axis powers, and studio heads anticipated a rush of profits free from overhead. The importation of American movies, however, conflicted with foreign countries' desires to nurture their own film companies and stop the outflow of money needed to rebuild after the war.

In 1947 the British government was the first to take action, placing limits on the amount of earnings American studios could extract from the country and freezing the rest within Great Britain. In the future, 75 percent of all profits earned in the United Kingdom by American film companies would be subject to taxation. The next year France and Italy, faced with postwar economic problems, followed suit.

The United Kingdom represented the studios' biggest export market, and its restrictions cut deep into Hollywood's profits. Distributors continued to exploit the Latin American market developed during the war and extended their markets in Asia and Africa, but the new profits did not compensate for the lost income from Europe.

In the panic over declining markets, studio executives attempted to reduce overheads by not renewing contracts with actors, directors, writers, and various craft workers who had been with them since the Depression. Performers who remained under contract were forbidden to appear on television, which meant a loss of revenue particularly for stars. Resentment against studio control and accusations of professional bondage, present since the late 1930s, began to mount. Actors and actresses came to feel that they would fare better under a freelance system, in which they could select better roles and negotiate higher fees for their services.

When Universal sought James Stewart for the lead in *Winchester 73* in 1949, his agent, Lew Wasserman, refused to allow him to sign until the studio agreed to pay the actor 50 percent of the picture's profits rather than his customary fee of $250,000. Stewart eventually made $600,000 from the movie, from which the agency representing him collected 10 percent. Stewart's arrangement with Universal set a precedent for stars no longer content to work for a salary; powerful agencies such as William Morris and MCA became the talent brokers in Hollywood.

But directors, too, had grown restless under the old contract system and sought greater control over their films. In 1946 directors Frank Capra, William Wyler, George Stevens, and producer Sam Briskin formed Liberty Films as an independent production company. "Our idea," said Wyler, "was that directors form their own units, look for material, get it financed by a studio, but control the whole project." The company's first effort was Capra's *It's a Wonderful Life* (1947), now a classic but not enough of a financial success at the time to keep Liberty Films in operation.

Meanwhile, director Lewis Milestone became disenchanted with the established studios and joined Enterprise Productions. The company made *Body and Soul* (1947), a successful boxing movie starring John Garfield, before Milestone directed Ingrid Bergman and Charles Boyer in *Arch of Triumph* (1948), a box office disaster, for Enterprise. "The mistake was the management's," Milestone said later. "I thought the motive should have been to be slightly different from the usual product that a major studio would put out. But they tried to do the same thing that every other studio was doing— make money, no matter how." Milestone directed one more film for Enterprise, and the company folded.

Despite these failures, actors and directors soon realized there were larger profits and tax advantages in setting up their own production units. In 1946 actress Rosalind Russell and her husband, producer Frederick Brisson, created Independent Artists with writer Dudley Nichols. A year later they made their first movie, *The Velvet Touch*, using facilities on the RKO lot. In 1948 actress Joan Bennett, producer Walter Wanger, and director Fritz Lang launched Diana Productions with *Secret beyond the Door*, made at Universal-International.

Actor Burt Lancaster and agent Harold Hecht also formed a company in 1948, later changing the name from Norma Productions to Hecht-Lancaster and turning out a string of box office and critical successes, including the Academy Award-winning *Marty* (1955). Humphrey Bogart named his company Santana Productions, after the star's yacht, and produced *Knock on Any Door* (1949) and several other pictures released through Columbia. In 1951 John Wayne set up his own company, which made *Hondo* (1953) and other movies with Wayne in the leading role.

In 1945 there were about 40 independent producers in Hollywood, 70 by 1946, 90 in 1947, and about 165 a decade later.

Most of the independents distributed their films through either one of the major studios or United Artists, Columbia, or Universal. The trend in financing independent productions shifted away from sole funding by banks toward an arrangement whereby the releasing studio put up as much as half of the budgeted cost. In return the studios gained the right to exercise certain controls.

Stanley Kramer, for example, the most adventurous of the postwar independent producers, brought his unit to Columbia in 1951. Kramer's company, Screen Plays Inc., had already made a series of modest-budget message pictures that had received critical acclaim, among them *Champion* and *Home of the Brave* (both 1949). The agreement with Columbia stipulated that Kramer could make no picture that cost more than $2 million or ran more than two hours in length. If he should, the studio had the right to take over.

With profits shrinking, banks grew cautious about loaning vast sums even to established filmmakers. When they did, they charged more and took an active interest in the details of production, beginning with the script. The power of the old Hollywood moguls, who had ruled their studios like caliphs, was eroded. Stockholders grew increasingly restive, despite continuing staff and budget cuts. Early in 1953 Warner Bros. announced a decrease in pay of up to 50 percent for its remaining employees.

As production declined, the studios no longer had the resources to keep stars in the limelight. The days when the Cocoanut Grove, the Mocambo, and other famous Hollywood nightclubs were packed with celebrities each night were coming to an end. With television, even stars found staying at home easier. When they entertained, it was more likely with a group of friends in private surroundings. Hollywood's glamour seemed to be fading.

Many of the reports from Hollywood that made headlines during the late 1940s and early 1950s were scandalous, destructive to the image studio publicists had worked to create. In 1948 actor Robert Mitchum was arrested for smoking marijuana in a home in Laurel Canyon; he was handcuffed and taken in a police car to the Los Angeles County jail. Mitchum's arrest posed a serious threat to his career, in part because of the media coverage the incident received.

Even more devastating was the announcement in December 1949 that actress Ingrid Bergman was expecting a baby fathered by Italian director Roberto Rossellini. Bergman was still the wife of Dr.

Peter Lindstrom; her pregnancy out of wedlock rocked Hollywood and shocked fans across the country. As news circulated that the actress planned to divorce her husband, forsake her daughter, and marry Rossellini, she was ridiculed by traditionalists as symbolic of the general moral decay taking place.

The playful, joyous atmosphere of Hollywood seemed to have vanished, what remained were indecency, perversion, and ruin. The new tabloids, led by *Confidential* and later the *National Enquirer*, told all—the sicker and more twisted the stories, the better. The old gods and goddesses of the silver screen were becoming relics of a bygone era. Producer David Selznick, whose *Gone with the Wind* (1939) had brought the greatest glory to the movie capital, viewed the destruction with despair. He told writer Ben Hecht in 1953 that Hollywood was like Egypt, "full of crumbled pyramids."

CONCLUSION

Throughout Hollywood's Golden Era, the studios had maintained a coherence within the movie industry despite basic contradictions: commerce versus art, formula versus originality, social commentary versus entertainment. By 1950 the big studio system, which had dominated the business for more than a quarter of a century, was starting to fracture. Internal friction present since the organization of the craft unions during the 1930s burst into open warfare in the months after the end of World War II. The purge of the House Un-American Activities Committee and the ensuing blacklist widened the split and weakened the industry's trust and confidence in itself, causing producers to turn cautious at a time when creative thinking was needed. Postwar movie audiences were more sophisticated than those of the previous generation, and Hollywood's conservative approach began to look naive and outmoded. The idealistic romances and slick adventure yarns that had won studios loyal fans during the Great Depression were too simplistic for a more complex world to accept.

Divorced from their theater chains by government decrees, the studios no longer enjoyed an assured market for their product. With the migration of the American middle class to the suburbs and the appearance of television, home entertainment became the postwar pattern. Inflation, the baby boom, and the distance from existing theaters reduced movie audiences and made them more selective in their choice of films. Between 1950 and 1953, 3,000 theaters closed as box office returns diminished at an accelerating rate. One wit suggested that exhibitors show their pictures in the streets, thereby driving people into the movie houses. But Hollywood's leaders were not amused.

Although the old moguls had attempted to enter the television field early in its development, recent court decisions prevented their doing so. To compete with the new medium, producers turned to technology and gimmicks, which proved merely temporary lures in attracting mass audiences. Fewer and better pictures seemed a wiser path, but with reduced output the contract players and large studio staff of former years had to be eliminated. Reduced markets would not support such immense overheads.

Actors and directors, resentful of the dictatorial methods of the old studio heads, were at first delighted with the freedom to select their own projects and negotiate for percentages of box office receipts generated by the movies they made. Later, many of them would complain about the loss of security that the old contract system had assured, but the trend toward deal making through powerful agents and independent production companies would become dominant in the years to come.

Faced with multiple shocks in quick succession, Hollywood's leaders felt victimized. Any one of the upheavals that shook the motion picture industry after World War II would have been traumatic; together they proved devastating. For more than two decades Hollywood had monopolized the American entertainment business and mirrored the nation's fundamental values. The Hollywood phenomenon, despite its hype and hyperbole, fit the mood of American culture and magnified its ideals. Audiences delighted in seeing enticing images of themselves on the screens of baroque movie palaces and fantasized that they would come true. Hollywood carried those images around the globe, creating mythic heroes, a conspicuous lifestyle, and fashions for the world to emulate. "Everybody wanted to come to America and see the streets of gold," said actor Robert Cummings, and many came expecting life in the United States to be what it was in the movies.

With the decline of the big studio system, much of the mechanism behind the Hollywood mystique disappeared. The loss involved more than a shrinkage of markets; the legendary stars, massive publicity campaigns, balanced patterns of production, and glossy stories faced extinction with the demise of Hollywood's glamour factories. Although independent producers and fresh talent would heap new laurels on the American movie industry, Hollywood around 1950 faced a precarious period of adjustment. The decades ahead would not be easy.

Gloria Swanson and William Holden in Sunset Boulevard *(1950).*

Chapter 2

A SEARCH FOR NEW MARKETS

Moods in the United States were changing. In 1950 Paramount released *Sunset Boulevard,* a film classic centered on an aging silent picture star who wallows in memories of past glories and an era that is dead. Directed and coscripted by Billy Wilder, *Sunset Boulevard* is arguably the most subtly philosophical movie about Hollywood ever made. It takes a hard look at the motion picture business and draws the conclusion that most of Hollywood's output has been vain and vaporous, that the highly publicized creations of one age, with few exceptions, will be crumbling celluloid in the next.

On the surface *Sunset Boulevard* seems to be about the grotesque eccentricities of Norma Desmond, a daft old silent picture queen living in the Hollywood of 1950. She was once a great, glamorous star, but for decades she has secluded herself in a musty mansion off Sunset Boulevard, protected by her faithful servant, Max, and absorbed with delusions of her continuing importance. Yet Norma Desmond is more than a living relic from an ostentatious and absurd past; she becomes an eerie reminder that glittering success in one generation may be dismissed as insignificant folly as values and tastes modify.

But the glimpses Billy Wilder shows in his film of contemporary Hollywood are no more appealing. Joe Gillis, an aspiring screenwriter down on his luck, is calculating and underhanded, devoid of either sentiment or compassion. As played by William Holden, Joe is as self-consumed as Norma, yet he is willing to debase himself for the comfort and luxuries she can provide. He ends by hurting not only Norma but also a young girl who falls in love with him when they collaborate on a script.

Sunset Boulevard places the past and the present side by side. Its fiction is haunted by truth, and the picture is filled with irony. Norma Desmond, portrayed in the movie by Gloria Swanson, herself a silent picture star, dreams of making a comeback as the teenage Salome under the direction of Cecil B. DeMille, with whom Norma had scored her greatest success. Swanson's own career advanced rapidly after DeMille cast her in a major role in 1918, and *Sunset Boulevard* was for her the stellar comeback that Norma Desmond fantasizes. Norma's favorite pastime is watching her old movies at home with Joe, while Max, her butler, former husband, and first director (brilliantly played by the great silent filmmaker Eric von Stroheim), serves as projectionist. The footage seen is a sequence from *Queen Kelley,* a Swanson movie that the legendary Stroheim directed in 1928. Yet loaded as it is with inducements to nostalgia, *Sunset Boulevard* is brutal in its suggestion that Hollywood's celebrity is mainly transient.

Perhaps the greatest irony is that the film anticipated by several years the demise of Hollywood's Golden Age—the breakup of the big studios, the end of the old star system, and the demolition of the movie palaces across the country. But *Sunset Boulevard* also reflects the depressed atmosphere in Hollywood at the time it was made. While the past is viewed by Wilder in decaying terms, the present is seen as fragile, uncertain, and ultimately desperate.

Sunset Boulevard is a superlative example of the motion picture genre known as *film noir,* a pervasive theme in Hollywood movies during and especially after World War II. Heavily indebted to German expressionism, film noir represents a crisis in values, a direct response by filmmakers to the troubled times of the 1940s. Its attitude is harsh, oppressive, fatalistic; its characters are without a firm moral base. A hallmark of film noir is the feeling of claustrophobia and entrapment; its people are immobilized by paranoia and fear, unable to tell truth from falsehood, good from evil. Its central characters are confused and weak, easily misled, while relationships often prove destructive. Alienation and loneliness dominate a dark world, in which love has been replaced by unrestrained desire and life is purposeless.

Women in film noir tend to be femmes fatales, determined to castrate or destroy male heroes, who are easily manipulated and victimized. Corruption and violence result, as misguided dreamers of the American Dream are tempted to seek fame and fortune through immoral or criminal acts. "You're no good and neither am I," Jane Greer tells Robert Mitchum in *Out of the Past* (1947). "We deserve each other."

The tone of film noir is ambiguous: murky and constricted, cynical and pessimistic. Filmmakers relied heavily on flashbacks, voice-over narration, dramatic camera angles, and shadowy, low-key lighting to create a convulsive, nightmare world. The look of the films is dark and gloomy, atmospheric yet riddled with evil.

The best examples of film noir were directed by European expatriates who fled to Hollywood with the rise of Fascism. Billy Wilder had grown up in Vienna, and his early work there was light-hearted and romantic. But the war changed all that. In 1944, under contract to Paramount, he directed *Double Indemnity,* a classic murder story with Barbara Stanwyck playing a temptress who leads Fred MacMurray to his ruin. A year later Wilder won critical acclaim with *The Lost Weekend,* a harrowing account of one man's battle against alcoholism.

Fritz Lang, who had established a reputation in Germany before the war, directed *The Woman in the Window* (1944) and *Scarlet Street* (1945), with Edward G. Robinson in both films playing a middle-aged man victimized by Joan Bennett. Otto Preminger, who had worked with stage director Max Reinhardt in Austria, contributed *Laura* (1944) and *Fallen Angel* (1945), two murder mysteries with ambiguous overtones, and Robert Siodmak, a German Jew forced into exile by the Nazi takeover in 1933, directed *Phantom Lady* (1944) and *The Spiral Staircase* (1946). Titles alone suggest the mood of film noir: *Dark Waters* (1944), *The Dark Mirror* (1946), *Dark Passage* (1947), and *Dark City* (1950).

In this murky world almost no one could be trusted; villains were as glamorous as they were deceitful and vile. Film noir captured the anxieties of the 1940s and early 1950s, when much was won, but nearly as much seemed lost. In addition to the Cold War with its fears of espionage, there was corruption in government. The traditional family structure appeared to be breaking down, as men rose on the corporate ladder and women assumed more active roles in society. There was strife over civil rights and charges that a traditional work ethic had been replaced by a redefined social ethic that encouraged conformity on the one hand, status seeking on the other. For many the vitality, sense of purpose, and consensus of prewar America appeared headed toward destruction.

For Hollywood, film noir represented a burst of creative energy, but also a means of chronicling and coping with the failings of contemporary life. By dwelling on these darker images, the sumptuous decor and pristine language characteristic of Hollywood in former years were abandoned; instead chaos, uncertainty, moral decay, irrationality, and alienation became keynotes.

The most lasting impact of film noir probably came from the British emigrant Alfred Hitchcock, who combined the genre's macabre themes with art, humor, and eroticism. Hitchcock directed his first Hollywood thriller, *Rebecca,* in 1940, then established himself as "the master of suspense" with such classics as *Shadow of a Doubt* (1943), *Spellbound* (1945), and *Notorious* (1946). He was fascinated with guilt and the bleaker shades of human behavior and indulged in a bewildering play with identities, implying that people are neither as good nor as bad as they seem. Above all, Hitchcock's films are consistently entertaining, and his success continued with *Rear Window* (1954), *To Catch a Thief* (1955), *North by Northwest* (1959), and *Psycho* (1960).

HOLLYWOOD IN DESPAIR

Despite annual successes, Hollywood had little reason for optimism during the 1950s. As the decade began, motion picture attendance in the United States was down more than 25 percent from its postwar peak, and by 1953 attendance had dropped to nearly half what it had been in 1946. In 1954 only 32 percent of domestic theaters were breaking even on box office receipts alone. Production shrank from 425 films in 1946 to 354 in 1953 and fewer than 300 in 1954. By 1960 Hollywood was making around 200 pictures a year.

Although *Photoplay* and the other fan magazines tried to preserve the illusion that Hollywood's magic remained intact, even small-town America began to have doubts. As the novelty of wide screens wore off, all but the first-run market proved disastrous. By 1963 the number of four-wall theaters had declined by 48 percent since 1947, and many towns were left with none at all. Wall Street meanwhile grew increasingly conservative about loaning the funds needed to make pictures unless a "bankable" star headed the cast.

The product in least demand was the low-budget film, which most nearly approximated television programming. As the market for double features evaporated, studio executives realized that the smaller picture business was finished. Monogram, one of the Poverty Row companies, reorganized itself into Allied Artists and tried to produce better films that could compete in first-run theaters. "They didn't cost as much as the A's being made by major companies," Monogram executive Walter Mirisch said, "but they cost a lot more than the second features we'd been making." Although Allied Artists enjoyed modest success with *Suspense* (1946) and *Bad Boy* (1949), which featured war hero Audie Murphy, the ploy soon failed.

Republic, which specialized in budget westerns and country musicals, suffered a loss of more than $1 million in 1957, with the result that the studio went out of business the following year. In 1948 eccentric billionaire Howard Hughes purchased RKO, the smallest of the major studios, but ran it capriciously, making only a few pictures after 1951. In 1954 RKO lost nearly $40 million; many observers were convinced that Hughes had bought the studio strictly as a tax liability. He sold it in 1955 to the General Tire and Rubber Company, which owned a television subsidiary.

From the large profits of the wartime years, Metro-Goldwyn-Mayer, the Tiffany of Hollywood studios, quickly suffered sharp reverses, beginning with a $6.5 million loss in 1948. MGM executives continued to maintain that the American public, burdened with the problems of a complex urban lifestyle, still wanted escapist entertainment and genteel vehicles with glamorous stars. But the studio's pictures began to seem old-fashioned in the postwar world, and its stockholders held Louis B. Mayer, MGM's head of production, responsible for the current deficit. Mayer was replaced in 1948 by Dore Schary, who favored more realistic movies.

Schary chose such stories as *Battleground* (1949) and *Asphalt Jungle* (1950) to launch his regime and dispensed with the lavish sets, beautiful costumes, and authentic jewelry that had won MGM its position of leadership. In 1952 Schary announced pay cuts for the studio's 4,000 employees, and for the next few years Metro-Goldwyn-Mayer showed a narrow profit. Then it went back into the red; by 1956 the studio's losses were $4.6 million, and Schary was fired.

Three years later Twentieth Century-Fox was teetering on the edge of bankruptcy, while Warner Bros. and Paramount had cut production sharply. By 1959 contract players in Hollywood were the exception rather than the rule, but salaries for major stars had soared astronomically. All the major studios had reduced personnel to a fraction of what they had employed a few years before. Movie shorts, cartoons, and newsreels were eliminated, as studios concentrated on fewer feature films. Backlots became playgrounds for jackrabbits, as more pictures were made on location. "I walk down a studio street at MGM, Warners, Twentieth—you name it," local movie critic Philip K. Scheuer said in 1960, "and I am all but alone in a ghost town."

By the late 1950s more than half of all films produced in Hollywood were made by independent companies, and more than half of those lost money. No longer were the studios self-contained factories with assembly lines turning out product. They had mainly become distributors for a growing number of independents. Many of the old stars turned to the stage, some went into television, others were forgotten. A new generation of Norma Desmonds ensconced themselves beside their telephones, waiting for a call from an agent. Some reminisced about the glory days with joy; more felt the pain of oblivion.

SPECTACLES AND DISTANT LOCATIONS

Prompted by the success of MGM's *Quo Vadis* (1951) and Paramount's *The Greatest Show on Earth* (1952), both of which broke box office records, studio heads decided to concentrate on a smaller number of pictures, channeling vast sums into projects that stood a chance of drawing mass audiences. These blockbusters were targeted for first-run theaters that had the seating capacity, location, and bargaining power to bid for them. Increased production costs necessitated higher admission prices if larger profits were to be achieved. To insure bigger returns, producers selected grander stories, packed them with stars, and lavished attention on special effects.

Historical epics provided the best opportunities for Hollywood filmmakers to show off the wide screen, exotic locations, and improved technical skills that had been born out of desperation. Cecil B. DeMille and other filmmakers had been making spectacles since the early silent era, but most of them, even as late as 1951, were photographed on the studio's backlot or some nearby location. A trip to Lone Pine, California, or Monument Valley, on the Arizona-Utah border, for filming westerns was a luxury awarded only to big pictures. Even DeMille's *Samson and Delilah* (1949) and Twentieth

Century-Fox's *David and Bathsheba* (1951), two biblical epics, were mainly filmed inside their studios. For *The Robe,* Twentieth Century-Fox reproduced the city of Jerusalem on its own lot.

By the mid-1950s, with audiences more sophisticated and selective, it became essential for film crews to travel to actual locations. No longer could Parisian streets be represented on a soundstage or Waterloo Bridge be built on the backlot. Since studio profits were frozen in numerous foreign countries and could be expended only there, travel proved convenient. Labor was cheaper in foreign countries, and crews could be kept to a minimum since there was no need to conform to Hollywood's union regulations. Living away from home for an extended period provided welcome tax breaks for stars, whereas employing international casts widened a movie's appeal on the world market.

MGM already owned a seldom-used studio in England, and Metro executives announced in 1951 that their upcoming production of *Ivanhoe* would be filmed there. Producer Pandro Berman remembered that his company had the facilities in England all to themselves and said they enjoyed being free of the hierarchy in Culver City. "It was $650,000 cheaper to make the picture in a British studio than it would have been had we stayed at home," Berman declared. "And, of course, it was infinitely better." The producer cast British actors in supporting roles, made use of the British countryside that was legitimate for the story, and employed English costume and set designers, all of which made for a more authentic film. "When I was in England, I concentrated on *that* picture," said Berman, "whereas at the studio I was always working on four or five at the same time."

The following year MGM planned to make *Knights of the Round Table* in England, using CinemaScope for the first time. Pandro Berman again produced. "We had some difficulty with the English unions," Berman recalled, "and I couldn't make the big battle scenes in England on account of the union demands. So we went over to Ireland. I got the use of the Irish army, and we made the big scenes there."

Paramount's *Roman Holiday* (1953) was among the first American movies filmed in Italy after the war. "It was an absolute joy to live there for six months and make that movie," remembered Gregory Peck, who starred in the picture opposite Audrey Hepburn. "You cannot reproduce the Trevi Fountain or the Spanish Steps on the backlot, or the crowds and the traffic. So we got right out and worked in the streets, which was a lot of fun because the Italians were used to seeing Italian filmmakers in the streets of Rome."

Soon Hollywood's cameras traveled all over the world. *Three Coins in the Fountain* was filmed in Rome in 1954, giving moviegoers their first CinemaScope tour of the Eternal City. *Summertime* (1955) was made in Venice, *Garden of Evil* (1954) in Mexico, *The African Queen* (1951) and *Mogambo* (1953) in Africa, *Soldier of Fortune* (1955) in Hong Kong, and *River of No Return* (1954) in British Columbia. In 1959 it was reported that thirty-two American pictures were currently being made in Italy, twenty-eight in France, and twenty in Great Britain.

Audiences began to expect a more realistic look from filmmakers, which reduced the need to build sets. Shooting motion pictures by the mid-1950s took longer than during the Golden Age to assure accuracy of detail. The six-week production schedules for the big pictures of the 1930s and 1940s gave way to three- and four-month schedules. Costs likewise skyrocketed. During the 1930s a major picture might cost $200,000 to $400,000; during the 1950s costs rose to $1 million to $3 million.

Not all the blockbusters proved successful; some were disasters. In 1959 MGM remade *Ben-Hur* at the extravagant cost of $15 million, with another $1.75 million for advertising. The film won the Academy Award for best picture that year and earned $96 million. Its success started an avalanche of epic remakes. MGM squandered much of its profits from *Ben-Hur* on a lavish reworking of *Mutiny on the Bounty* (1962), a troubled picture that ended the reign of Sol Siegel as studio head. *Four Horsemen of the Apocalypse* (1962) cost $7.8 million and was another catastrophe.

Yet the trend toward spectacles continued: *War and Peace* (1956), *Solomon and Sheba* (1959), *Spartacus* (1960), *El Cid* (1961), and *Lawrence of Arabia* (1962). *The Ten Commandments* (1956), made at a record cost of $13.5 million, had grossed $45 million by 1959 and is still shown on prime-time television every year. Directed by David Lean, *Lawrence of Arabia,* which tastefully intimated Lawrence's sexual confusion, won the Academy Award for best picture. There were exceptions, but most Hollywood spectacles were more popular with the public than with critics. In 1964 *The Fall of the Roman Empire* was almost universally judged a bore, despite its spectacle and all-star cast. Biblical epics frequently became ludicrous: *The Greatest Story Ever Told* (1965) had John Wayne as a Roman centurion supervising Christ's crucifixion, and *The Bible* (1966) found director John Huston alternating between the role of Noah and the voice of God.

Hollywood's most notorious debacle with gigantic productions came with a remake of *Cleopatra* (1963). In 1959 producer Walter Wanger informed Spyros Skouras, president of Twentieth Century-Fox, that he had a sensational idea that would rescue the studio from its current financial doldrums—an extravaganza based on the Roman romances of Cleopatra starring Elizabeth Taylor. Skouras not only accepted the notion, but *Cleopatra* became his obsession, and he approved an initial budget of $5 million for the project.

Toward the end of 1959 Elizabeth Taylor was signed for the title role at an unprecedented fee of $1.75 million. The picture's budget already had swollen to $10 million. Filming began in London during the fall of 1960 with Rouben Mamoulian as director, Stephen Boyd as Mark Antony, and Peter Finch as Caesar. Then Taylor became critically ill, and the production came to a halt. When work resumed almost a year later, the location had shifted to Rome; Joseph L. Mankiewicz was directing a rewritten screenplay, Rex Harrison was playing Caesar, and Richard Burton was Antony. Footage shot earlier had to be scrapped.

By November 1961, *Cleopatra* was again in trouble. Torrential rain and wind made location shooting impossible, while production costs reached $12.5 million. Publicity was endless, most of it centering around the off-screen romance of Elizabeth Taylor and Richard Burton, both of whom were married—Taylor to singer Eddie Fisher, whom she had recently lured away from actress Debbie Reynolds. Gossip columnists had a field day, turning the Taylor-Burton affair into the biggest scandal Hollywood had faced since Ingrid Bergman's pregnancy out of wedlock.

Still the production dragged on; by the close of 1961 costs on *Cleopatra* had reached $24 million. Twentieth Century-Fox, near financial ruin, defaulted on its bank loans. There was nothing to do but sell off the studio's extensive backlot, a valuable piece of commercial real estate that became Century City. Finally on July 24, 1962, filming on *Cleopatra* ended in Egypt. Total costs were estimated at $44 million, almost nine times the original budget. The disaster marked the end for Spyros Skouras, who was dismissed as the company's president by shareholders.

The original film ran more than three hours in length, before astute editors trimmed its running time by thirty-three minutes. *Cleopatra* opened to tepid reviews at the Rivoli Theatre in New York and at the Pantages in Los Angeles during June 1963, four years after its inception. Exhibitors agreed to pay Twentieth Century-Fox a $20 million guarantee, which just about covered the interest on bank loans. "The cost of that film was a disgrace," said veteran editor Elmo Williams, who worked on the picture. *Cleopatra* was a flawed spectacle at best and signaled the pitfalls of run-away productions, which more than once pushed Hollywood's studios to the brink during the decades ahead.

THE CHALLENGE FROM FOREIGN FILMS AND ART HOUSES

British filmmakers, led by Alexander Korda and J. Arthur Rank, began to challenge Hollywood's domestic market shortly after the close of World War II. *The Seventh Veil* (1945), *Black Narcissus* (1946), *Odd Man Out* (1947), and *The Blue Lagoon* (1949) became popular pictures with sophisticated American audiences, along with such English stars as Deborah Kerr, James Mason, Jean Simmons, and Stewart Granger. As the British film industry expanded after 1947, *Kind Hearts and Coronets* (1949), *The Man in the White Suit* (1952), and other comedies featuring Alec Guinness developed a cult following within the United States, as did pictures directed by Carol Reed and David Lean.

Postwar Italian realism in films, first seen in Roberto Rossellini's *Open City* (1945), made an impression not only on thoughtful American audiences, but also on Hollywood filmmakers. Rossellini's *Paisan* followed in 1946. The director seemed to create a newsreel-like immediacy in his films, using people off the street in key roles. Vittorio DeSica's *Shoeshine* (1946) and *The Bicycle Thief* (1948) continued the trend toward harsh reality in their depiction of life in postwar urban Italy. Federico Fellini's *La Strada* (1954) and *La Dolce Vita* (1961) reached a wider public, since Hollywood distributors by then had gained control of American rights to the pictures.

Japanese films, beginning with the ambiguous but strikingly original *Rashomon* in 1951, caused American audiences and critics to take notice. *Gate of Hell* and *Seven Samurai* (both 1954) also made strong impacts, enough that Hollywood remade the latter as *The Magnificent Seven* (1960), with Yul Brynner in the leading role.

The work of Swedish director Ingmar Bergman cut an even deeper impression with intelligent American audiences. *Smiles of a Summer Night* (1955), *Wild Strawberries* (1957), and *The Virgin*

Spring (1959) all found an enthusiastic following in the United States, while critics hailed Bergman as a visual poet of love.

One Summer of Happiness (1951), another Swedish film, created excitement when it was first shown in American theaters, because a couple was seen bathing nude in a lake, then photographed from the waist up during lovemaking. Five years later *And God Created Woman,* a French movie directed by Roger Vadim, proved a phenomenal success mainly because it showed actress Brigitte Bardot in the nude. Although controversial, both movies suggested that mass audiences in America might be ready for broader parameters of eroticism.

World War II, the atomic bomb, and the Cold War had forced the United States into closer community with other nations of the world. The imported European and Japanese films became models for a coterie of American intelligentsia who frequented theaters specializing in more artistic fare. By the early 1950s the movie-going public had begun to fragment; a split developed between those who saw movies as entertainment and those who saw them as art. Small independent movie theaters that had previously played fourth runs converted to foreign features and more artistic domestic productions to survive. Audiences there were selective, mainly college-educated adults, who became known in the business as "the art-house crowd." Not satisfied by repetitious television programming or the routine movies Hollywood continued to turn out, these sophisticated patrons came to be viewed as a "lost audience." Managers of intimate inner-city and neighborhood theaters, faced with the difficulty of luring suburbanites back into town for an evening's entertainment, carved out a niche for themselves by appealing to this elite.

Many of the art houses were located in college or university communities. Coffee, rare teas, and Swiss chocolates were sometimes sold in the lobbies where works of local artists were on display. Some theaters presented a mix of foreign films, documentaries, American classics, and avant-garde shorts. Charles Chaplin's *Monsieur Verdoux* (1947), which was boycotted by the major chains during the HUAC investigations, played mostly in art houses, grossing only $325,000 in the United States, although far more abroad. A number of the films exhibited in art houses were more sexually explicit than Hollywood's Production Code permitted, but many of them also contained deeper social messages.

In 1950 there were only eighty-three art houses in the United States, but by 1966 the number had increased to 664. New York

City and Los Angeles had twenty-five art houses each, and those theaters launched most of the new releases. The majority of the art houses were individually owned. They drew a consistent audience during the 1950s, reached their peak in the mid-1960s, and enjoyed major success with such acclaimed imports as *Never on Sunday* (1961), *Tom Jones* (1963), and *Blow-Up* (1967).

REACHING FOR MATURE AUDIENCES

The challenge for Hollywood was to find a way of satisfying the new art-house crowd without losing moviegoers looking for pure entertainment. Producers first tried to combine franker portrayals of American life with old-fashioned storytelling, turning out a number of problem pictures, realistically filmed. *Kiss of Death* (1947) dealt with gangsterism; *Body and Soul* (1948) drew a parallel between professional boxing and capitalism; *A Foreign Affair* (1948) offered a sardonic look at Congressmen on an investigation of occupied Berlin, as well as American military personnel; and *City Across the River* (1949) treated juvenile delinquency. All were photographed in stark black and white, yet none departed far from the Hollywood norm.

More adventuresome American filmmakers, taking their cue from the Italian neorealists, felt the need for an even more accurate look in their postwar pictures. *The House on 92nd Street* (1945) and *Call Northside 777* (1948) achieved authenticity by using actual settings.

To attract mature audiences Hollywood producers invested in best-selling novels, which provided stories that were pretested and presold. Robert Penn Warren's *All the King's Men* (1949) took a hard look at political corruption. The movie version of James Jones's *From Here to Eternity* (1953) is best remembered for its beach scene, with Burt Lancaster and Deborah Kerr making love amid breaking waves and torrential ocean spray. Harper Lee's *To Kill a Mockingbird* (1962) presented racial injustice in the South at a time when the civil rights movement was reaching a height.

Recent Broadway hits, including some with controversial themes, were purchased and made into movies to gratify adult tastes. Hollywood still contended with the limitations of censorship imposed by the Production Code Administration. Hints of homosexuality had to be eliminated from the screen versions of Tennessee Williams's *A Streetcar Named Desire* (1951) and *Cat on a Hot Tin*

Roof (1958). When *Tea and Sympathy* (1956) was filmed, the teacher's wife had to pay for her adultery, despite the kindness behind her act. Garson Kanin's *Born Yesterday* (1950), Arthur Miller's *Death of a Salesman* (1951), William Inge's *Picnic* (1955), and Eugene O'Neill's *Long Day's Journey into Night* (1962) were all successful plays before Hollywood made them into motion pictures. Nor were the classics forgotten; *Hamlet,* a British production released through an American distributor, won the Academy Award for best picture of 1948, and *Cyrano de Bergerac* earned Jose Ferrer the best actor award in 1950.

Original screenplays were also written with more sophisticated tastes in mind. Joseph L. Mankiewicz won double Academy Awards two years in a row for writing and directing *A Letter to Three Wives* (1949) and *All About Eve* (1950). Even westerns were reshaped into adult fare, most notably *High Noon* (1952) and *Shane* (1953). Director John Ford's famous cavalry trilogy reflected contemporary attitudes on the Cold War, moving from the conciliatory tone of *Fort Apache* (1948) to a more aggressive stance against marauding Apaches in *Rio Grande* (1950). The latter reached theaters soon after the outbreak of the Korean War and mirrored the MacArthur-Truman controversy then making headlines.

The investigations of the House Un-American Activities Committee continued to haunt Hollywood. *High Noon,* written by blacklisted writer Carl Foreman, was a parable of the Committee's attack on Hollywood and the movie colony's timidity in defending itself. Sheriff Will Kane, ironically played in the picture by friendly witness Gary Cooper, is threatened by a gang of ruffians (HUAC), who are on their way to Hadleyville (a fictionalized name for Hollywood). Kane has to fight the gunmen alone, since he is unable to find allies bold enough to stand with him.

Johnny Guitar (1954), which cast Joan Crawford as an unlikely western heroine, was another allegory of the McCarthy era. Suspected subversives (Crawford and her allies) are pitted against local vigilantes, with the final shootout a symbolic battle between intolerant upholders of conformity against nonconformists. As with *High Noon,* the atrocities of McCarthyism were viewed within the relative safety of a traditional western format.

In contrast, *On the Waterfront* (1954) attempted to vindicate the cooperative witnesses who had named names by emphasizing the valor of informers. The screenplay, which dealt with trade unionism and racketeering, was written by Budd Schulberg and directed by Elia Kazan, both of whom had named colleagues when they testified before HUAC in 1951 and 1952, respectively.

Although McCarthy fell from grace during his televised debate with the U.S. Army in 1954, the Hollywood blacklist continued until 1960. Actors and actresses listed in *Red Channels* remained barred from films, whereas blacklisted writers often worked under assumed names. Dalton Trumbo, one of the Hollywood Ten, won the Academy Award for best screenplay in 1956 under the alias Robert Rich. Rich was not present to accept his award, but insiders knew who he was. Still, the hypocrisy continued. The script for *The Bridge on the River Kwai* (1957), an award-winning box office sensation, was attributed to Pierre Boule, author of the novel on which the movie was based. Boule, however, spoke no English; the screenplay was actually the work of Carl Foreman and Michael Wilson, both blacklisted writers.

Finally in 1960 director Otto Preminger courageously announced his hiring of Dalton Trumbo to write the script for his next picture, *Exodus*. That same year actor-producer Kirk Douglas dared to give Trumbo screen credit for his clandestine work in writing *Spartacus*.

Already observers were lamenting that too much of Hollywood's output was negative in content. Of the fifteen top films in 1959, all were judged to be preponderantly bitter or cynical, including the one comedy, *Some Like It Hot*. Two years later, *Films in Review* claimed that 1961 would be remembered in motion picture history as the year that "even reputable producers exploited vice and degeneracy in feature films without shame or hindrance."

BREAKING WITH TRADITION

During the postwar effort to heighten reality in motion pictures, "method" acting made a major impact on Hollywood. The "method" began in Russia with Konstantin Stanislavski at the Moscow Art Theatre and placed emphasis on psychological realism. In America, the Group Theatre of the 1930s had adopted the more naturalistic approach to acting that Stanislavski advocated, but Hollywood's initial exposure to "method" acting came from John Garfield and Lee J. Cobb, both products of the Group Theatre. Garfield's moody performance in *The Postman Always Rings Twice* (1946) anticipated what would come later from actors trained at the Actors Studio, soon the center of the "method" approach in America.

The Actors Studio opened in New York on October 5, 1947, under the direction of Elia Kazan, Robert Lewis, and Cheryl Crawford, all former Group Theatre members. In the 1950s Lee Strasberg, another Group stalwart, became the backbone of the Actors Studio, as the "method" established itself as the dominant acting style on the contemporary Broadway stage.

Over the next decade a new generation of young actors appeared in Hollywood, embodying a sensitivity, anguish, and estrangement shared by much of the postwar youth. Montgomery Clift, Marlon Brando, and James Dean were among the first, followed by Paul Newman, Julie Harris, Rod Steiger, Joanne Woodward, and Eva Marie Saint. Montgomery Clift, a handsome actor tormented by sexual confusion, made his screen debut in *The Search* (1948), then rocketed to fame in *Red River* (later in 1948), playing opposite John Wayne. Clift spoke naturally, showed tremendous vulnerability, and pulled from within himself intense emotions that he conveyed with power and lyricism. Brando had the body of an animal, but like Clift possessed the face of a poet and the ability to communicate a wide range of emotions.

Spencer Tracy and other established Hollywood actors denounced the "method" as nonsense, yet it became the vogue for a younger generation. Dustin Hoffman, Steve McQueen, Robert Redford, Shelley Winters, and Geraldine Page all spent their formative years at the Actors Studio and were molded by the "method" approach.

But Hollywood's maturity was impeded as long as pictures still had to acquire the approval of the Production Code Administration to play in major theaters. The Production Code had been devised during the 1930s to assure exhibitors that films would have nothing distasteful or immoral about them, nor were they to be advertised in a salacious way. The gap between the screen image of life and present-day reality had unmistakably widened. Hollywood's false depiction of American life was out of sync with the contemporary mood and stood as an obstacle to mature drama. At their worst the old Hollywood fairy tales about success and prosperity, pristine virtue, and endless happiness appeared ludicrous, if not downright insulting, to postwar audiences.

The first serious challenge to Hollywood's production and advertising codes came in 1946 when Howard Hughes's *The Outlaw* finally reached the theaters after a long dispute with the censors. Joseph Breen, head of the Production Code Administration, objected strongly to "the countless shots of Rio (played in the film by Jane Russell, an actress of heroic physical proportions), in which her breasts are not fully covered." Hughes refused to alter his movie, which included scenes of sadism and others with homosexual overtones. He hired Russell Birdwell, the publicist who had handled the promotional campaign for *Gone with the Wind* (1939), and instructed Birdwell to flood the press and billboards across the nation with provocative pictures of Jane Russell lying in a haystack. "How would you like to tussle with Russell?" the advertisements read.

When *The Outlaw* was released by United Artists, a number of independent theaters were willing to exhibit it even though the film lacked a seal of approval from the Production Code Administration. Hughes's prolonged battle with the censors had a salutary effect on the box office; by 1948 his western had earned more than $3 million.

Otto Preminger's comedy *The Moon Is Blue* was denied approval by the Breen office in 1953 because the script dealt with adulterous conduct and contained such phrases as "professional virgin." Preminger refused to sanitize his picture, determined to present to movie audiences essentially the same play that theater patrons had enjoyed for more than two years on Broadway. *The Moon Is Blue* was issued by United Artists without a Production Code seal; it played in first-run theaters and returned $8.5 million within twenty-one weeks. Albert Van Schmus, a member of the censorship office, later said:

> *The Moon Is Blue* did violate the [Production Code's] sections on sex, but that didn't make it wrong or offensive. Preminger was a very tasteful man.

In 1954 the Production Code Administration objected to Jane Russell's "violent wiggling" in *The French Line,* which the censors found "grossly obscene, suggestive, and indecent." RKO announced its intention of releasing the picture without a Production Code seal, which it did with no apparent loss of business. The next year Otto Preminger began work on *The Man with the Golden Arm,* a film dealing with drug addiction, a subject specifically forbidden by the censorship office. The picture, released in 1956 without the seal of approval, was a box office success for major theater chains, and won praise from most critics.

In December 1956 a modernized Production Code went into effect, which allowed a broader freedom of expression. The new censorship guidelines permitted filmmakers to show prostitution, drug deals, kidnapping, and abortion, none of which had been tolerated under the old system. Subjects that would have been verboten earlier soon appeared on the screen. *Baby Doll* (1956) cast Carroll Baker as the child-wife of middle-aged Karl Malden; the girl sleeps in a crib, sucks her thumb, and has not yet consummated her marriage with her lusting husband. Billy Wilder's *The Apartment* (1960) portrayed with acid wit amoral ambition, executive-level adultery, and male chauvinism. In 1961 William Wyler remade Lillian Hellman's *The Children's Hour,* this time giving frank attention to the story's lesbian theme. In *Advise and Consent,* produced and directed by Otto Preminger in 1962, a U.S. Senator is accused of homosexuality and a fleeting glimpse of a gay bar is shown. *The Chapman Report* (also 1962) was a fictionalized story about a Kinsey-type team researching sexual practices in the United States. Suddenly American life did not seem as tidy or as neatly resolved as it had been portrayed during Hollywood's Golden Age.

APPEALING TO THE TEENAGE MARKET

During the early 1950s an estimated 70 to 75 percent of the American film industry's audience was less than thirty years of age, with the greater portion coming from the fourteen to twenty-five-year-old bracket. With one-third of the urban population living in the suburbs by 1960, Hollywood responded with movies centering around the new lifestyle. *Father of the Bride* (1950) and *Father's Little Dividend* (1951) aimed at depicting a typical American suburban family.

Not only were teenagers becoming more numerous, they were also more independent and affluent than formerly. As suburban teenagers grew older, home became a place they seemed to want to escape. Most of the youngsters had cars, money, freedom in dating, and they preferred to build a separate life among their own age group. The "rock 'n' roll culture" emerged, in revolt against the conformity, materialism, and the conventional thinking of their elders. Teenagers wanted entertainment designed especially for them and movies that reflected their values and contemporary vogues. By the mid-1950s every studio in Hollywood was producing pictures targeted mainly at young audiences.

The Wild One (1954), *The Blackboard Jungle* (1955), and *Rebel Without a Cause* (1955) were among the first to deal with teenage

James Dean, Hollywood's symbol of rebellious youth in the 1950s.

problems. Whereas weekly television series, such as *Father Knows Best* (1954-1960) and *Leave It to Beaver* (1957-1963), showed idealized family units, the features Hollywood produced for the youth market during the 1950s more often focused on splintered, disintegrating families and juvenile delinquency. *The Wild One* found Marlon Brando as the leader of a motorcycle gang and pictured the clash between hipster America and traditional middle-class mores. *The Blackboard Jungle* linked teenage rebellion to rock 'n' roll and featured Bill Haley's "Rock Around the Clock" on the soundtrack. *Rebel Without a Cause,* an even bigger hit because of the presence of James Dean, portrayed bored, misunderstood, angry adolescents who reject the sterile, unctuous world of their parents, yet have found no meaningful substitute.

For adult viewers these films confirmed what they read in the newspapers—that America's youth was disaffected, rebellious, and "running wild." The new styles in dress and grooming seemed to prove the point: the greasy look, ducktail haircuts, black leather jackets, T-shirts with a package of cigarettes rolled up in one sleeve. There was a new vocabulary many found distasteful—words like "cool," "cat," "chick," and "hip." But worst of all was the music, the loud rock 'n' roll beat and libidinous lyrics that the big band generation found difficult to fathom.

Teenagers meanwhile welcomed the changes as part of *their* culture and looked for a figurehead to symbolize the rebellion taking place. At first their hero seemed to be Marlon Brando, but when Brando put on a suit and sang and danced in the movie version of *Guys and Dolls* (1955), he began to look too much like Dad. That was a betrayal. What the teen cult wanted was a hero who would remain permanently young, someone as confused and as inarticulate as they were. And if he or she became a martyr, so much the better.

When the twenty-four-year-old actor James Dean was killed in an automobile collision on September 30, 1955, he became the icon teenage America had been waiting for. Dean made only three films, and only one of those—*East of Eden* (1955)—had been released before his death. When *Rebel Without a Cause* appeared in the theaters, he had been dead four weeks. Suddenly, teenage boys from coast to coast began combing their hair the way Dean had, wore jeans and jackets like his, and tried to smoke as he had. Fan clubs sprang up across the country, and Dean's brooding image seemed to be everywhere—inside high school lockers and taped to covers of loose-leaf notebooks. Girls claimed to be pregnant by him, and dozens of songs were written about him: "Hymn to James Dean," "Goodbye, My Jamie Boy," even "James Dean's Christmas in Heaven."

During his short life Dean exhibited many of the characteristics members of his cult admired. A charismatic "method" actor who drew from his own experience, he conveyed insecurity and vulnerability, yet was rebellious and unconventional in his public behavior. When he arrived in Hollywood, he played the young iconoclast, shocking and confusing the old guard. Julie Harris, Dean's costar in *East of Eden,* said:

> To me he was the personification of Tom Sawyer. Like Peter Pan, he didn't want to grow up. "Where's the next adventure?" is what I would put on Jimmy's tombstone. It was thrilling to be around somebody who was so alive and perceptive and engaged life with such appetite and enthusiasm. Jimmy was an extraordinary person.

A new batch of teenage idols appeared on the screen during the early 1950s—Tony Curtis, Robert Wagner, and Tab Hunter among others—yet none would equal the impact James Dean made. "Movie personalities were emerging who looked and acted very much like the kids in my neighborhood," screen actor John Saxon said later, himself a teenage heartthrob of those years. "Suddenly there was a class of movie star that was very identifiable to kids— unlike Gable and the older stars—and seemed to be close to us in manners and mores and dress."

After Dean's death, rock star Elvis Presley was crowned "the king" by teenage audiences. Presley's first movie, *Love Me Tender* (1956), set box office records across the country. Producer Hal Wallis, who had the singer under contract, quickly found scripts that cast him as the sensitive outsider, yet allowed for his sensual rock 'n' roll music. Throughout the decade Presley's pictures had an assured following. Said actress Lizabeth Scott, who starred opposite him in *Loving You* (1957):

> Elvis was so talented. I shall never forget his eyes, so mature and so exquisite. He was the most polite young man, but untouchable. He always had an entourage around him. Yet he was a simple man, a little boy actually.

The studios did their best to satiate the youth market with movies within Hollywood's established parameters. Clean-cut singer Pat Boone appeared in *Bernardine* and *April Love* (both 1957), revealing the eagerness of producers to exploit current teenage idols. Debbie Reynolds, a girl-next-door type, starred with success in *Tammy and the Bachelor* (also 1957), and later there was a series of inane, yet highly profitable Muscle Beach pictures featuring Frankie Avalon and Annette Funicello, beginning with *Beach Party* (1963). But traditional movies that offered a teenage star or two were not enough.

Although most suburban adolescents had access to automobiles by the time they reached high school, many of them were reluctant to drive into the urban center on dates and add parking fees onto ticket prices to see a movie. Still, there were few movie houses, if any, in their neighborhoods. The quickest and cheapest way of constructing theaters within easy reach of the suburbs was for exhibitors to acquire a piece of land on the outskirts of a city, build a screen at one end, add a sound system and a projection booth in the middle, and open a drive-in, where patrons could watch a movie from parked cars. Couples with small children could take their kids along, and most drive-ins provided a playground where youngsters could amuse themselves before the show started. Some had picnic areas, laundry facilities, miniature golf courses, and bottle-warming services. There was little need to dress up, and the cost was modest, usually around two dollars a carload, no matter how many people squeezed inside. Teenagers particularly found drive-ins appealing. They were cheap, gave minors a place to drink beer without being caught, and allowed dating couples enough privacy to make love in relative seclusion and safety.

The drive-in concept had been launched in 1933, but at the close of World War II fewer than 300 outdoor theaters were operating in the United States. By 1950 the number had grown to more than 2,000 and by 1958 to 4,700, nearly one-third of all movie theaters in the country. Construction costs were a fraction of what it took to build new four-wall theaters, and returns could be high. Although attendance at drive-ins was limited to a thirty-week season in most parts of the country, in the South and Southwest the theaters stayed open all year long. In 1958, with indoor movie houses closing at a rate of roughly two a day, drive-ins accounted for 25 percent of all domestic film rentals.

Much of the income for drive-in owners came from concession stands. By 1955 outdoor theaters sold about four times as much candy, popcorn, and soft drinks as indoor theaters did. But drive-ins also sold pizza, barbecue, french fries, onion rings, and hot dogs. Carhops frequently moved from car to car taking orders.

Adults began to complain about unreliable sound systems, noise from "wild" teenagers in adjacent cars, and the general discomfort of seeing movies from behind the dashboard of an automobile.

Gradually the high school crowd dominated the drive-in business, and, as that happened, management noted that young people favored movies tailored especially to them, much as they preferred music that was predominantly theirs.

The need for "teenpics," as these exploitation films were called, was met by a few small production companies newly arrived on the Hollywood scene. American International Pictures (AIP), which released its first feature, a drag-racing movie called *The Fast and the Furious* (1954), led the way and thrived on the drive-in market. Budgets on "teenpics" were kept to a minimum, shooting schedules were short, and the tawdry pictures were usually shown on a double or triple bill with movies similar in length, budget, and kind. Productions looked amateurish, but they were filled with action, thrills, and gore. Mamie Van Doren, usually seen in a white cashmere sweater several sizes too small, was a frequent star, yet any number of actors and actresses learned their craft in the cheap exploitation films of the late 1950s and early 1960s. Titles are indicative of content: *Teenage Crime Wave* (1955), *Hot Rod Girl* (1956), *Untamed Youth* (1957), *High School Confidential* (1958), and *Sex Kittens Go to College* (1960).

ROGER CORMAN, NEW KING OF THE B'S

American International Pictures's premier producer-director, Roger Corman, mastered low-budget filmmaking techniques and made movies that sold on their topicality and sensationalism rather than on stars and production values. Corman directed forty-nine features between 1955 and 1970 and produced at least four times that many, demonstrating speed, economy, and a keen sense of the youth market. "The whole idea," said Corman, "was to tell an interesting, visually entertaining story that would draw young people to the drive-ins and hardtop cinemas, and not take yourself too seriously along the way."

His first picture was a science fiction thriller called *Monster from the Ocean Floor* (1954), which the twenty-seven-year-old filmmaker shot on location in Malibu in six days at a cost of $12,000. The movie returned a profit of $110,000. The next year Corman directed *The Day the World Ended* on a ten-day shooting schedule for $96,000. *Attack of the Crab Monsters* (1957), which combined humor with horror, cost $70,000 and took in more than $1 million at the box office. "To me, the horror film is essentially the re-creation of childhood fear," said Corman.

He churned out eight seventy-minute features in 1956 and nine in 1957, capitalizing on teenage anxieties, violence, and horror. *Teenage Doll* (1957) was Corman's first picture about juvenile delinquency, followed that same year by *Sorority Girl.* During production he knew a shortcut for everything and expected performers to come to work prepared. "When I made movies with Roger Corman," character actor Dick Miller said, "the only way you did a second take was if the camera fell over." Casts worked long hours and usually went home exhausted. "I call it the 'blood and guts' kind of moviemaking," said actress Beverly Garland, who appeared in several of Corman's films. "We did them fast, but we all cared terribly about our work. It was the best training in the world."

Corman wrote of his schedule in 1961: "*Blood Island* finished on a Saturday and I started *Last Woman* on Monday. Two Saturdays later we wrapped *Last Woman* and were ready to start *Creature from the Haunted Sea* the following Monday—one day of preproduction per picture." His speed, the director claimed, allowed him more freedom to experiment than would have been possible on big-budget movies.

Roger Corman was always a businessman first; not one of his pictures lost money, and he exploited current events and contemporary trends. On October 4, 1957, Americans were stunned when the Russians successfully launched their satellite *Sputnik.* Three months later Corman had *War of the Satellites* on drive-in screens. It was one of the fastest movies ever produced. The script was written in less than two weeks, but Corman understood that there was cash in the satellite craze if he moved quickly.

Corman made westerns, gangster pictures, and movies about outsiders and misfits, and in time attempted social comment. *Machine Gun Kelly* (1958), starring Charles Bronson, and *Bloody Mama* (1969), with Shelley Winters as Kate Barker, stand out among his gangster films. "It's a free country, but unless you're rich. you ain't free," said Ma Barker. "I aim to be freer than the rest of the people." Of the features Corman directed, *The Little Shop of Horrors* (1960) has probably attracted the widest cult following. Principal photography on the picture was completed in two days and an evening on a vacant soundstage, but *The Little Shop of Horrors* began a new genre: the black-comedy horror film. *The Wild Angels* (1966) dealt with motorcycle gangs at the height of public awareness of the notorious Hell's Angels. *The Trip* (1967) focused on the drug subculture then making headlines and starred Peter Fonda and Dennis Hopper.

Corman's most aesthetic achievement came with a series of eight relatively big-budget movies adapted from the stories of Edgar Allan Poe, all of which Corman directed himself. He had enjoyed Poe's stories and poems as a boy and launched his cycle in 1960 with *The Fall of the House of Usher.* The film returned $3.5 million and created a new audience for actor Vincent Price, who starred in the series. *The Pit and the Pendulum* (1961) cost $200,000 but did even better than its predecessor at the box office. *The Tomb of Ligeia* (1964) brought the cycle to a close, but all eight films proved lucrative and lifted AIP's product to a level of respectability.

Corman's work, including the Poe series, was dismissed by contemporary critics as lowbrow, although his reputation abroad became stronger than in the United States. His characters dwell in a bleak world, surrounded by failing social institutions and death. In Corman's view, life seems pointless, empty, and absurd. Many of his people attempt to withdraw into an artificial, self-created environment, but even that is in constant danger of collapse. When asked about the dreariness of his output, the filmmaker replied, "You reflect what you see around you."

Corman's skill and personality were reflected in every aspect of the films he made. As Beverly Garland recalled:

> Roger was the boss. He put the package together and did the writing. Roger did it all. If the cameraman had had a heart attack, he probably would have pushed him to the side and taken over the camera. That's how Roger was; he could do everything.

Corman's success enabled AIP to expand its operations during the 1960s and produce an average of twenty pictures a year between 1963 and 1973, mostly designed for young audiences. Since the major studios were no longer making budget films, AIP filled a void, placing its product in theaters that lacked the resources to bid for potential blockbusters.

THE SCIENCE FICTION CRAZE

Much of AIP's income came from science fiction, beginning with the company's first big moneymaker, *The Beast with 1,000 Eyes* (1954).

World War II, with its technological advances (especially in weaponry and rockets), the atomic bomb, and the Cold War all stimulated an interest in science fiction, and during the 1950s the "sci-fi" boom reached major proportions. Many of the decade's monster pictures stemmed from fears about nuclear testing and anxieties over the possibility of atomic warfare. Another factor behind the craze was the paranoia that swept the country with the "flying saucer" scare that started in 1947 and persisted for more than a decade.

The postwar interest in filmed science fiction was demonstrated with *Destination Moon* (1950) and *When Worlds Collide* (1951), medium-budget films that were highly successful. In *The Day the Earth Stood Still* (1951), a better movie than the others, earthlings are warned by a superior force from outer space to mend their ways or face destruction.

The Beast from 20,000 Fathoms (1953) was Hollywood's first movie to pose the dangers of nuclear testing. In the picture a nuclear explosion in the Arctic melts an iceberg that releases a "rhedosaurus" frozen inside. The beast heads for New York, where it wreaks havoc on Manhattan and destroys Coney Island. The military eventually kills the monster by firing a nuclear missile into its mouth. The film's message apparently is that nuclear weapons can resolve problems they create, but the public controversy over further testing continued.

Invasion of the Body Snatchers (1956) touched on the issue of conformity, which many felt had replaced individuality as the key to success in contemporary America. The movie shows giant pods taking over people's bodies; the pods are regimented and emotionless, yet tranquil and obedient. They have become technological monsters, which some feared could become a reality. *Invasion of the Body Snatchers* has been regarded by some film scholars as a masterpiece of social commentary; for certain it reflects the tensions of the period in which it was made.

The Creature from the Black Lagoon (1954) was another huge success, also becoming a cult classic. Screenwriter Harry Essex admitted:

> When I was assigned by the studio to *Creature from the Black Lagoon,* I wanted to quit. I was embarrassed. Then I realized that it was "Beauty and the Beast," a story that has worked for hundreds of years.

The creature in the movie was purposely designed to look like the Academy Awards' Oscar, and Julie Adams, who starred in the movie, remembered that the monster was played by two performers: one inside the suit for underwater scenes and another to carry her around on land.

The Gamma People (1956) was followed by *The Incredible Shrinking Man* (1957) and *I Married a Monster from Outer Space* (1958). Scores of "sci-fi" stories began after the bomb, and their exploitation titles earned them frequent scorn from Parent-Teacher Associations across the country. Still, they continued to fare well at the box office, appealing especially to younger audiences.

Science fiction plots often were combined with elements from the classic horror films. *I Was a Teenage Werewolf* (1957), part teenage problem picture, part horror movie, introduced Michael Landon as a high school student who sprouts fangs. Director Gene Fowler, Jr., read the script he had been assigned and initially thought it was terrible. Without consulting his producer, Herman Cohen, Fowler started rewriting. "I made Landon a fellow who really had the good of the world at heart," the director said. "We were shooting so fast that Cohen never knew I was rewriting the script." *I Was a Teenage Werewolf* cost $82,000 and earned back its cost within two weeks; it went on to gross $14 million, an unprecedented return for an AIP film. *I Was a Teenage Frankenstein* followed within a few months.

But the final word on the atom bomb came not from an inexpensive exploitation film, but from producer-director Stanley Kramer. Kramer's *On the Beach* (1959) portrayed the bomb as a deadly force capable of destroying the world. In Kramer's picture an atomic war has annihilated life in every part of the planet except southernmost Australia. A radioactive shroud moves down from the north, as Melbourne prepares for the end. Whereas Hollywood tended to portray the American military as infallible in the decade's earlier movies, after the release of *On the Beach* the tone became more critical. Stanley Kubrick's satire *Dr. Strangelove or: How I Learned to Stop Worrying and Love the Bomb* (1964) views the bomb as lacking any redeeming features, while both Russian and American military and governmental leaders are pictured as incompetent warmongers.

RECOGNITION OF BLACK AUDIENCES

The fantasy world represented by studios during Hollywood's Golden Era was basically a world populated by whites. The classic American films were produced by whites for whites. When black people appeared on screen, which was rare, they were stereotyped as loyal servants or entertainers. Almost never were they pictured as mature individuals with fully formed lives of their own. A few films were made with all-black casts—*Hallelujah!* (1929), *Green Pastures* (1936), *Cabin in the Sky* and *Stormy Weather* (both 1943)—and a handful of black actors and actresses achieved international recognition—Paul Robeson, Lena Horne, Canada Lee, Stepin' Fetchit, Hattie McDaniel, and Butterfly McQueen among them. But the roles they played in movies were either subservient or in no way a threat to white domination.

Black filmmakers had existed in the United States since 1910, but their work was virtually unknown to whites. They labored against tremendous odds to make independent features for black audiences. During the 1930s and 1940s the black community, sensitive to the stereotypes being presented to the general public, frequented such African American–made movies as *Murder in Harlem* (1935), *Bronze Venus* (1938), and *Juke Joint* (1947), shown in exclusively black theaters in larger towns.

Although these films had little or no interference from white backers, they contained their own stereotypes. Light-skinned actors with straight hair and "Aryan" looks tended to play leading and romantic roles, while darker-skinned, kinky-haired performers with "African" looks most often played comic, parental, or less important parts. Drinking, fighting, and gambling were viewed as characteristic of "low-life" types in black films.

With the integration movement of the 1950s and the advances in civil rights during the 1960s, separate black theaters died out. When blacks were able to attend any theater or restaurant they chose and gained the freedom to apply to whatever college they wanted, they entered the American mainstream in a fuller sense. After 1948 Hollywood paid more attention to blacks and consciously tried to avoid depictions that would offend minorities.

A plea for tolerance and racial justice paved the way for movies holding greater appeal for African American audiences without alienating liberal whites. In *Home of the Brave* (1949) an educated, emotionally disturbed black soldier is cured of psychosomatic paralysis by a white psychiatrist. The black hero is easily accepted since he exemplifies values no different from professional whites. But *Home of the Brave* made an enormous impact and established a trend toward well-intentioned problem movies, limited nonetheless by neat Hollywood formulas.

Lost Boundaries (1949) was produced by documentary film-maker Louis de Rochemont and employed a largely nonprofessional cast. Based on a true story, *Lost Boundaries* told of a black doctor and his wife, both light-skinned and well-educated, who succeed in passing for white. Although members of the black press criticized de Rochemont for using white actors to play black family members, the movie was greeted with wide enthusiasm.

The title character in *Pinky* (1949) is a black nurse light-skinned enough to pass for white. Pinky (played by Caucasian actress Jeanne Crain) becomes romantically involved with a white doctor who is unaware of her background. When he proposes marriage, she grows frightened and returns home in confusion, ultimately deciding to stay there and open a clinic and training center for black nurses.

Intruder in the Dust (still 1949), based on a novel by William Faulkner, graphically depicted the discrimination blacks faced in the South, and *No Way Out* (1950), the last in this series of black problem pictures from major studios, pressed its point harder by showing a brutal race riot, a warning of things to come should America remain racially divided.

No Way Out introduced actor Sidney Poitier in films, playing a gentle black doctor fighting against racial prejudice. Poitier's robust, friendly personality endeared him to general audiences, and his roles were written so that sexual overtones were eliminated. With *Lilies of the Field* (1963) he became the first black to win an Academy Award for best actor. Poitier later commented on the "one-dimensional, middle-class imagery" he embodied throughout his early career. "I knew that however inadequate my step appeared," he said, "it was important that we make it."

By the 1960s there were noticeable improvements in Hollywood's depiction of blacks. Lorraine Hansberry's *A Raisin in the Sun,* a classic of black theater made into a movie in 1961, marked a noteworthy attempt to deal with the African American experience from inside with honesty. As the decade progressed, blacks more frequently were cast as doctors, nurses, lawyers, teachers, and business executives. In *Paris Blues* (1961) American jazzmen abroad are presented as articulate, interracial soulmates. Greater numbers of black actors and actresses appeared on the screen, among them Dorothy Dandridge, Harry Belafonte, Ossie Davis, and Ruby Dee. As Poitier wrote, "The image of the black man just scratching his head was changing."

THE MARRIAGE WITH TELEVISION

During the early 1950s most prime-time television programming originated in New York City and was broadcast live. Hollywood moguls faced competition from the new medium by inserting provisions in their contracts with actors forbidding them to appear on television shows. Studio executives tended to dismiss early video programming as slipshod and unworthy of serious consideration. When Marilyn Monroe asks George Sanders in *All About Eve* if they have auditions for television, Sanders (playing an acid-tongued critic) replies, "Auditions, my dear, are *all* they have on television."

With Hollywood's talent largely unavailable for television, broadcasters turned to older performers from vaudeville, burlesque, and nightclubs, such as Milton Berle and Pinky Lee, as well as established radio personalities like Jack Benny, George Burns, and Gracie Allen. For dramatic shows they relied on stage actors or stars no longer bound by exclusive contracts to a Hollywood studio. When Metro-Goldwyn-Mayer failed to renew Keenan Wynn's contract, for example, the character player moved to New York and launched a significant career in weekly dramatic anthologies. "Live television saved my life," said Wynn, "because I was rediscovered as an actor."

Early television's prestigious live dramas, such as *General Electric Theatre, DuPont Theatre,* and *Schlitz Playhouse of the Stars* contributed mightily to what is now considered the medium's Golden Age. *Studio One* was CBS's long-running dramatic anthology series, but the network also offered exceptional plays on *Playhouse 90,* an hour-and-a-half show, and *Climax.* NBC's premier dramatic series was the *Philco/Goodyear Playhouse,* a half-hour show that rehearsed for four days and went on the air the fifth. Since television studios were located on the edge of the Broadway theater district, producers drew mainly from that pool of talent. "Actors were shuttling from theater plays at night to television rehearsals during the day," director Paul Bogart remembered. "When the television show aired, actors would simply miss their stage show that night." Occasionally performers were rushed from a nearby television studio to a theater where the curtain was being held for their arrival.

Most players found the pressure of live television frightening, since millions of people were watching. Opening night on the dramatic anthologies was also closing night, and disasters frequently happened as performers moved from one set to another. Preparation time was limited, there was always a scramble for enough suitable scripts, and production staffs were small. Delbert Mann, who directed both the television and movie versions of *Marty,* was one of two directors on the *Philco Playhouse* for three years. "You simply had to grind it out and wing it," said Mann. "But live television was a fantastic training ground for actors, writers, and directors."

A new generation of actors and actresses emerged from early television: Paul Newman, Anne Bancroft, Steve McQueen, Grace Kelly, Rod Steiger, and Eva Marie Saint, all of whom solidified their reputations in motion pictures later. Such future film directors as George Roy Hill, Sydney Pollack, Arthur Penn, Sidney Lumet, and Sam Peckinpah learned their craft in live television. And television writers, led by Paddy Chayefsky, Horton Foote, and Rod Serling, soon found their way to Hollywood and adjusted their styles to the big screen.

Paddy Chayefsky observed:

> The physical limitations of live television production necessitated a certain kind of writing. In television we were doing miniatures. I used to call them "dramatic portraits," very intimate material. We were writing for the small screen and a small audience, maybe two or three people in a room. Live television presented middle-class drama, small little problems inside the normal home, the problems of the audience that watched the shows.

In 1955 agent-producer Harold Hecht, in partnership with actor Burt Lancaster, decided to transfer Chayefsky's *Marty* to the screen, the first television show expanded into a filmed feature. It was an enormous gamble. *Marty* was a low-key story about a shy Bronx butcher and his unglamorous girlfriend. "I think Hecht-Lancaster did it against the advice of almost everybody in Hollywood," said director Delbert Mann. "But Harold was from the Bronx and identified with the character." The realism of the modest production drew attention, and the picture proved an enormous success, winning the Academy Award for best picture of the year.

Suddenly there was a demand for other inexpensive films based on television plays. Chayefsky's *The Catered Affair* reached the screen in 1956, starring Bette Davis. *Twelve Angry Men,* directed by Sidney Lumet, followed in 1957 and starred Henry Fonda.

By then most prime-time television programming had moved to Hollywood, and nearly all of it was on film. Heads of networks soon realized that filmed shows offered multiple advantages over live productions, especially in the airing of weekly series. Telefilms could be photographed outdoors and aired at convenient times— earlier on the East Coast, later in the far west. Most important, they would generate additional revenue from reruns and foreign distribution. Hollywood possessed the facilities, which New York did not, to ensure a continuous supply of telefilms, including empty soundstages and an abundance of trained technicians. Both NBC and CBS built extensive production facilities in Los Angeles during 1951, but by the mid-1950s Hollywood's major studios had moved headlong into the television market and soon produced the bulk of network programming.

With the appearance of telefilms, the distinction between motion pictures and the television medium became less distinct. Action-adventure series quickly outnumbered dramatic anthologies in network schedules, destroying for many the aesthetic promise that television had shown earlier. With the decline in the number of feature films, three-quarters of the work force in Hollywood studios was employed on prime-time television shows by the early 1960s.

United Artists set up a television arm as early as 1948, whereas Eagle-Lion Studios, a small postwar operation, vanished within a few years and its facilities were converted to television programming. In 1949 Columbia Pictures formed a subsidiary, Screen Gems Inc., to produce television shows and commercials. Three years later Columbia announced a $1 million agreement with the Ford Motor Company to make thirty-nine half-hour films for NBC's *Ford Theatre*, using Hollywood actors. In 1955 Warner Bros. launched a weekly series for ABC, consisting of hour-long episodes based on Warner's classics *Casablanca* and *King's Row.* Soon Metro-Goldwyn-Mayer and Fox entered the field with *The MGM Parade,* a half-hour program of shorts, and *The Twentieth Century-Fox Theatre,* which premiered with a remake of Fox's *The Ox-Bow Incident* (1943).

Toward the end of the decade, television production was keeping most of the studios afloat. Screen Gems scored a popular hit with *Father Knows Best,* a weekly comedy show that starred Robert Young and remained on the air for five seasons. Warner Bros. Television did well with 77 *Sunset Strip, Maverick,* and *Cheyenne,* using stock footage from their vast film library. In 1959 twenty-three television series were made at the Warner Bros. studio, while most of the feature films were shot on location.

By then Desilu, an independent television production company headed by Desi Arnaz and Lucille Ball, held a controlling interest in the old RKO studio, where *I Love Lucy, Our Miss Brooks,* and *December Bride* were filmed, all comedy series with top ratings. Republic Studios was sold for television programming in 1958. Paramount earlier had spent $2 million to turn the old Warner Bros. studio on Sunset Boulevard into facilities for station KTLA, and the studio itself became active in television production. In 1953 United Paramount Theatres, the theater chain detached from Paramount Pictures as a result of the divorcement decrees, merged with the American Broadcasting Company, the third-ranking network behind CBS and NBC.

As live prime-time programming declined, Hollywood became the supplier in commercial broadcasting, while New York remained the exhibitor. Weekly series with continuing characters were modeled after the old budget movies and employed some of the same directors. Much of the technical personnel released by the demise of the big studio system found themselves working again. Television production might be less glamorous and less well publicized than making movies for theaters, but it was more dependable and had the advantage of residuals. By 1963 Hollywood produced almost 70 percent of the prime-time network programming.

Studio heads soon discovered that weekly television shows could be used to promote current theatrical features. Walt Disney began the trend in 1954 when his studio contracted with ABC to produce a weekly hour-long show called *Disneyland,* which advertised the Disneyland theme park that opened in Anaheim the next year. Disney adroitly exploited the merchandising possibilities offered by his series, beginning with the Davy Crockett rage of 1955, when coonskin caps, an assortment of toys, lunch boxes, tablets, T-shirts, and many other items bearing the frontiersman's screen likeness flooded the market for several months.

Music Corporation of America (MCA) entered the field of television production early in the 1950s through its subsidiary Revue, which enjoyed major success with such weekly shows as *Alfred Hitchcock Presents, Wagon Train,* and *Bachelor Father.* By 1959, with Revue becoming the largest producer of telefilms, MCA bought Universal's studio facilities and continued its spectacular growth, earning an immediate return from its investment by renting space back to Universal for filming its own productions.

Television companies began raiding the ranks of Hollywood's stars. Loretta Young signed for a weekly series in 1952, Bob Cummings two years later. By the end of the decade Ann Sothern, Barbara Stanwyck, Groucho Marx, Donna Reed, Ronald Reagan, Raymond Burr, and even Lassie had their own network shows. Before long, producers of important movies took note of popular series when casting. Warner Bros. sought to broaden the appeal of the John Wayne western *Rio Bravo* (1959) by adding teenage heart-throb Ricky Nelson to its cast of veteran players. The nineteen-year-old Nelson had recently won a large following on *The Adventures of Ozzie and Harriet,* a family sitcom. James Garner, Charles Bronson, and Clint Eastwood, who established their reputations first on television, soon qualified as major Hollywood stars.

By the early 1960s Hollywood had become more of a television town than a movie town. Work on weekly series required economy and compromise, since budgets were limited and production schedules short. "I couldn't plan ahead as I did when making a feature film," said director Gene Fowler, Jr., "nor could I have a set specially designed for something I had in mind." In his television work Fowler developed a practice of concentrating on three key scenes, doing a good job with those, and sloughing the rest. "I tried to space them evenly," he said. "Audiences are very forgiving; they basically want to like what they see."

Beginning in the fall of 1965 NBC committed to a complete prime-time lineup in color, and the other networks were quick to follow. Hollywood studios had little choice but to do likewise with feature films; within three years black-and-white movies had become a rarity, except for an occasional documentary.

The war with television was over. Studios were earning some $300 million a year from television production, a third of their total revenue, and had adjusted to the constraints of network programming. They had also discovered a lucrative market in television for their film libraries and recent releases, once the newer pictures had finished their run in the theaters.

The first studios to sell their inventory of films to broadcasters were Republic and Monogram, the leading producers of low-budget pictures. During the early 1950s the Hopalong Cassidy westerns appeared on television and demonstrated how profitable merchandising could be when linked with video exposure. Upon its dissolution in 1955, RKO sold 740 features and 1,000 shorts to General Teleradio, a subsidiary of General Tire and Rubber

Company. The sale marked the first time that movies made by a major studio were available for syndication on television, and by 1957 General Teleradio had earned an estimated $25 million from the arrangement.

The transfer of RKO's pictures to a television distributor signaled a breakthrough. Early in 1956 Columbia Pictures released 104 movies to its subsidiary, Screen Gems, for distribution to broadcasters. Later that year Warner Bros. sold 850 of its pre-1948 films to television for $21 million, and MGM contracted to lease to broadcasters 725 features and 900 shorts from its library. Still later in 1956, Twentieth Century-Fox made 450 pictures available to National Telefilm Associates, in return for $30 million and 50 percent interest in the telefilm company. Two years later Paramount sold 750 of its pre-1948 backlog to MCA for $50 million.

By 1958 all the major studios had negotiated for their pre-1948 films to be shown on television, and *The Late Show* had become a national pastime. The studios were free to dispose of their pre-1948 films, since they controlled all auxiliary rights to those pictures. But the Screen Actors Guild, the Directors Guild of America, and the Writers Guild of America demanded residual compensation to guild members credited in features made after August 1, 1948.

The television networks did not utilize feature films until September 23, 1961, when NBC launched its *Saturday Night at the Movies* with Twentieth Century-Fox's *How to Marry a Millionaire.* The series aired a package of thirty-one recent pictures that NBC leased from Fox for $25 million. Newer features had become available to television after a 1960 agreement between the film industry and the major motion picture guilds. Ratings for *Saturday Night at the Movies* ran high, with the result that feature films soon became a prime-time staple.

ABC was the second network to offer a weekly movie series, when it began *Hollywood Special* on Sunday nights in 1962. Three years later CBS added a Thursday night feature film series. As the demand for pictures increased, studios charged broadcasters higher prices. In 1961 the average feature leased to the networks for prime-time airing brought $150,000; by 1965 the fee had risen to $400,000. In 1966 ABC paid Columbia $2 million to show *The Bridge on the River Kwai* (1957), but the movie attracted an estimated audience of 60 million. Fox soon leased *Cleopatra* to ABC for $5 million, which eliminated some of the loss the studio had suffered on the film.

In part, the sales and rentals to television were motivated by necessity; in many instances studios would have closed the year in the red financially without the bonus from broadcasters. But the mid-1950s witnessed a new configuration of the motion picture and television industries. No longer would films be made without producers having television rentals in mind. By the early 1960s five times more movie footage was shown on television each year than was released annually as feature films by the studios, and network programming had become an accepted secondary market for theatrical movies.

MAKING THE MOST OF LESS

Despite the postwar efforts of foreign governments to limit the importation of motion pictures, in 1953 box office returns from abroad surpassed Hollywood's domestic business for the first time. Foreign receipts accounted for 60 percent of the total, with 80 percent of that earned in Europe. During the 1960s the appetite for American popular culture around the globe intensified dramatically, and Hollywood films dominated foreign screens. Soon the world saw nearly all American movies, although action-packed, simply plotted pictures scored best in markets abroad.

Musicals fared well in foreign countries, as they continued to do at home throughout the 1950s and early 1960s. MGM led the way with such innovative musicals as *An American in Paris* (1951) and *Singin' in the Rain* (1952). But by the mid-1950s budget cuts necessitated less spectacular films; *Brigadoon* (1954), for example, had to be filmed on an MGM soundstage rather than in Scotland as originally planned. Internationally presold subjects, such as *The Glenn Miller Story* (1954) or Marilyn Monroe in *Gentlemen Prefer Blondes* (1953), were preferred. At the close of the decade, almost all screen musicals were adaptations of successful Broadway shows: *Damn Yankees* (1958), *West Side Story* (1961), *The Music Man* (1962), and *Bye Bye Birdie* (1963).

Musicals offered the advantage of a soundtrack album, which became part of the merchandising scheme, although scores from dramatic films also sold well in record shops around the world. Hit songs, particularly title songs, became recognized as an effective means of advertising films. *Unchained* (1955) was an inexpensive, offbeat movie about a prison without walls. Film composer Alex North wrote a song for the film called "Unchained Melody," which remains a standard, even though the movie is largely forgotten. "The song saved the picture," declared actress Barbara Hale, who headed the cast.

"Every producer wanted a title song," said Bill Stinson, former head of Paramount's music department, "because that was a means of exploiting a picture." Henry Mancini wrote "Moon River" as a theme song for Paramount's *Breakfast at Tiffany's*, but it was not a title song and therefore not readily identified with the picture. Stinson invited 500 California disc jockeys who broadcast on radio stations between Bakersfield and San Diego to come to the studio and view the picture. They returned home and began plugging "Moon River" and *Breakfast at Tiffany's* on their radio programs. "Our New York office saw what I had done," said Stinson, "and they arranged similar screenings throughout the country."

The Doris Day pictures, even her comedies and dramatic shows, usually benefited from a popular song by the singer on the soundtrack. Beginning in the late 1950s, the star's movies frequently portrayed the wholesome actress fending off sexual advances from her costar, while she coaxed him into marriage. In an era when many of Hollywood's films were downbeat—dramas ranging from *Paths of Glory* (1957), Stanley Kubrick's cynical antiwar film, to Blake Edward's *Days of Wine and Roses* (1962), the story of a husband and wife who are alcoholics—the Doris Day comedies, such as *Pillow Talk* (1959) and *Lover Come Back* (1962), were a lighthearted change. The actress was seen wearing real jewels, magnificent clothes, and chic hairstyles, and she played opposite some of the screen's most handsome leading men.

Producer Ross Hunter acknowledged that these films were against the trend. Yet he believed that the way to lure audiences back into the theaters was to return to the glamour of Hollywood's Golden Era. "I wanted to go back," said Hunter, "and make pictures about the beautiful people for a change. The old days in Hollywood were exciting years. They were the years that made fantasy come true."

By 1963 the movie capital seemed pale in comparison with the fabled days of the past. Weekly movie attendance was down to 21 million, a quarter of what it had been in 1946. Even though fans still gathered at four o'clock in the morning outside whatever theater was hosting the annual Academy Awards ceremony, hoping to secure a place from which to see stars as they arrived that evening, the legendary aura seemed to be missing, as Hollywood sank into the doldrums.

Although the movie colony had always been plagued by periodic scandals, many of the earlier ones had been hushed up by adept publicity departments. The scandals of the 1950s and early 1960s seemed rawer and involved celebrities heretofore held as America's aristocracy. In December 1951 a calendar went on sale revealing current sex symbol Marilyn Monroe completely nude. The nude photographs eventually became collectors' items, but they were considered shocking at the time by most fans. In April 1952 the distinguished movie producer Walter Wanger was sentenced to four months in prison for shooting agent Jennings Lang in a private part of his anatomy, over Lang's supposed affair with Wanger's wife, actress Joan Bennett. Partly in revenge Wanger produced *I Want to Live!* in 1958, a grim tale about a prostitute-crook who, according to the script, is framed for murder and unjustly sent to the gas chamber. That same year actress Lana Turner's daughter, Cheryl Crane, stabbed and killed her mother's lover, Johnny Stompanato, during an argument in Turner's bedroom. The episode found its way into the 1964 movie *Where Love Has Gone*, based on a Harold Robbins novel. The line between reality and fantasy appeared to be growing dimmer, but life among the movie idols seemed shabby if compared with the decades when romance and glamour reigned.

Ironically, as Hollywood's glory began to fade, the cinema emerged as a serious subject of criticism and scholarship in Europe and later the United States. Film departments became more evident in respected American universities, while film courses found their way into the college curriculum—proof to some that Hollywood was dead.

CONCLUSION

In the early 1950s television gained the mass audience that movies had enjoyed for more than two decades. To meet the challenge of television and the loss of a guaranteed market, Hollywood first tried to emphasize what home screens could not—giant spectacles filmed on location at exorbitant costs. But movie executives also recognized a mature audience that wanted more sophisticated pictures and some of the reality found in newer foreign films. To compete with the recently converted art houses, Hollywood attempted a selection of serious films that dealt candidly with social issues. As theater attendance continued to decline, producers came to rely heavily on presold material—scripts based on best-selling novels, successful Broadway plays, Bible stories, the lives of famous personalities, sequels, remakes, and, eventually, popular television shows.

Out of necessity Hollywood became more innovative. New technology was developed, special effects were improved, a new acting style emerged, the censorship code was revised, and new markets were explored. Among the most profitable was the youth market, which relished sensationalized images of teenagers, horror films, action movies with car chases, and science fiction thrillers. With racial integration, a previously underdeveloped black audience was acknowledged, and a more favorable depiction of minorities began.

In the mid-1950s major television production moved to Hollywood, as live broadcasting gave way to filmed programming. With a decline in the number of theatrical movies being made, the major studios were soon more heavily engaged in the production of weekly television series than with the making of feature films. Hollywood offered the actors, the craftsmen, and the technique for turning out television shows quickly and inexpensively, with an acceptable level of professionalism. The family audience for television, the need for likable characters as the central focus of popular series, and the power of advertisers often contributed to a blandness in television fare, but most professionals in Hollywood accepted the commercial nature of their business and the compromises that were necessary. With rare exceptions the status of working on weekly series was less than working on feature films, but the opportunities were more reliable.

Also during the mid-1950s studio executives found a lucrative market for their film libraries in television programming. Local stations were desperate to fill up airtime, and Hollywood had the product ready and available. The union between the motion picture industry and the networks was finalized when arrangements were made for showing recent movie releases on national television during prime hours.

If Hollywood seemed less bewitching than it had once been, all of its major studios except RKO had survived a difficult transition period. By 1960 MGM, Paramount, Warner Bros., and Twentieth Century-Fox had undergone revision, but they were soon to experience wholesale reorganization. Universal's facilities had already been bought by MCA, and similar takeovers became the wave of the future.

Display of items to be sold at the MGM auction in May 1970.

Chapter 3

——

TANGLES OF CONGLOMERATES

During the 1950s the old moguls began to depart from the Hollywood scene, and the basic structure of the movie kingdom soon became permanently altered. Darryl Zanuck resigned as Twentieth Century-Fox's chief of production in 1956, planning to spend most of his time in Europe; he would return later to bail the studio out of its difficulties during the making of *Cleopatra.* Louis B. Mayer died in 1957, six years after being forced out as production head at Metro-Goldwyn-Mayer. Harry Cohn, the indomitable founder of Columbia, died in 1958. The following year Samuel Goldwyn produced his last film, *Porgy and Bess.* The moguls had been the galvanizing force behind the big studio system, but their successors demonstrated neither the style nor power of the industry's founders. By the early 1960s only the names of the great studios remained.

Although the motion picture business stayed within the control of the established studios, by the late 1950s more than half the pictures Hollywood released were independent productions. The important factor behind the rise of the independent companies was the decreased demand for feature films, which made the big studios' approach to production outmoded. As the industry rebuilt during the 1960s, the studios became distributors more than producers of motion pictures, functioning as bankers that loaned money to the independent producers to whom they rented space and equipment. As financiers the studios retained the right of approval over details of production and held sufficient power to exercise fiscal controls. The studios decided which pictures went before the cameras and which television shows would be developed, but their decisions were influenced by investment bankers and corporate attorneys.

Until the early 1970s motion picture distributors financed the bulk of the industry's production costs. As expenses mounted, the distribution company might supply partial funds, but the remainder usually came from bank loans or individual investors. The Bank of America freely loaned money to producers during the 1970s, yet insisted on specified restrictions to protect the bank's investment. Bankers depended on distributors to oversee the development of scripts, shooting schedules, and expenditures during production. Studios therefore served as deputies for the banks involved.

Although the larger studios continued to produce their own movies, they also kept their distribution machinery occupied by releasing an assortment of films made by other companies. Independent producers who moved onto the lot became tenants rather than employees of the studio; they were more or less free to make their pictures in their own way, as long as they abided by strictures set down by the bank financing the project and gained periodic approval from the distributor. With the demise of the old contract system, actors, writers, and most technicians became free agents, no longer tied to a single studio, nor sheltered by them. Picturemaking became piecemeal rather than the assembly-line approach that once had operated. And the making of feature films, for the most part, was a sideline to the production of television programs.

As Hollywood's old feudal system reached its end, agents became increasingly powerful, emerging as the industry's prime movers. A talent agency would most likely be the force in the packaging of deals for film and television productions, taking 10 percent of the sale price for putting the package together. It was to an agency's advantage to combine a writer, director, and actors that the company currently represented, thereby extracting the largest possible commission. Eventually, agents came to determine what stories would be made into movies, selected the talent to develop screenplays, cast projects, and often arranged for the financing of films. In doing so, they took over work that formerly had been done by studio executives. In such cases the main function of the studios would be the actual distribution of pictures to theaters.

William Morris, International Creative Management, and Creative Artists Agency rank as the giants among the Hollywood talent agencies, although Music Corporation of America (MCA) was a power in the field until antitrust problems forced the company to divorce itself from the agency business. Although William Morris has declined over recent years, International Creative Management and Creative Artists Agency have thrived. CAA's president, Michael Ovitz, by the 1980s was spoken of as the single most influential person in the motion picture business. The top three agencies dominate the supply of talent, providing story material and artistic personnel for Hollywood's television shows and feature films.

Since the 1970s a majority of the industry's producers have been either agents or lawyers. Superagents have come to rule the movie business as firmly as the old moguls did earlier. Unlike Hollywood's founding fathers who were dedicated filmmakers, sensitive to the pulse of their public, the talent agencies are comprised of outsiders, who form lucrative packages centered around their clients. Whether or not a movie is successful, the agents, attorneys, and accountants involved will make money off the package they present to the studio.

In the late 1960s and 1970s the studios themselves were taken over by huge conglomerates with business activities far more diverse than just the making of motion pictures. The massive entertainment combines that developed owned television networks, publishing houses, record and video companies, theme parks, holiday resorts, and toy companies. Even though the division between marketing the various forms of entertainment became blurred, profit remained the unifying link. Following the trend set in other industries, Hollywood's movie studios, one by one, were bought by domestic and foreign conglomerates that placed the production and distribution of motion pictures under a larger corporate umbrella.

From a financial standpoint these conglomerations offer advantages; they serve as banks, reinvesting windfall profits from one company into the production and marketing activities of others. The major limitation from the creative viewpoint is that motion picture studios are now run by corporate executives, lawyers, and accountants who are usually ignorant of the filmmaking process and sometimes apathetic to movies as a popular art form. Size is often mistaken for strength, quantity confused with quality, and ambition substituted for imagination.

Yet through all of the changes, readjustments, and retrench-
ments, the major Hollywood studios maintained their dominance
over the production and marketing of feature films, despite no
longer owning theaters. In 1975 Paramount, Warner Bros., and
Twentieth Century-Fox still ranked among Hollywood's leading studios, while Universal, Columbia, United Artists, and Walt Disney
had been elevated to top status. Metro-Goldwyn-Mayer, once the
industry's giant, had temporarily dropped out of production but
would return in a different guise.

MCA AND UNIVERSAL

In 1958 Universal Studios, owned by Decca Records since 1952,
suffered a $2 million loss. Revue Productions, the television sub-
sidiary of Music Corporation of America, on the other hand, had
become the world's leading producer and distributor of filmed television series, responsible for such successes as *Wagon Train,*
Dragnet, Alfred Hitchcock Presents, The Adventures of Ozzie and
Harriet, and *Leave It to Beaver.* When Decca merged with MCA
in 1959, Universal became the pacesetter in television production.
Revue was supplying the networks with a third of their prime-time
programming.

MCA also ranked among the most powerful talent agencies at
the time. It acquired the 423-acre Universal lot (but not Universal's
production and distribution company) for $11 million. Headed by
former agent Lew Wasserman, MCA modernized the studio at a cost
of $110 million and expanded its operation, while other companies
were forced to cut back. Wasserman was the first of a new breed of
studio executive, one whose background was in the agency business
rather than film production. With MCA's takeover of Universal, the
initial crack in the old Hollywood power structure became evident.
The new pattern would involve mergers that led to a cross-media
industry.

In 1961, under scrutiny of Robert Kennedy and the Justice
Department, MCA was forced to decide between being a talent
agency or being an employer of talent, since the dual role was
deemed a conflict of interests. The following year MCA agreed to
divest itself of its talent agency. By then the choice was clear; television production had become far more lucrative.

In 1962 MCA started construction on the black tower that would become the studio's corporate command center and its famous landmark. Universal's television production became the most efficient in Hollywood, while the studio also gained strength during the late 1960s from its feature films. Ross Hunter's production of *Airport* (1970) alone grossed $80 million in domestic revenues.

In July 1965 tours of the Universal studio were resumed and through the decades have increased in popularity. Trams carry paying visitors around the lot, and guides lead them through sound stages and into demonstration areas. The taking of photographs is permitted, and fans are occasionally rewarded by a glimpse of a favorite star. Income from the tours proved far from negligible, by 1969 earning Universal $5.5 million a year.

After the renovation and expansion of the studio, MCA employed 3,200 people. In 1966 the corporation grossed nearly $225 million from its television productions, movies, records, real estate investments, and related interests. The next year the parent company began building a twenty-one-story hotel on the outskirts of Universal City. Yet in 1969, with conglomerate takeovers the trend on Wall Street, MCA nearly became a division of Firestone Tires.

Universal in 1970 earned almost as much from its musical sidelines as from the distribution of films. The soft-spoken but aggressive Lew Wasserman had become one of the most powerful men in the motion picture business; in 1973 he was made chairman of MCA's board. Universal by that time was the biggest and busiest movie studio in the world, employing 6,000 people in 1975.

Ten years later MCA was a $2 billion empire, owning companies in book and music publishing, a major record company, home video marketing, recreation services, transportation systems, a savings and loan company, real estate, mail-order purchasing, data processing, retail store merchandising, and cable television. In 1990 Matsushita, a Japanese electronic hardware manufacturer, bought control of MCA/Universal for $6.1 billion in the largest single takeover of an American corporation by a foreign concern. Within two years, reports spoke of growing tension between MCA executives and the parent company, but the liaison continued until 1995. In April of that year, MCA president, Sidney Sheinberg, argued that the Japanese electronics giant was destroying the entertainment combine. Matsushita then sold MCA to the Seagram Company.

PARAMOUNT AND GULF + WESTERN

In 1966 Gulf + Western Industries, a vastly diversified insurance trust, bought Paramount Pictures. A year later the corporation added Desilu Productions, Paramount's next-door neighbor, which had been the old RKO lot. Charles G. Bluhdorn, the bombastic, Austrian-born chairman of Gulf + Western, became chairman of Paramount's new board, while Robert Evans, a former garment tycoon, was named head of production. Evans proved tremendously hardworking, yet suffered the failure of *Paint Your Wagon, Darling Lili,* and other expensive Paramount films in 1969. Although Gulf + Western possessed sufficient cash reserves to ride out the crisis, the studio was forced to sell off some of its real estate.

Bluhdorn reveled in the glamour of his film company and pumped millions into Paramount. Fortunately the studio's luck improved with the release of *Love Story* (1970). *The Godfather* (1972), an instant financial success, restored the board's confidence in feature films, while Paramount also became a major supplier of television programming.

Gulf + Western's operations included a variety of companies that had nothing to do with entertainment and little in common. Only the trade section known as the Leisure Time Division was relevant to motion pictures. Leisure Time by no means provided the conglomerate with its chief source of revenue; only 11 percent of Gulf + Western's income in 1977 came from that division. Paramount was only part of Leisure Time, which consisted of various lines of entertainment: the production of films for television and cinema, the production of records and magnetic tape, an electric guitar factory, and many other operations. The eleven additional divisions of the conglomerate dealt in everything from zinc mines to the manufacture of automobile parts.

During the 1970s, after Robert Evans's success with *Love Story* and *The Godfather,* the Paramount production chief seemed to do no wrong. He made *Chinatown* (1974) under a personal arrangement with the studio, married actress Ali MacGraw, and lived amid lordly accoutrements. Like other executives of his station, Evans enjoyed having private jet planes at his disposal, suites in the fanciest hotels, the best tables in posh restaurants, and the company of celebrities.

The 1980s proved a sadder story, however. Evans was arrested for possession of cocaine, and a murder was linked with the production of his box office disaster *The Cotton Club* (1984). He contemplated suicide, escaped from a mental hospital, and in 1994 published his memoirs detailing his tumultuous personal life.

By the 1980s the conglomerate structure was proving too unwieldy for Gulf + Western to manage. Corporation heads responded by downsizing their operations, shedding more than fifty companies and focusing on selected activities. After restructuring, the organization's goal was to become a global communications and entertainment giant. In 1989, with the entertainment industry enjoying a record boom, Gulf + Western changed its name to Paramount Communications, intending to divide its energies between entertainment and publishing, most visibly Simon and Schuster. That year Paramount, Disney, Time Warner, MCA, and Columbia together grossed more than $500 million at the box office.

In 1993 a $16.5 billion megamerger of entertainment giants was approved by the directors of Paramount Communications and Viacom International. Paramount television promised a "new experience" in its promotional campaign but the conglomerate merger behind that experience followed a trend fast becoming the norm.

FROM WARNER BROS. TO TIME WARNER

Jack Warner was the last of the old Hollywood moguls to surrender his uninterrupted position of leadership, remaining head of production at Warner Bros. until 1967. The studio's biggest success during the 1950s had come from the making of television series; ten years later, feature releases at Warner Bros. were almost entirely independent productions. In 1967 Warner merged with Seven Arts Productions, a Canadian-based television packaging company, while Jack Warner himself joined the ranks of independent producers. His studio was shortly christened the Burbank Studio, although the Warner name was never completely erased.

Two years after Seven Arts took over, the studio was sold to Kinney National Services, Inc. Based in New York and headed by Steven J. Ross, Kinney National was not the industrial giant that Gulf + Western was, but the corporation operated on the same principle of diversification. Its holdings included *Mad* and eighteen other magazines, parking lots, janitorial services, funeral parlors, and an automobile rental company. Kinney acquired Warner Bros. for the value of its equipment, its installations, and its production capacity for television and cinema; the market value of its music section, which published scores and produced records; the studio's extensive library of films; Warner's cartoon characters and the right to use them in advertising; and the studio's 250-acre lot in Burbank.

Later renamed the National Kinney Corporation, the company split in two in July 1971, with the leisure-time section transformed into Warner Communications Corporation. Falling under this leisure-time division were Atlantic Records, Panavision, several cable television companies, as well as film and video releases. In 1972, to lessen operating costs, Warner and Columbia became joint owners of the Burbank Studio.

Warner had a disastrous experience with Atari video games in 1983 and lost $300 million. The company sold off subsidiaries in cosmetics and sports, and the decision was made to concentrate on film and television production and distribution, along with music and publishing. Six years later Steve Ross masterminded the purchase of Warner Communications by Time Inc., on terms that were extremely favorable to Warner. Time Warner aligned Time's magazine and cable television channels with Warner's films, records, studio, and worldwide distribution facilities to become the largest communications and media conglomerate in the world. Ross served as Time Warner's chairman until his death in 1992.

The trend toward megamergers dominated the Hollywood scene in the 1990s, as media conglomerates oriented toward serving a global market earned unprecedented profits. Hollywood's movies and television shows are currently distributed around the world, generating a burst of spin-off merchandising—compact discs, books, T-shirts, posters, and toys. Soon after the Time Warner merger, its studio released the $35 million movie *Batman.* The film triggered a market for tapes and recordings, books and comic books, video cassettes, wearing apparel, and countless incidentals—all made by companies under the parentage of Warner. *Batman's* success would be imitated time and again, while Warner Bros. retail stores appeared in major American cities from New York to Honolulu.

COLUMBIA, COCA-COLA, AND SONY

Following the death of Harry Cohn, Columbia Pictures faced a number of lean years, although the studio's television subsidiary, Screen Gems, consistently showed high profits. While Screen Gems earned $4.5 million in 1966, the rest of the studio suffered a deficit of $2.2

Window display of merchandise at Time Warner shop in New York, 1989.

million. Losses continued in the early 1970s, with such miscalculations as *Young Winston* (1972) and *Lost Horizon* (1973), making Columbia ripe for a corporate takeover.

In 1973, after three bad years in succession, Allen and Company, a Wall Street investment banking firm, gained control of the ailing studio and undertook its financial rehabilitation. David Begelman, a flamboyant talent agent whose clients included Paul Newman, Barbra Streisand, Robert Redford, Judy Garland, and Cliff Robertson, became Columbia's head of production. Begelman demanded budget cuts and took a watchful attitude toward producers in an effort to restore the company's financial health. Columbia soon was identified with successful and trendy pictures such as *Shampoo* (1975), *Taxi Driver* (1976), and *Close Encounters of the Third Kind* (1977).

A poor boy from the Bronx, Begelman had a reputation in Hollywood as one of the most skillful negotiators of deals in the

David Begelman (left), former president of Columbia Pictures, in court on grand theft charges.

business. In his tailor-made suits and polished Rolls Royce, Begelman exuded a regal style. Under his guidance Columbia again showed profits, and there were plans for expansion. *Close Encounters of the Third Kind* was the most expensive and ambitious movie the company had ever made, and it proved one of the biggest box office hits of all time.

In 1977 the Begelman bubble burst amid scandal. The exposure began when actor Cliff Robertson received his 1976 income statement from the Internal Revenue Service. Robertson could not remember receiving a check for $10,000 from Columbia, nor could he recall having done any work for the studio to warrant such payment, yet the amount appeared on his tax statement. Upon investigating the matter, the actor was presented with a series of evasive explanations from Columbia personnel, but he finally succeeded in tracing the check. It had been made out to him, but cashed by someone else. His signature had been forged on the back by none other than David Begelman.

An FBI investigation disclosed that Begelman had embezzled $60,000 of Columbia's funds by falsely signing bogus checks. Although his annual salary was $300,000, he spent extravagantly and lived beyond his means. The studio announced in October 1977 that Begelman was taking a leave of absence, as the "Begelman affair" rocked Hollywood. The movie executive's crimes might easily have put him in prison, but Judge Thomas C. Murphy of Burbank Municipal Court decided instead on a fine of $5,000 and three years' probation.

For a time the film capital was viewed as the seat of another Watergate, and a furor swelled concerning Hollywood's business practices and so-called creative accounting. In the wake of Begelman's disgrace, Alan J. Hirschfield, the president of Columbia's parent company, was ousted. At the same time a number of others left the studio: Daniel Melnick, a Begelman assistant; Robert Cort, who had been in charge of publicity and advertising; Norman Levy, the head of sales and therefore responsible for putting Columbia's movies into the best theaters; and Peter Guber, producer of two of the studio's biggest hits.

Ironically Cliff Robertson, who discovered Begelman's forgery, was subsequently blackballed in Hollywood for four years. David Begelman, on the other hand, received a standing ovation when he entered a fashionable Beverly Hills restaurant. He was soon hired by Kirk Kerkorian, the controlling shareholder of Metro-Goldwyn-Mayer, who put Begelman in charge of production at MGM for a short time. Kerkorian meanwhile purchased a 25-percent interest in Columbia and attempted to take control of the studio. A bitter struggle ensued before Kerkorian backed off, selling his Columbia stock for a profit of nearly $60 million.

Under Begelman's successor, Frank Price, a former television writer, the studio turned out such hits as *California Suite* (1978), *Kramer vs. Kramer* (1979), and *Absence of Malice* (1981). Columbia again became a well-oiled unit, still under the parentage of Allen and Company, and the studio's financial condition appeared solid. Then in January 1982 Coca-Cola, faced with a leveling off of its soft drink business, purchased Columbia for $700 million, intending to diversify the studio's activities by entering the cable and pay television fields.

To secure a greater market, Coca-Cola quickly created Tri-Star Pictures, owned jointly by Columbia, Home Box Office (HBO), and CBS. Tri-Star's goal was to produce movies that would be distributed to the theaters by Columbia, to pay television by HBO, and to network television by CBS. Coca-Cola also began plugging its products in the pictures Columbia and Tri-Star produced.

In 1986 the corporation announced that it was importing the distinguished British producer David Puttnam to run Columbia. Puttnam had been responsible for such hits as *Chariots of Fire* (1981) and *The Killing Fields* (1984). A crusader for excellence, the British producer vowed to reduce excessive spending. Puttnam said:

> The studios made a terrible mistake six or seven years ago when they somehow allowed themselves to be talked into mega-salaries on top of a percentage of the box office gross. It was the greatest single folly they ever got embroiled in.

What Puttnam envisioned was a more artistic studio that turned out medium-priced pictures. He wanted to move away from what he called "the Tsar approach" of Frank Price and eliminate overpaid producers, stars, and directors. "I was quite convinced," Puttnam later remarked, "that there was room for one studio that set out to do a different job." He intended to create a new ethos at Columbia by abandoning the mega-budget productions that made Hollywood studios so vulnerable. "My plan," said Puttnam, "was to strip back and start again with the studio, and to try to come up with a new generation of directors, writers and, in some cases, stars."

Puttnam felt that those running the Hollywood studios did not tend to be idea people. "Everyone is copying hits," he said, "or just slavishly adhering to what someone who has had a hit wants to do." He objected to an underlying nastiness in contemporary films and to the cynicism that had become fashionable. His strong opinions alienated many of the industry's important names, and within fifteen months Puttnam was out.

He understood too late that power and profit were the unyielding motives in the Hollywood game. Columbia had developed into one of the top distribution networks in a worldwide market; its chief resource was money, large volumes of money. "I was responsible for a company the standing overhead of which was $55,000,000," Puttnam said. "That was just to open the door in the U.S. To open the door in the rest of the world was around $100,000,000."

Puttnam's departure from Columbia left behind a cadre of confused followers and a studio in disarray. What the controlling interests wanted was a regime with more commercial instincts, one savvy about the market-research techniques that had become the mode in Hollywood. They selected as Puttnam's replacement Dawn Steel, the first woman to be placed in charge of a major studio. Steel lasted until 1989 when Columbia and Tri-Star were bought for $3.4 billion by Sony, the Japanese electronics giant.

Sony had begun shopping for a Hollywood studio shortly after buying CBS Records. Coca-Cola meanwhile had become eager to back out of the movie business, particularly when Sony offered to assume Columbia's $1.5 billion debt. Japan had been a major force in American banking since the mid-1980s, and Sony's purchase of Columbia prompted widespread fears of a foreign invasion of Hollywood and the loss of American cultural identity. Three years after the buyout, however, virtually no Japanese employee had taken on any role of importance in either Columbia or Tri-Star.

After purchasing the film companies, Sony embarked on a search for established Hollywood executives to run them, finally enticing Peter Guber and his partner, Jon Peters, to leave Warner for Columbia. Guber was a lawyer before becoming a movie producer, whereas the flamboyant Peters was best known as Barbra Streisand's former hairdresser and lover. Peters had made his first million dollars before he turned thirty through his chain of high-fashion hair salons, but had been fascinated with Hollywood since the age of ten when he worked as an extra in Cecil B. DeMille's *The Ten Commandments.* Neither Guber nor Peters had ever headed a studio, but both were men of great drive and neither was intimidated by powerful figures in the movie business. Their company's success with *Batman* (1989), financed and distributed by Warner, had made them extremely visible.

Sony acquired the services of Peter Guber and Jon Peters by paying $200 million to buy out the Guber-Peters Entertainment Company and, under threat of a massive lawsuit, compensating Warner with another $500 million, since the move to Columbia meant that Guber and Peters would be breaking a long-term agreement they had with the Burbank studio. Upon agreeing to head Columbia, the two executives were each awarded a base salary of $2.75 million a year for five years.

Guber and Peters evidently decided that they needed more experienced heads to supervise the actual running of Columbia and Tri-Star, so Frank Price, who for the past three years had been at Universal, was brought back to head production at Columbia, while

Michael Medavoy, cofounder of Orion Pictures, was hired to head Tri-Star. As part of the settlement with Warner, Sony agreed to trade Columbia's interest in the Burbank Studio for the old MGM facility in Culver City. With the Metro-Goldwyn-Mayer lot no longer used for production, the once mammoth studio was badly in need of renovation, which Guber and Peters sanctioned at a cost of $100 million. Warner also secured the right to distribute Columbia's film library to cable television.

When Columbia took over the MGM lot, the former administration building there was redone in an Art Moderne style, and its executive offices were refurnished lavishly. Under instructions from Guber and Peters the studio bought its own florist shop, so that executives could have fresh flowers in their offices every day. Jon Peters drew a great deal of criticism for his extravagant use of Columbia's jets and for the size of his estate in Colorado, which he had stocked with wild animals.

In March 1990 at an annual business meeting in New York, budgetary constraints were imposed on Columbia, and Sony's operations in Hollywood were restructured. The new austerity program soon claimed casualties in management, beginning with Jon Peters. In May 1991, a little more than a year after he and Guber accepted the invitation from Sony, Peters was removed from his administrative position and given production rights on the Culver City lot instead.

The next head to roll was that of Frank Price, who ran afoul of Guber over style and output. Price had been responsible for such major hits as *Tootsie* (1982) and *Back to the Future* (1985), and his buyout, estimated at between $15 to 20 million, resulted in confusion at Columbia and embarrassment for Sony. Price remained at the studio as a producer, but he was replaced as production head by Mark Canton, a former Warner Bros. executive.

After Price's removal Guber grew frustrated with Michael Medavoy, Price's counterpart at Tri-Star Pictures. Tri-Star had not performed well, and Medavoy left the company in January 1994.

The previous year had been a difficult one for Sony Corporation; its profits fell by half. During the summer of 1993 Columbia, despite a few modest box office successes, suffered a string of commercial failures. Sony's acquisitions in Hollywood were proving a financial drain, and it was clear that all or part of Columbia and Tri-Star were for sale at the right price.

THE ECLIPSE OF MGM

Metro-Goldwyn-Mayer began contracting with independent producers after 1956, the year L. B. Mayer's successor, Dore Schary, left the
studio. For distributing independent productions, MGM would claim
30 to 35 percent of the net box office receipts after theaters had taken
their share. Yet with Schary's departure MGM went through a series
of management changes, at one point experiencing three turnovers
within a single year. "The studio really lost its ability to function,"
veteran producer Pandro Berman said; "everything began to fall apart.
After Schary's replacement, it continued to go down, down, down."
Berman put much of the blame on the company's East Coast office:

> I would call the president of the company in New York on some
> important matter and not get an answer for a week. The New York
> office had become a group, and that group, like most groups, func-
> tioned poorly. It needed *a person* to make decisions. Metro was no
> longer Metro.

The once-glorious studio began selling off its backlots, which
had become worth more as real estate than as sets for filmmaking.
Late in 1968 the company, with debts in excess of $85 million, was
on the verge of defaulting on its bank loans.

A year later Kirk Kerkorian took command by purchasing 40 percent of MGM for $80 million. The son of an immigrant Armenian
farmer, Kerkorian possessed an eighth-grade education, had been
an airline pilot, and as a boy never expected to own anything more
exalted than a secondhand plane. But he was a gambler who operated by instinct, and he became a millionaire. By 1969 he was the
largest shareholder in Western Airlines and the owner of two large
hotels and gambling casinos in Las Vegas—the Flamingo and the
International. In his youth Kerkorian had worked at MGM as a day
laborer and was excited at the prospect of ruling the mythic kingdom, once the domain of Louis B. Mayer and Irving Thalberg. He had
neither taste nor knowledge of the motion picture business; what
interested him, aside from the prestige of ownership, was the bot-
tom line on MGM's financial report.

Kerkorian selected James T. Aubrey, former president of CBS,
to head his studio. The son of wealthy parents and educated at
Princeton, Aubrey was a product of network television and had
never made a movie. Known as "the Smiling Cobra," the new head

ran Metro-Goldwyn-Mayer like a dictator, closed its studio in London, reduced the staff in Culver City from 6,200 to 1,200, discontinued production on several films, set a maximum budget for future projects at $2 million, and destroyed the studio's morale.

In January 1970, at an annual stockholders' meeting, Aubrey announced that the company had incurred a deficit of $35 million the previous year, but promised drastic changes. He proceeded to sell off more of the studio's 187-acre lot, at prices lower than market value, and announced a massive auction of the props and costumes that MGM had collected over nearly half a century. Accessories from more than 2,000 movies were sold in May 1970, including Clark Gable's trenchcoat, the shoes worn by Judy Garland in *The Wizard of Oz* (1939), Elizabeth Taylor's wedding veil from *Father of the Bride* (1950), the velvet suit Greta Garbo wore in *Queen Christina* (1933), as well as swords, armor, spears, branding irons, peace pipes, powder horns, antique organs, radiators, brass hair-curlers, Egyptian plaques, and vintage cars. The auction lasted for eighteen days, during which the studio was stripped of its more expensive props. Many of the items, particularly the furniture and chandeliers, sold at undervalued prices, since they were not reproductions but genuine antiques.

"I don't want to hear any more bullshit about the old MGM," Aubrey snapped. "The old MGM is gone." As if to demonstrate the point, he had the Thalberg Building renamed the Administration Building and a bust of Irving Thalberg removed. MGM's East Coast offices were shut down so that marketing could be centralized in Culver City. Aubrey's high-handed, contentious attitude alienated a number of Hollywood's top directors and producers. Some refused to work at the studio, and those who did found themselves repeatedly challenged and at war with the MGM management. By 1972 the studio faced a number of lawsuits from directors who claimed undue interference with pictures they had made on the lot.

Aubrey insisted that the days of spectacles like *Doctor Zhivago* (1965) were over at MGM. Two of the movies he sanctioned were *Shaft* (1971), an exploitation film about a black private detective, and *Kansas City Bomber* (1972), which featured Raquel Welch as a roller-derby queen. For Aubrey, movies should be made inexpensively and appeal to a clearly defined audience. Those with sex and violence, he seemed to feel, stood the best chances for success. Although *Skyjacked* (1972), *Soylent Green,* and *The Man Who Loved Cat Dancing* (both 1973) were made at MGM under his regime, most of the pictures filmed there during Aubrey's four years as studio head did poorly at the box office.

With discontent boiling, Kerkorian fired the callous Aubrey in October 1973 and replaced him with Frank E. Rosenfelt, a former lawyer. "The Kerkorian-Aubrey management," critic Vincent Canby wrote, "was the realization of everyone's worst fears of what would happen to Hollywood when the money-men take over."

By 1973 Kerkorian's emphasis had shifted from the Culver City studio back to his gambling interests in Las Vegas, where he was building the MGM Grand. The site for his projected hotel and casino had been purchased in 1971 for $5 million, and groundbreaking had taken place the next year. The $110 million MGM Grand opened late in 1973, with talent from the studio lined up to perform there. It now became the function of MGM to serve Las Vegas. Foragers rummaged the lot in search of souvenirs missed by the auctioneers to stock the MGM Grand's gift shop. Jack Haley, Jr., a dedicated cinephile who served as MGM's vice president for creative affairs, visited the hotel and discovered William Wyler's shooting script of *Mrs. Miniver* (1942), complete with the award-winning director's notes and stage directions, on sale there. Haley bought the script for twelve dollars.

Meanwhile the studio itself was languishing; nothing worked. Critics liked *Slither* (1973), but audiences failed to respond. Workers on the lot began greeting one another with shrugs. When a producer presented an MGM executive with a script that seemed promising, he was told, "I don't think we'll be buying anything for a while." For the rest of the decade the studio turned out four to seven movies a year, but kept their budgets between $3 and 5 million.

By the middle of 1974 the MGM Grand claimed to be "the most profitable hotel in the world." Rather than channeling its profits into picturemaking, Kerkorian decided to build another MGM Grand in Reno. The Reno hotel and casino opened in 1978; two years later the Las Vegas Grand was engulfed in flames. Eighty-four people died in the fire and 600 were injured. With typical bravura Kerkorian announced that he would rebuild the hotel on an even grander scale.

In May 1981 Kerkorian startled Hollywood by announcing that he had acquired troubled United Artists for $380 million, picking up the valuable James Bond movies and the *Rocky* sequels in the process. To add to the surprise, he recruited David Begelman, recently discredited at Columbia, to supervise an ambitious program of films to be released under the combined banner of MGM/UA. Since United Artists had pay-or-play commitments with a number of actors and actresses, efforts were made to develop pictures for them. Yet the slate of movies approved by Begelman was expensive and performed poorly at the box office, with the result that he was dismissed in July 1982.

With Begelman's departure, a power vacuum existed at MGM/UA. The company suffered from duplicate management— Freddie Fields heading production at MGM, Paula Weinstein serving as his equivalent at UA—but neither had the confidence of top management. Kirk Kerkorian found himself faced with a gigantic bank debt, an array of unprofitable films, an assemblage of feuding executives, furious stockholders, and hostile critics. In 1982 he sold MGM's music division for $62 million, which was almost immediately resold for twice that amount. From Hollywood's viewpoint the mysterious Kerkorian had exploited his filmmaking enterprises to bolster his gambling empire in Reno and Las Vegas.

Frank Yablans was appointed the next president of MGM/UA, but the studio remained in deep financial trouble. When Yablans departed in 1985, Alan Ladd, Jr., a Hollywood name that carried weight in the banking and investment community, was placed in charge of the merged studios. But by the end of the year the two once-great companies had become a mere logo. Ted Turner, a rich man's son from Georgia who had scored with CNN cable television, bought MGM/UA in 1985 mainly for its library of movies, which consisted of some 3,500 titles, including *Gone with the Wind* (1939). Turner quickly sold MGM's lot in Culver City, by then reduced to forty-four acres, for $190 million to its principal tenant, Lorimar-Telepictures, who in turn sold it to Warner.

Before Columbia took over the facilities, the huge MGM sign atop the studio's water tower was dismantled; only Leo the Lion, the MGM logo, remained on Ted Turner's video releases and an occasional new feature for the theaters. In 1989 MGM/UA Communications reported an annual loss of $75 million. Within two years the company was barely in business; *Thelma and Louise* was its only major release. When a reporter asked Ted Turner if he regretted contributing to the dismemberment of the legendary studio, he said, "MGM died long before I came along." And indeed it had.

UNITED ARTISTS AND TRANSAMERICA

In February 1951 United Artists was reorganized by Arthur Krim and Robert Benjamin, two young lawyers. To increase the company's film inventory quickly, the new management bought distribution rights to the 300 movies produced by the short-lived Eagle-Lion Studio, which had been created shortly after World War II. United Artists then adopted a policy of financing motion pictures made by independent producers, guaranteeing them promotion and distribution. Profits were evenly divided—half to the production company who made the film, half to UA for distributing it.

Under Krim and Benjamin, United Artists was reborn. The company diversified by forming United Artists Records, entering the music publishing business, and in 1960 purchasing Ziv Television Programs. UA became visible again and economically successful, earning annual profits in the late 1960s of approximately $20 million.

But in April 1967 Krim and Benjamin sold out to Transamerica Corporation, a mammoth financial services company based in San Francisco. Originating in Bank of America, Transamerica sold various lines of insurance, but also dealt in investment loans and the building and management of hotels and motels. The corporation's stock in 1967 was stable but sluggish; Transamerica's hope was that the glamour of a Hollywood subsidiary would enhance the company's appeal with investors.

Within four years, however, United Artists announced a net annual loss of $52 million. A series of routine pictures and lackluster years followed, but ironically the making of *The Missouri Breaks* (1976) turned the company around, opening doors that had been closed during UA's doldrums. The picture was a box office disaster, but the prestige of having Arthur Penn as director and Marlon Brando and Jack Nicholson as the picture's stars proved a powerful package. The picture cost United Artists millions, but suddenly the company could again attract major talent for important films.

In 1978 five of UA's top executives quit the company and formed Orion Pictures. Arthur Krim became Orion's chairman, and an arrangement was made for Warner to distribute the new organization's movies. Although Orion kept control over publicity, advertising, and booking of its films, the agreement with Warner cost the company $100 million.

Meanwhile UA's relationship with Transamerica had become strained. Having lost its top management, United Artists scrambled for product and took chances on untried directors. In need of a blockbuster, the studio signed Michael Cimino to direct *Heaven's Gate* (1980), awarding him unprecedented directorial freedom and a projected budget of $7.8 million. The film ended up costing the company $40 million and proved one of the most notorious critical and financial disasters in Hollywood history. Bruised and beaten, UA in 1981 was receptive to Kirk Kerkorian's offer to merge with MGM.

Under Kerkorian, Jerry Weintraub became head of United Artists. As a boy Weintraub had ushered at Loew's Paradise in the Bronx and fallen in love with movies. He became an apprentice agent at MCA, graduated to movie producer, and with the success of *Karate Kid* (1984) won a foothold in Hollywood's proprietary class. But Weintraub headed UA for only five months. When the merger with MGM foundered, the studio wound up in the hands of Pathe Communications, an Italian-French company.

TWENTIETH CENTURY-FOX, THE LAST INDEPENDENT MAJOR

The Darryl Zanuck era at Twentieth Century-Fox came to an abrupt halt in 1956, when Zanuck, eager to free himself of domestic entanglements, moved to Europe with the intention of making films as an independent producer. The long-time chief of production had served his studio tirelessly and involved himself in every aspect of moviemaking. Zanuck understood the picturemaking process, demonstrated a keen sense of story development, had an instinct for film construction, and was sensitive to the commercial market. His successor at Fox, Buddy Adler, proved far less satisfactory, and during the regime of Spyros Skouras the studio ran into serious financial trouble, in large measure stemming from the *Cleopatra* disaster.

When Skouras was dismissed as president by the company's shareholders in 1962, Darryl Zanuck was invited back. His current success with *The Longest Day* (1962) had made him visible again in Hollywood, and Zanuck agreed to end his voluntary exile in Paris. Upon his return to Fox, he took charge of editing the unwieldy *Cleopatra*, which initially ran more than five hours, aware that the studio's future depended on the success or failure of that one picture.

With *Cleopatra* in release, the energetic Zanuck embarked on a policy of blockbusters designed to increase the company's profits. His schedule for 1964–1965 included such wide-screen productions as *The Agony and the Ecstasy, The Sand Pebbles,* and *The Sound of Music,* all shown in the theaters on roadshow bookings. Once Zanuck held firm control of the reins, he opted to handle the studio's business affairs from New York, putting his twenty-eight-year-old son, Richard, in charge of production on the West Coast.

The elder Zanuck planned to remain at the head of Twentieth Century-Fox for three years, then turn the company over to his son. For a time the Zanuck policies were successful, and the studio enjoyed a brief boom. But too much money was spent on big pictures that failed to win favor with the public. In 1966–1967 the company lost $47.5 million, and its board of directors began to complain about the Zanucks' reckless policies. Yet father and son saw things differently, and their paths began to part. Richard favored more sexually explicit films. When the company's board objected, Darryl Zanuck was forced to reprimand his son. "They got into some arguments about production," film editor Elmo Williams said. "Dick was pretty cocky and told his dad that he was old-fashioned and out of step. When I made *Tora! Tora! Tora!* (1970), I got caught between father and son."

By 1967–1968 much depended on the success of *Dr. Dolittle* and *Star!*. Both were expensive films, and both were disasters. Twentieth Century-Fox's losses in 1969 were $52 million; in 1970 they rose to $77 million. With his position in the studio shaky, Darryl Zanuck decided to act before the storm broke. In August 1969 he asked to be relieved as the company's president, but stayed on as chairman of the board. He proposed that Richard be named president of the company, as well as chief of production, and the board meekly agreed.

Then in late 1970 lightning struck. With Twentieth Century-Fox's stock falling on the New York exchange, Chase Manhattan Bank and Morgan Guaranty Bank, the studio's two principal creditors, demanded drastic changes in policy. Faced with dire circumstances, Darryl Zanuck sacrificed his son, firing Richard on December 31, 1970. The humiliation for the younger Zanuck was painful:

> My car was parked at the curb with my name along the side in front of the building. I couldn't get into the car because the painter was down on his knees in front of the thing, painting my name out. I couldn't open the door without asking him to stand up so I could drive off.

A few months later Richard Zanuck and his production partner, David Brown, joined Warner Bros. After a year with Warner, they left for Universal, where they rebuilt their careers with *The Sting* (1973); *Sugarland Express* (1974), the first movie directed by Steven Spielberg;

and *Jaws* (1975). Six months after his son's dismissal from Twentieth Century-Fox, Darryl Zanuck stepped down as chairman of the board. He had lost touch with the company and realized that his enemies had mobilized against him. Not wanting a fight that was sure to end in his defeat, he resigned on the eve of the annual shareholders' meeting in September 1971. His departure symbolized the close of an era.

Despite its heavy losses, Twentieth Century-Fox had remained in business through returns from its smaller releases. *Butch Cassidy and the Sundance Kid* (1969), *Patton* (1970), and *The French Connection* (1971) had all proved highly successful. In 1972 *The Poseidon Adventure* scored big at the box office. But like other Hollywood studios, Twentieth Century-Fox had been kept alive in large part through television production; it had also been rescued during the *Cleopatra* debacle by the sale of its 640-acre backlot to Alcoa for $43 million. Then, following MGM's example, an auction of Fox's costumes and props was held in 1971.

After Richard Zanuck's demise Dennis Stanfill, who had come to dominate the company's board, was made Twentieth Century-Fox's president. Under Stanfill's supervision 2,000 studio employees were either fired, retired, or furloughed. In 1973 Alan Ladd, Jr., joined the company as vice president for creative affairs. Ladd got off to a rocky start with such fiascoes as *At Long Last Love* (1975) and a remake of *The Blue Bird* (1976), but he redeemed himself by giving a green light to *Star Wars* (1977), whose domestic rentals alone would total upwards to $175 million. Meanwhile, *The Omen* (1976) opened to smash returns, and Mel Brooks's *Silent Movie* (1976) continued the winning trend. Ladd solidified his reputation and demonstrated his ability to attract top talent by pairing Jane Fonda and Vanessa Redgrave in *Julia* and Shirley MacLaine and Anne Bancroft in *The Turning Point* (both 1977), but he left the studio in 1979 after being denied a larger share of the company's profits. He moved to Warner Bros., where he set up his own production unit.

News of Ladd's departure caused Fox's stock to drop from $40.63 to $38.87 in one day. Then in June 1981 Marvin Davis, a Denver oil billionaire, bought Twentieth Century-Fox for $720 million; it was the first time since Howard Hughes's purchase of RKO that an individual had acquired ownership of a major Hollywood film company. Of the old studios, Twentieth Century-Fox remained the only one still independently owned and operated. In 1981 Fox was the sole studio among the majors whose primary interest was the making of feature films and television entertainment.

For three years Sherry Lansing headed production at Twentieth Century-Fox, but there was a dearth of hits during the years of Marvin Davis's ownership. Between 1982 and 1985 the studio lost $189 million. Early in 1985 Davis sold 50-percent interest in the company to Rupert Murdoch, an Australian-born international newspaper magnate, for $575 million. Murdoch, however, saw Twentieth Century-Fox as more than a producer of films and television shows. With the assistance of Barry Diller, the company's chairman and chief executive officer, Murdoch and Davis spent $2 billion buying Metromedia Television. By then Murdoch had taken American citizenship; he promptly bought out Davis and created Fox Broadcasting Company, which soon challenged the three established networks.

But when film director Joe Roth became head of Twentieth Century-Fox in 1989, the studio had made only seven feature movies in the past year. Roth was the fifth person to head the studio in less than a decade; he lasted until late 1992.

NEW DIRECTIONS FOR DISNEY

Beginning in 1955 with the opening of Disneyland, Walt Disney Productions made millions from the amusement parks the company peopled with familiar characters from Disney films. By the early 1960s Disney focused more attention on real estate than movies. Disney World opened in Florida in October 1971, followed by Epcot and Disney theme parks in Europe. The company's profits in 1973 were $47 million, with more than 60 percent of its revenue coming from amusement parks.

The Disney studio in Burbank, however, continued to make films, reaching a commercial peak in 1964 with *Mary Poppins.* In the 1980s Disney's movies remained so consistently profitable that the studio took its place among the Hollywood majors. But in 1984 Roy Disney, Walt's nephew, resigned from the board. The stock of Disney Productions fell to a level below the value of the company's assets.

That same year financier Saul Steinberg, who had a reputation as a feared corporate raider, announced his intention of a hostile takeover of Disney. Steinberg planned to gain control of the company, split it apart, sell the Disney studio, and dispense with some of its other real estate; he would keep and operate Disneyland and Disney World. To the company's executives, Steinberg's scheme was ruthless profiteering, while much of the public viewed it as down-right un-American. Yet Steinberg was prepared to pay more than ten dollars per share higher than the current selling price of Disney stock. A substantial portion of that stock was in the hands of institutional investors, who handled the portfolios of banks, insurance companies, and pension funds, and were obligated to seek the best possible returns on their clients' money. Steinberg did not succeed in his plan, because the Bass brothers from Texas and other new investors bought into the company and reinvigorated it. Within two years after Steinberg's attempted takeover, Disney stock reached its highest level in history.

By that time the company had changed directions in film production. The branch of the Disney family that had controlled the studio for nearly sixty years was no longer in power, and a new team of executives had taken control. At their behest Touchstone Pictures was formed as a second division of Disney Studios. Touchstone, which debuted with *Splash* (1984) starring Daryl Hannah, would make movies for adult audiences rather than the family entertainment the public had come to expect from Disney.

The studio quickly expanded its operation, turning out a series of hits such as *Down and Out in Beverly Hills* (1985), the company's first R-rated film; *Three Men and a Baby* (1987); and *Who Framed Roger Rabbit?* (1988). Disney also resumed animation with such megahits as *Beauty and the Beast* (1991) and *The Lion King* (1994), reissued its classic films on home video, produced such successful television shows as *Golden Girls,* and added Hollywood Pictures. In 1990 the studio's profits had risen to around $650 million.

Five years later Disney bought ABC's network and cable channels for $19 billion, becoming the biggest entertainment company in the world.

THE APPEARANCE OF MINI-MAJORS

Standing between the independent producers, who negotiate each deal separately, and the major studios, which are backed by a more or less steady stream of corporate money, is a more recent group known as the mini-majors. These companies produce or finance movies outside the formal studio structure, do not own real estate, usually rent office space, yet have been responsible for an increasing number of box office hits. Among them have been Orion

Pictures, Lorimar, the Cannon Group, the Ladd Company, the Dino De Laurentiis Entertainment Group, and First Artists.

For fourteen years Orion proved the most successful of the mini-majors. Formed in 1978 by a management team that had previously headed United Artists, Orion scored big in 1986 when three of its pictures—*Platoon, Hannah and Her Sisters,* and *Hoosiers*—received eighteen Academy Award nominations. Orion became the sanctuary for such creative filmmakers as Woody Allen and also diversified into television production, making the long-running *Cagney and Lacey* series. In 1990 the company had spectacular success with *Dances with Wolves* and *The Silence of the Lambs,* both award-winning features, but suffered from debts of nearly $700 million incurred during the late 1980s. Despite its recent triumphs, Orion in 1992 was forced to declare bankruptcy.

Making motion pictures has always been a high-risk business, but it is especially risky for smaller companies. The fickleness of the market, huge investments in scripts, and maintaining the necessary staff of artists, readers, publicists, accountants, and lawyers all work against newer firms. The mini-majors engage exclusively in the production of feature films, yet they do not have the teams of salespeople with established contacts that major studios have developed over the years. The bigger studios and theater owners divide box office returns on films equally. But smaller outfits, since they do not have their own distribution networks, are expected to pay 15 to 20 percent of their cut to the studios that circulate their product.

Hazardous though the movie business may be, three of Hollywood's most powerful figures announced in October 1994 that they were joining to form their own entertainment company, to be called DreamWorks SKG. The three-man team consisted of Steven Spielberg, recently Hollywood's most successful movie director, with an estimated net worth of $600 million; Jeffrey Katzenberg, former head of Disney Studio, who had helped perfect that company's modern style of animation; and David Geffen, a billionaire music and movie entrepreneur who had discovered and recorded such popular singers as Elton John and Linda Ronstadt.

"We want to back our own movies," Spielberg said, "be the owners of our own dreams." The plan was that Katzenberg would run the studio and that the emphasis would be on motion picture and television production, animation, recording, and new interactive media. Initial funding came from the company's three founders, with the probability that their films would be released through Universal.

Spielberg insisted that the goal of the new company would be creative freedom, although he himself kept the right to direct outside projects. "I'd like to find ways to ensure filmmakers have a home they feel comfortable in," he said.

By the early 1990s mini-majors had begun to eat into the market of the established studios. The major companies' share of domestic profits fell from 94 percent in 1992 to 86 percent in 1993, and the projection was that the drop would continue.

CONCLUSION

During Hollywood's Golden Era the major studios operated like self-contained city-states, in absolute control of the means of film production and distribution. The old moguls possessed near-complete authority over their domains and based their decisions on years of moviemaking experience and keen instincts for what the public wanted in entertainment. But toward the end of the 1950s, Hollywood's major producing and distributing organizations, following contemporary trends in international business, were taken over by conglomerates whose purpose was cross media ownership. Their aim was full employment of current marketing concepts on a global scale.

Although many of the new corporate heads were attracted to the glamour of the entertainment world, they often knew little about show business, yet intended for their movie subsidiaries to earn substantial profits. Studio chiefs were expected to score quickly at the box office or suffer the consequences. As a result there have been constant changes in leadership, and hundreds of millions of dollars were dispensed time and again to acquire the services of potential winners. Power in Hollywood remains as elusive as the acclaim leading to it. Even though studio executives have traditionally earned vast salaries, the amounts have grown to astronomical proportions. The pressure on leaders to succeed, however, has increased since the conglomerate takeovers, and few of the current crop expect to hold their positions for very long.

The primary responsibility of the person who heads a studio is to select the pictures that the company will make, but those selected must make money. Costs not only for stars, directors, and writers, but also for cinematographers, editors, and other skilled technicians have spiraled in recent years, so that an increasing number of movies fall into the $100 million category. The more expensive films are the ones that stand the greatest chance of influencing the company's net profits and therefore the value of its stock. A new studio boss will inherit several films that went into production during the previous regime. Since it requires about a year and a half for new projects to be made ready for release, a studio head may be fired before the productions he or she has selected reach fruition.

The passion for movies demonstrated by the old moguls is less evident among today's leaders in Hollywood than a reliance on computerized market research. Keith Barish, producer of *Sophie's Choice* (1982), said:

> As the larger and larger companies take over studios, they start treating film as a product no different than soda pop or potato chips. Same cost controls, same reporting structure, same market testing.

Yet conglomeration has become a given in both the production and distribution of films, with the parent company serving as the bank for its motion picture component. In an earlier period of American history, such titanic combines might have been targets for new antitrust suits, but during the years of Ronald Reagan's economic policies the government showed less interest in restraining corporate consolidation. Whereas the old movie companies had developed into vertical trusts (controlling production, distribution, and exhibition), the present conglomerates have expanded into horizontal ones, embracing a broad sweep of the entertainment business—motion pictures, network, cable, and pay television; home videos; music and records; theme parks; resorts; electronic games; books, magazines, and newspapers; and all varieties of related merchandising.

By the late 1980s the physical size of many of Hollywood's studios had diminished, as valuable real estate was sold for housing developments and shopping centers, leaving shells of what the industry's founders had built. Although work on the major lots remains continuous, most of the activity over recent years is more concerned with television production than with feature films. Instead of the balanced package of theater releases turned out by the old moguls, each of today's movies has to be developed, financed, and produced as a separate entity. Most films are made by independent companies, many of which are short-lived.

Amid the instability and turmoil of contemporary Hollywood, there have been gains, but also losses. Excellent pictures are produced every year, and screen acting has grown more realistic. Motion picture technology has shown remarkable advances, particularly in the area of special effects. Younger studio heads are more receptive to women as executives, producers, and directors, although sexism continues to exist. While sophisticated movies on diverse subjects are made, scripts with simple plots and familiar characters are still preferred over those with complex ideas or unusual story lines.

To win the approval of financial backers, a film must have a star with proven box office potential at the top of its credits. A handful of "bankable" actors but fewer actresses have gained tremendous power in Hollywood, and those can command gigantic fees in addition to a percentage of their films' profits. Studio intrigues are rife, and nothing in Hollywood seems to happen easily, making for a tense and insecure community. A constant complaint is that studios cheat filmmakers through "creative accounting" and "Byzantine bookkeeping," and the feeling is widespread that the only money a creative team member is likely to see is that gotten "up front" (that is, the amount paid when the deal is negotiated).

Concern over foreign control of Hollywood has grown in recent years, especially with the rapid increase of Japanese investments. By 1992 over a third of the 138 pictures made by the major studios were financed by Japanese capital. The total Japanese investment in the industry was estimated to exceed $20 billion. On the other hand, Japan emerged as the largest foreign market for American movies.

In today's Hollywood, filmmakers move, not always easily, between studio pictures, independent productions, series for television, network and cable movies, commercials, and music videos. Producers have become more like agents or packagers who put together deals and take them to a studio for financing and distribution. "The producer has abdicated his function as the creative person in the set-up," said Pandro Berman. Meanwhile veteran actors complain about the depersonalization of their industry. Actress Beverly Garland said:

> Today you're working for Coca-Cola, you're working for Federated, you're working for the Bank of Whatever, you're working for Tokyo. You don't know who the guy at the top is; it's a conglomerate. Everything is business.

Yet the motion picture industry has always been a business, with earnings more important than the production of quality entertainment or lasting art. Despite the bewildering shifts that have taken place in Hollywood's studios over the past decades, and the more recent game of musical chairs affecting top executives, the movie industry in the mid-1990s had again become dynamic and profitable, reaching a diversified market and setting box office records at the theaters.

Julie Andrews and children in the blockbuster musical The Sound of Music *(1965).*

Chapter 4

POPULAR CULTURE TO
COUNTERCULTURE AND BACK

In the years following the assassination of John F. Kennedy, America experienced social unrest, student demonstrations, and violent protests against national policy. "The times they are a-changin'," a contemporary song stated, and the changes came with lightning speed. The upheaval seemed to reverse many of the values and goals on which the country had been built, even making patriotism itself suspect. The decade after Kennedy's death was a time of introspection for Americans, but also a period of piercing criticism and destruction, the ramifications of which are debated still.

In 1965 *The Sound of Music*, a sentimental musical about the von Trapp family singers, became the highest grossing film up to that time, topping the longstanding leader, *Gone with the Wind*. Although critics found the musical silly and unrealistic, the picture became a favorite at the box office for exactly those reasons. Majestically filmed in the Austrian Alps, *The Sound of Music* starred Julie Andrews in the infectious role Mary Martin created on Broadway, featured Richard Rodgers's delicious music and Oscar Hammerstein's appealing lyrics, and added up to pure fun and amusement.

Set during World War II, the musical centers around the German occupation of Austria. When Baron von Trapp refuses to serve as a military specialist for the Nazis, his family flees over the mountains to freedom in Switzerland. But the horrors of Nazi occupation are minimized in the picture; instead a melodious Technicolor dream world unfolds, where "raindrops on roses and whiskers on kittens" rank high among the von Trapp children's favorite things.

Even some disenchanted cast members, who initially referred to the saccharine story as "The Sound of Mucus," changed their attitudes during the ten weeks director Robert Wise filmed around Salzburg. Actress Anna Lee remembered the experience as heaven, and editor William Reynolds found the movie a dream assignment. Lee said:

> The rushes started coming in, and we used to go down to a little theater after shooting and see them. We suddenly realized what a perfectly glorious, beautiful picture this was. *The Sound of Music* was a joy from beginning to end, because it was a happy picture.

The movie cost $10 million and grossed nearly $100 million in rentals, encouraging Hollywood to launch a succession of big pictures. "The worst thing that ever happened to this business was *The Sound of Music*," director Alfred Hitchcock said. "That film stimulated everybody into making expensive films."

For a brief time in the mid-1960s, it looked as if lighthearted, family entertainment was still in demand. Warner Bros.'s stylish screen version of the Lerner and Loewe musical *My Fair Lady* (1964) was a smashing success, and MGM's spectacular *Dr. Zhivago* (1965) became the fourth highest grossing picture in the industry's history to date. But most of the lavish movies that followed in the wake of *The Sound of Music* failed. *Dr. Dolittle* (1967), *Star!* (1968), and *Hello, Dolly!* (1969) all lost big money. Although increased production costs were partly to blame, the major reason for their failure lay in changing tastes of audiences. The generation that dominated movie attendance during the late 1960s and early 1970s expected realism and social comment; suddenly overblown musicals and vapid spectacles seemed old-fashioned and out of touch with the rebellious attitudes of a growing counterculture.

THE DARKENING MOOD

The year after *The Sound of Music*'s unprecedented success, Warner Bros. released its film adaptation of playwright Edward Albee's emotionally brutal *Who's Afraid of Virginia Woolf?* (1966). Directed by Broadway's Mike Nichols and starring Elizabeth Taylor and Richard Burton, the film introduced a new vocabulary to the screen. Shocking though the expletives traded by Burton and Taylor were, the frenzied intensity of *Who's Afraid of Virginia Woolf?* and its searing view of marriage proved no less startling to audiences accustomed to movies filtered through the Production Code. By testing new waters in such depth, *Who's Afraid of Virginia Woolf?* became a landmark and thrust Hollywood into a new era.

By 1967 the mood of the country, particularly among America's youth, had changed drastically. An angry, antiestablishment outlook was developing that demanded a redefinition of freedom, a reexamination of traditional values, and the right to explore untried paths. The existential hero, or antihero, became a model, while the search for deeper meaning led to experimentation with drugs, alternative sex, communal living, and a probing of dark corners of the mind. Ugliness became a sign of inner beauty, disobedience a mark of social responsibility, and permissiveness a mirage for liberty. Yet through it all ran a pessimistic, cynical strain that accepted futility and glorified defeat.

In motion pictures Paul Newman and Steve McQueen emerged as popular antiheroes, for they assumed the kind of roles that Humphrey Bogart had pioneered during the 1940s. In *Cool Hand Luke* (1967) Newman plays a chain gang loner who refuses to submit to authority, and McQueen in *Nevada Smith* (1966) seeks revenge on the killers who tortured his parents to death, only to discover that he runs the risk of becoming as sadistic as they were. Mainly the antihero was at war against a social and political system that no longer defended the individual who dared to be different. "The old heroes used to protect society from its enemies," Paul Newman said. "Now it's society itself that's the enemy."

Hollywood's old formulas no longer seemed to work. Shifting moods and altered values necessitated a different approach, one that explored contemporary themes and reflected current notions of art and worth. The adjustment did not come easily nor without pain, since producers were forced to readjust their critical assumptions. Yet along with an inclination toward pessimism and gloom, Hollywood's films in the late 1960s and early 1970s were significantly reshaped and repositioned, perhaps more than in any period since the advent of sound.

To the new breed nothing was sacred. In 1967 the hero of *The Graduate,* brilliantly played by Dustin Hoffman, is in limbo about his future after college. While coming to terms with adulthood, he engages in an adulterous affair with the seductive wife of his father's business partner. John Boorman's *Deliverance* (1972) found four Atlanta businessmen seeking redemption on a weekend canoe trip, yet instead of tranquility in nature they find sodomy, terror, maiming, and death.

Stanley Kubrick's *2001: A Space Odyssey* (1968) showed humankind's tendency to become more like machines, while machines become more like human beings. Kubrick, always a maverick in Hollywood, earlier had directed *Dr. Strangelove or: How I Learned to Stop Worrying and Love the Bomb* (1964), a nightmare comedy in which an accidental nuclear war is presented as a joke. *2001* is a more poetic film, dealing with human contact with superior extraterrestrial intelligence, yet it raises questions about reality that the viewer is left to answer. Kubrick employed visual rather than narrative language to express his ideas, so that *2001* is vivid with psychedelic impressions. The air in movie theaters during 1968 often grew dense with marijuana smoke, as youthful audiences "turned on" to the universe.

Kubrick emerged as the undisputed leader in imaginative science fiction. Intellectual and stubbornly independent, he exiled himself to England and insisted on total control over his productions. *A Clockwork Orange* (1971), based on the novel by Anthony Burgess, portrays a society in the immediate future based on power and brings an explosion of violence to the screen. In this bizarre society— devoid of religion, art, entertainment, and moral values—the young form brutal street gangs primarily because they have no other outlet for their energies. *A Clockwork Orange* is a frightening look at what life could become, but it found a ready audience among the disenchanted, skeptical youth of the early 1970s.

Technical excellence is a hallmark of Kubrick's films, and there could be little doubt that the director was truly innovative. He constantly returned to what he considered the great dilemma of modern industrial society—the gap between humankind's scientific and technological knowledge and humanity's social, political, and moral ineptitude. In each of his examples this fatal flaw wrought disaster.

No longer did actors and actresses look like glamorous movie stars; they acted characters on the screen rather than bigger-than-life personalities. "I'm not a movie star," Academy Award-winner Gene Hackman insisted; "I'm an actor!" The grand old names of

Hollywood were fast disappearing. Most of the new crowd prided themselves on their stage experience and professional versatility, although many came from television. Movies of the period focused on men more than women (perhaps a reaction to the women's movement), and many of the popular arrivals were ethnic actors: Dustin Hoffman, Al Pacino, Robert DeNiro, among others. Some stars shared the jaundiced view of society that was becoming a prevailing mode, while most accepted the directorial nonconformity that resulted in a looser, freer kind of film.

NEW WAVE INFLUENCES

Although the international market for American movies expanded during the early 1960s, Hollywood filmmakers also came to be strongly influenced by new techniques from Europe, particularly what became known as the "New Wave" originating in France. In 1960 American audiences experienced two imports from abroad that affected both the shape and content of future Hollywood films: Jean-Luc Godard's *Breathless* and Francois Truffaut's *The Four Hundred Blows*. Godard and Truffaut were among France's most innovative directors, at the front of the New Wave movement. Their approach was improvisational, casual about plot, contemporary in tone, and full of personal touches. New Wave films were filled with profanity, sex, and violence. A new look in picturemaking was introduced through such techniques as ultrarapid cutting, hand-held cameras, zoom lenses, dramatic use of slow motion, helicopter shooting, brief flashes lasting only a fraction of a second, and freeze-frame endings. The intent was to create an atmosphere of supercharged realism, although critics accused the New Wave directors of emotional dryness.

By 1965 the New Wave impact was hailed by some as a revolution. For others the new approach wiped away skills Hollywood professionals had worked to develop over the past fifty years, substituting rank amateurism instead. Curiously enough, the unrehearsed look characteristic of New Wave films owed a great deal to American B movies, which were shot fast and without much rehearsal. Many of the impromptu techniques were first evident in the United States in television production; later they were transferred to the big screen by such former television directors as Sidney Lumet, Robert Mulligan, and John Frankenheimer. At their best the New Wave methods added a welcome freshness to Hollywood's movies.

Bonnie and Clyde (1967) incorporated a potpourri of New Wave effects and aroused more controversy than perhaps any film of the decade. The movie lifted two petty Southwestern bank robbers, Clyde Barrow and Bonnie Parker, into poetic folk heroes. An intense, often violent physicality pervades the picture, which juxtaposes farce and horror. By lauding unconventional morality, *Bonnie and Clyde* appealed to the insurrectionary spirit of the late 1960s and was particularly popular among the youth. Its populist heroes were seen almost as precursors to the growing counterculture, innocent rebels at odds with an unjust social order. The boredom and outrage then current in the nation's young people were cinematically articulated through a pair of mythologized outlaws.

Director Arthur Penn took great pains to reconstruct the atmo-sphere of the 1930s as authentically as possible in *Bonnie and Clyde,* yet its issues took on a contemporary flavor, defining the pre-sent as it evoked the past. The romance between Clyde Barrow and Bonnie Parker, played by Warren Beatty and Faye Dunaway, served as the movie's subplot. Although Clyde is impotent at the outset, his sexual prowess grows as his skill and fame as a bank robber develop.

Barrow and Parker were killed in 1934 in a police ambush in Louisiana, cut down by ninety-four bullets in a blood bath. In Penn's film their slaughter becomes a ballet of death, with slow motion used effectively to heighten the drama. *Bonnie and Clyde* is full of tension on multiple levels, some of which stemmed from the on-the-set fights between the director and Warren Beatty, who also produced the movie. "It was a very dynamic situation," remembered Estelle Parsons, who won an Academy Award for her role in the film. "Warren and Arthur Penn fought all the time; every single shot they fought about how it should be done. But I think it created a certain energy, not only between them, but among those of us in the cast." Despite the turmoil that *Bonnie and Clyde* unleashed at the time of its release, most critics agreed the movie represented a watershed for the American cinema.

Robert Altman, another of the Hollywood directors influenced by the New Wave, aimed at providing movie audiences with open-ended experiences, intending to implicate viewers in the creative process. After serving an apprenticeship in television, Altman turned to feature films, soon becoming a master at the casual, loosely constructed kind of film that the French innovators had pioneered. Altman's *M*A*S*H* (1970), a black comedy centering around an American medical unit during the Korean War, introduced camera and editing techniques that significantly altered the pace and format of Hollywood movies. The film's antiwar, anti-establishment attitude won cheers from counterculture audiences, who delighted in its often cruel wit directed at the government, the military, organized religion, and conventional morality.

Nashville (1975) represented a high-water mark for Altman, although it signals the death of the American dream. The film uses the country music industry as a metaphor for big business and offers a pessimistic view of the nation's goals and values. In Altman's vision the country's social institutions are decayed, its celebrities cardboard, its liberals either foolish or hypocritical. Business and politics have become deceptive and corrupt, motivated by lust and greed, while the great American majority remain apathetic to their manipulation.

Released on the eve of the nation's bicentennial, *Nashville* was admired but controversial. Altman saw diversity in American society and showed multiple points of view without resolution. Like most of his work, *Nashville* is a difficult film, not easily interpreted. Altman's production techniques proved highly innovative; he encouraged actors to improvise dialogue, write their own songs, and adjust the script as they formed their characters, drawing on aspects of their own lives. His goal was spontaneity and collective involvement.

Robert Altman's *McCabe and Mrs. Miller* (1971) and Arthur Penn's *The Missouri Breaks* (1976) both took a revisionist look at the American West, showing the underside of the frontier experience and a darker view of the nation's creation myth. Theirs was not the heroic West of popular fiction, but a West of hired guns, exploitation, and violence. In *McCabe and Mrs. Miller* corporations greedily divide the riches of the frontier and stifle individual freedom.

Both Altman and Penn challenged simple truths and conventional morality. Theirs is a far more complex world, a world in which solitary antiheroes, buddies, and communities of men (more frequently than women) are in search of themselves. Together with other directors influenced by the New Wave, Altman and Penn inserted bold techniques into American filmmaking, so that the screen between *Bonnie and Clyde* and *Nashville* exploded with some of the freshest, wildest innovations Hollywood had ever experienced.

THE NEW RATING SYSTEM

With revolutionary changes taking place in Hollywood's movies, the old Production Code seemed increasingly antiquated. Society's values were changing; experimentation and radical thinking became characteristic of a turbulent period in which youth played a conspicuous role. Although the Production Code had suffered severe blows during the 1950s, *Tom Jones* (1963), a lusty British import, ruptured most of the remaining precepts. Audiences received the movie with whoops of joy, and the film won the Academy Award for best picture of the year. Clearly there was a fundamental hypocrisy surrounding a Code that supported a sanctimonious attitude no longer in vogue.

In 1966 the Supreme Court declared precensorship to be unconstitutional and put an end to municipal censorship boards. At last Hollywood was free of the Production Code's strictures, yet public debate over obscenity in movies continued. In April 1968 the Supreme Court on the same day handed down two decisions that allowed communities to establish their own guidelines and create a rating system.

On October 7, 1968, Jack Valenti, president of the Motion Picture Association of America, unveiled a national rating system, which went into effect the following month. Under Valenti's arrangement each film produced or distributed would be submitted to MPAA for rating prior to its commercial release. Modeled after the British system, the categories Valenti introduced were G for general audiences; M for mature audiences (later changed to PG, parental guidance suggested); R for restricted audiences, persons under seventeen not admitted without a parent or guardian; and X, no one under eighteen admitted. The new rating scheme shifted responsibility for what minors could see away from filmmakers, distributors, and theater managers to parents.

The years immediately following the end of the old Production Code saw a flurry of superb, challenging, iconoclastic films, many of which contained explicit sex, graphic violence, blasphemous language, and themes that earlier would have been taboo. Hollywood's movies delved deep into sexuality, unorthodox passions, and what heretofore had been considered perversions.

In Paul Mazursky's *Bob and Carol and Ted and Alice* (1969), a middle-class couple attend a sensitivity institute and vow to expand their capacity for love and understanding by sharing everything with each other. So intense is their enthusiasm that they decide to include their closest friends, an uptight married couple. The foursome conclude that final barriers will be broken if they all sleep together. Since mate-swapping was openly discussed in sophisticated circles at the time, *Bob and Carol and Ted and Alice* reflected the sexual revolution currently in vogue, along with the belief that the fulfillment of sexual longings was essential for self-expression and self-awareness.

Carnal Knowledge (1971) is an even franker exploration of contemporary sexual mores. The film chronicles the sexual and emotional confusion of two male characters and meets sexism head on. Its protagonists are full of self-contempt and self-doubt, incapable of understanding what goes into a healthy sexual or romantic relationship. *Last Tango in Paris* (1973) probes the extremes of sexual fantasy. A burnt-out widower, played by Marlon Brando, is driven to assert his masculinity, venting his frustrations and aggressions on a twenty-two-year-old girl. He demands from her total subservience to his sexual wishes, including sodomy. *Last Tango in Paris* proved an enormously sensual film—praised by some critics, denounced by others.

In *Shampoo* (1975) Warren Beatty plays a Beverly Hills hairdresser who is a heterosexual Don Juan. The movie opens the night before Richard Nixon's reelection in 1972, and it exposes the excesses of recent sexual practices, as well as the prostitution of self within corporate America. Beatty's hairdresser wants to be a star, schemes to own his own shop, tempers his ambition by having sex with every beautiful woman he meets, yet in the end he stands alone, unhappy and unfulfilled.

The isolation and moral vacuum of contemporary urban life is vividly depicted in *Midnight Cowboy* (1969) and *Klute* (1971). In the first, Joe Buck, a semiliterate idler, leaves his small Texas hometown and moves to New York City, where he becomes a male hustler. *Midnight Cowboy* took advantage of the new freedom granted Hollywood to treat a sordid slice of American life, yet the picture remains as moving as it is tragic. It won the Academy Award for best movie of the year. *Klute,* on the other hand, is a detective-thriller with Jane Fonda playing a sophisticated New York call girl, the role for which she won her first Oscar for best actress.

During the late 1960s pop artist Andy Warhol became an underground filmmaker and popular culture icon, turning out avant-garde movies such as *Flesh* (1968) and *Trash* (1970). Warhol's pictures have a random quality and reflect the then-current practices of absolute sexual freedom. "There was never any script for the films," said Joe Dallesandro, Warhol's perennial male lead. "The dialogues were improvised." Nudity abounded in Warhol's movies, as the filmmaker wound his way through a variety of heterosexual and homosexual experiences.

By the early 1970s even hard-core pornography received nation-wide distribution for general adult audiences. *Deep Throat* (1972), starring Linda Lovelace, played in seventy American cities and grossed in excess of $3 million by January 1973. The movie was made in six days on a budget of $25,000 and featured actual copula-tion, cunnilingus, and fellatio, with close-ups of genitals. *The Devil in Miss Jones* (1973) pretended to be arty but ranked as pornography and benefited from mass-media attention. By 1975 explicit homo-sexual movies had also become common, especially in larger cities.

The removal of censorship also meant that unbridled violence could be shown on the screen. In 1969 violence in movies reached unprecedented heights, with director Sam Peckinpah leading the way. Peckinpah, who began his career in television, was convinced that violence is an inherent characteristic in all human beings; he believed that individuals must recognize and come to terms with that fact. His emphasis was always on harsh reality, and along with Robert Altman and Arthur Penn, he helped put an end to the traditional western.

Through all of his films, Peckinpah's central concern is the con-flict between individual dignity and survival. In *The Wild Bunch* (1969) the director focused on a theme he had sounded earlier in *Ride the High Country* (1962)—proud individuals overwhelmed by changing times. His outlaw band is violently at war with a corrupt social order that threatens personal freedom. Set in Mexico during the Pancho Villa rampage, *The Wild Bunch* contains scenes of limit-less brutality, showing blood spurting from bullet wounds and gush-ing from cut throats. The picture was shot and edited during the spring and summer of 1968—a violent time in American history, which saw the assassination of Martin Luther King, Jr., the burning of sections of the nation's cities, the murder of Robert Kennedy, the beating and arrest of students, the Tet offensive, and the chaos of the Democratic national convention in Chicago. Released at the close of one of the most turbulent decades in history, Peckinpah's film tore down most of the remaining barriers to graphic violence on the screen. The director added power to his brutality by splicing together film shot at varying speeds, ranging from normal to extreme slow motion. The juxtaposition created an internal tension, while his detail and pace served to intensify the ferocity of horror heaped upon horror.

Peckinpah's obsession with violence continued in *Straw Dogs* (1971), his first feature set in the present. Although he saw the ambiguity of life, Peckinpah's theme is again the individual's standing up against injustice. *Straw Dogs* contained another Peckinpah bloodbath and, like most of his films, proved highly controversial.

In the early 1970s filmmakers' fascination with violence led to a new genre, the "splatter" movie, far less profound than Peckinpah's films but popular with younger audiences. *The Texas Chainsaw Massacre* (1974) is a terrifying picture, grimly realistic, but it was a huge box office success and superior to the spate of imitations that followed.

THE YOUTH MARKET

As the youth of the late 1960s grew more demonstrative in their alienation, they wanted movies that incorporated their point of view. The better-educated preferred films that were both intellectually stimulating and emotionally fulfilling. *The Graduate,* among the era's undisputed classics, captures much of the younger generation's quandary in the form of a social comedy. Benjamin Braddock, the film's antihero, the role that skyrocketed Dustin Hoffman to fame, is not ready to accept adult life, which he views as dominated by values and goals that do not make sense. His seductress—Mrs. Robinson, played by Anne Bancroft—is a comic yet tragic symbol of the acquisitive, never-satisfied, bored, upper-middle-class matron. Benjamin sees her lifestyle and that of his parents as sterile and suffocating. Even though he is not openly rebellious, neither is he willing to conform to his family's expectations.

Benjamin's dilemma was one that the youth of the late 1960s and early 1970s mouthed endlessly in a voice that grew increasingly hostile. For the counterculture, compromise was a dirty word, associated with middle-class standards they were determined to escape. The crumbling of established values resulted in a plethora of films projecting a fragmented America, no longer certain of its identity. More and more, the motif of American cinema came to be disintegration and breakdown, as capitalistic society was construed as ideologically rotten to the core.

Peter Fonda as Captain America in Easy Rider *(1969).*

With *Easy Rider* (1969) the counterculture was featured for the first time in a major motion picture. Produced by Peter Fonda and directed by Dennis Hopper, who also starred in the picture, *Easy Rider* marked the beginning of a new era in Hollywood, a time when young filmmakers not only became more prominent, but demanded greater freedom of artistic expression. With the youth cult reaching its height, movie producers suddenly wore love beads rather than diamond rings and smoked marijuana rather than cigars. Like other young filmmakers of the time, Peter Fonda and Dennis Hopper were motivated by different rules from what Hollywood had known in the past. They addressed their movie to a relatively narrow but growing segment of the total population and captured the rebellious spirit of the generation that was challenging basic tenets of American life.

Easy Rider centers around two hip drug dealers, who after concluding a lucrative deal in Mexico take off on their motorbikes to see America. They want to live a free life, experience the beauty of the land, and have fun at Mardi Gras. Because of their long hair and unorthodox dress, however, they find themselves surrounded by enemies who refuse to accommodate them in motels or serve them in rural cafes. Along the way they visit a hippie commune, smoke dope, and are thrown in jail, where they meet George Hanson, a small-town, alcoholic lawyer out of step with his prominent Southern family and stifling environment. George, played by Jack Nicholson, joins the two bikers and reveals himself as something of a philosopher. "You know, this used to be a hell of a good country," George tells his counterculture friends. "I don't know what happened to it."

In New Orleans, after George has been killed by redneck townspeople who resent any deviation from the accepted rules, Hopper and Fonda's characters pick up two prostitutes and wander through the streets filled with Mardi Gras revelers. In a cemetery the four of them take acid, whereupon the film shows their drug experience in purposely chaotic, distorted sequences that give insight into the characters' emotions and fears.

Easy Rider often seems improvised, disjointed, and even incoherent, for Hopper placed little emphasis on a straight-line narrative. "The script was left flexible enough that we could add to it or change it as we traveled," the director said. Hopper used flash-forwards and, instead of dissolving from one scene to the next, flashes of an upcoming scene are intercut into the previous one before it ends.

The film cost less than $600,000 and grossed more than $60 million, proving an enormous success in the capitals of Western Europe. Although not a wholesale endorsement of the counterculture, *Easy Rider* was welcomed by the nonconformist youth of the late 1960s as an anthem of freedom. A later generation would find the hippie philosophy, with its sexual revolution and casual acceptance of drug use, shallow and fraught with dangers. But for a time Hollywood executives scrambled for ways to devise scripts that the alienated youth of the period would accept and pay money to see on the screen.

In 1969 it was estimated that 50 percent of American filmgoers were between ages sixteen and twenty-four. If nothing else, the financial success of *Easy Rider* proved the box office potential of a specialized youth market. Movie moguls rushed to install young executives who they hoped had the capacity to fashion more movies to which nonconformists of the Age of Aquarius could relate. A new generation of directors arrived on the scene, determined to "tell it like it is" in films of intense realism. Untried talent invaded the studios, eager to retire traditional character models in favor of alternate types and a lifestyle that would appeal to a fractured society. Romance all but disappeared from the screen, as a new crop of

Hollywood filmmakers focused on the loss of consensus and the death of the American dream.

For a while, looser formats and counterculture messages seemed to possess elements of freshness. For *Alice's Restaurant* (1969) director Arthur Penn used nonprofessional actors and avoided stylized scenes, deliberately giving his gritty film a rambling, homespun, sometimes crude look. Penn's movie celebrates the virtues of communal living, lashes out at bureaucracy and social hypocrisy, and severely criticizes the Johnson-Nixon position on the war in Vietnam. *Alice's Restaurant* is a more coherent look at the contemporary counterculture than *Easy Rider,* but it portrays the same kind of personal freedom, idealized by a collectivist lifestyle.

In *I Love You Alice B. Toklas* (1968), a comedy starring Peter Sellers, a mild-mannered, middle-aged lawyer freaks out and becomes a hippie. *Woodstock* (1970), on the other hand, is a documentary of the famous 1969 pop music festival in upstate New York. Filmed cheaply and released by Warner Bros., *Woodstock* celebrates a counterculture that was rapidly becoming a mass phenomenon. The flower children who flocked to Woodstock advocated love and peace at a time when antagonism and opposition was deepening in the country. The documentary of the rock festival brought in millions at the box office and again proved the power of the growing youth market.

In *Five Easy Pieces* (1970) Jack Nicholson plays another dissatisfied rover, unable to find his place in society. Staying for long in any situation brings him distress; commitment is impossible for him. Out of touch with his feelings and rebelling against a dysfunctional family, Nicholson's character has little insight into his own identity. He wants autonomy, yet suffers from loneliness. So he finds himself on the road, sacrificing his own promise in an endless quest for freedom.

The drug subculture made headlines in 1970; dropping out and turning on became revered as an alternative to a materialistic, emotionally constipated, corrupt establishment. In *Getting Straight* (1970) Elliott Gould and Candice Bergen are graduate students unable to decide whether to drop in or drop out of a hypocritical society. *The Strawberry Statement* (1970), based on riots at Columbia University that had recently occurred, reflects the attitudes of a generation immersed in social strife, but *American Graffiti* (1973) looks back on the previous era, when life was simpler, with genuine affection.

THE DISCOVERY OF MINORITIES

In the late 1960s with American audiences for movies shrinking and advances in the civil rights movement underway, Hollywood began catering more to black people. Although *Guess Who's Coming to Dinner* (1967) was made by the white establishment primarily for white audiences, it remains a landmark film, since the movie sympathetically portrays a romance between an accomplished black doctor and a white girl. With clean-cut Sidney Poitier playing the doctor and Spencer Tracy and Katharine Hepburn as the girl's parents, *Guess Who's Coming to Dinner* won critical acclaim and became a box office success.

Hollywood studios still offered few opportunities to black actors, and jobs behind the camera for blacks were virtually nonexistent. Only a handful of African Americans belonged to the craft guilds, even though the National Association for the Advancement of Colored People had formed a Hollywood–Beverly Hills chapter in 1962 with the intent of pressing for greater employment of blacks within the motion picture industry and demanding more accurate depictions of their race on the screen. But studio executives remained fearful of offending white audiences, particularly in the South, and were slow to break with accepted racial stereotypes.

In the Heat of the Night (1967), another film featuring Sidney Poitier, makes a strong statement about race relations behind the facade of an exciting melodrama. "We felt we were doing a picture that was going to entertain and that also said a lot of things we thought should be said," producer Walter Mirisch declared. *In the Heat of the Night* won the Academy Award for best picture of the year and was popular with both black and white audiences.

Likewise, crossover films such as *Lady Sings the Blues* and *Sounder* (both 1972) were targeted for general audiences. In the former Diana Ross plays singer Billie Holiday, while in the latter Cicely Tyson is a black, Southern sharecropper during the Great Depression. As in Sidney Poitier's movies where his role is that of an idealized hero, neither film posed a serious threat to middle-class values. By 1970, however, studios discovered that blacks would turn out in numbers for movies that featured black performers and were sprinkled with sex and violence. Between 1970 and 1972 some fifty pictures were aimed specifically at the black community.

Referred to as "blaxploitation," these movies were geared to a previously untapped market. *Shaft* (1971), starring Richard

Roundtree and directed by Gordon Parks, a black director, centers around an African American detective. The story is full of thrilling incidents, with the charming Shaft invariably coming out on top. Whites in the movie are either villains or blundering and inept. The picture was particularly popular among black urban males and was followed the next year by *Shaft's Big Score* and *Superfly.*

Cotton Comes to Harlem (1970) proved a commercial success beyond the most optimistic expectations, with an estimated 70 percent of its rentals coming from the black sector. Based on Chester Himes's detective novel, *Cotton Comes to Harlem* marked the film debut of Ossie Davis, a black director and actor; the film skillfully combined action with comedy.

For a brief period it seemed that black audiences were hungry for entertainment cast in their own image. Jim Brown starred in *Slaughter* and *Black Gunn* (both 1972) as a new type of macho hero, seen beating up white Mafia members. *Watermelon Man* (1970) is a comedy that explores racist attitudes when a bigoted white man wakes up one morning to discover that he's turned black; John Berry's *Claudine* (1974), another comedy, centers around a black family on welfare. The latter two films were made for general audiences; by 1974 the number of pictures concerned with black cultural identity was greatly reduced.

The civil rights movement sparked an awareness of other minorities, but Hispanic material in Hollywood's movies remained stereotypical until well into the 1970s. Arthur Penn's *The Left-Handed Gun* (1958) and Sam Peckinpah's *Pat Garrett and Billy the Kid* (1973) perpetuate the legend of Billy the Kid as the friend of oppressed Hispanics and the enemy of Anglo cattle barons, whereas *Viva Max!* (1970) depicts in opera-buffa style Chicanos retaking the Alamo. By the mid-1970s it was common for at least one Latino worker to appear in office scenes, whereas classroom sequences might have a López or a Gómez among the students shown.

The shift in Hollywood's portrayal of Native Americans came sooner and was far more sweeping. *Broken Arrow* (1950) began the trend toward a sympathetic treatment of the Indian, although the movie's plea for racial tolerance seemed to transform Native Americans into model whites rather than acknowledging their distinctive culture. With a script written by Alvah Bessie, one of the imprisoned Hollywood Ten, *Broken Arrow* reversed the pattern of earlier westerns by showing armed conflict from the Indian point of view. This revisionist trend continued in the decades ahead, reaching an apex in Arthur Penn's *Little Big Man* (1970), in which the Indians became the heroes and General George Armstrong Custer was seen as a pompous buffoon.

Billy Jack (1971), on the other hand, was the first commercial movie to present the contemporary American Indian and quickly became a cult film. Its title character is a half-breed Southwesterner whose fighting skills stemmed from his experiences in Vietnam. Billy Jack, violence prone and anxiety ridden, emerges as a counterculture hero who attacks the system and wins by losing.

Men and male bonding dominated the screen during the late 1960s and early 1970s, with women appearing in marginal roles. Barbra Streisand emerged as one of the few female superstars in the years after Elizabeth Taylor's popularity faded, although Faye Dunaway, Jane Fonda, and Vanessa Redgrave played a succession of liberated women and were considered bankable stars. Most female roles during the period remained reactionary by feminist standards.

Alice Doesn't Live Here Anymore (1975), about a young mother's search for self and happiness after her husband dies leaving her penniless, signaled a change in the portrayal of women and was soon hailed as a feminist classic. In 1977 *An Unmarried Woman, The Turning Point, Annie Hall,* and *Looking for Mr. Goodbar* all had female protagonists and addressed some of the issues raised by the women's movement. *Norma Rae* (1979) focused on a female textile worker who turns labor activist in a depressed Southern factory town. By the end of the decade the message from Hollywood seemed clear: Meaningful work was no less essential for women than men.

The aged also came in for a sympathetic reevaluation. In Hal Ashby's *Harold and Maude* (1972) a seventy-nine-year-old woman teaches a twenty-year-old male to love life rather than death, and in Paul Mazursky's *Harry and Tonto* (1974), an old man is featured on a cross-country trip with only his cat as companion.

Until the mid-1960s homosexuality was seldom hinted at in American films. Both *Staircase* (1969) and *Death in Venice* (1971), however, picture males attracted to their own sex, while *The Killing of Sister George* (1968) and *Once Is Not Enough* (1975) treat lesbianism with frankness. *Sunday, Bloody Sunday* (1971) presents homosexuality as part of the human condition, rather than as a curiosity, and shows a passionate kiss between men. Such mainstream films were addressed to the majority more than to gays and often brought protests from gay activists. *The Boys in the Band*

(1970) drew a particularly negative response, since the film portrays homosexual life as inherently miserable.

In June 1969, barely a week before *The Boys in the Band* went before the cameras, patrons at Stonewall, a gay bar in Greenwich Village, got into a fight with New York police making a harassment raid. A week of demonstrations followed, as the gay rights movement in America took form. The decade that followed saw major changes in public awareness of homosexuals, with more Hollywood films coming to depict facets of gay life, not always in a favorable light.

In July 1979 director William Friedkin began filming *Cruising* in and around New York's leather bars, creating major controversy. In the movie Al Pacino plays an undercover cop seeking a vicious killer of gay men. When *Cruising* was released, many agreed that it was a distorted look at the gay community and a potentially dangerous film.

PROTESTS AGAINST THE VIETNAM WAR

The participation of the United States in the Vietnam War increased in 1965 with the commitment of American ground troops. In a turbulent decade of inflation, race riots, assassinations, counterculture dissent, and student demonstrations, American involvement in the Asian war became the single most divisive issue. Rick Halperin, a student at George Washington University during the late 1960s, said:

> My undergraduate schooling was accomplished in the streets, not in the classroom. My most vivid memories are of spending three successive years, virtually month after month, demonstrating against the war in Vietnam.

Brutal clashes took place between unarmed protesters and police employing clubs, tear gas, and mace to restore order. Peter Delisle, a student at the University of Connecticut in 1968, signed up for ROTC at the beginning of his freshman year. "When I graduated four years later," said Delisle, "we were commissioned behind locked doors because school administrators were afraid some kind of violence might be done."

Disagreement over Vietnam split the nation into hawks and doves, those favoring American involvement in the war and those opposing it. Screen hero John Wayne, an outspoken hawk, made a tour of Vietnam and returned home to make *The Green Berets* (1968), a salute to American forces fighting in southeast Asia. With polarization over the war reaching its height, *Patton* (1970) won applause from both sides, since the World War II warrior was depicted as an ambiguous, multidimensioned hero.

After 1975, when American military involvement officially ended, the Vietnam War became the subject of a cycle of hard-hitting films that depicted the havoc caused by the decade-long conflict. *Coming Home* (1978) deals with a Marine officer's wife who falls in love with a paraplegic veteran. Michael Cimino's *The Deer Hunter* (1978) shows the destruction and terror of the war through the metaphor of Russian roulette. Although the image has no basis in fact, it captures the risk, insanity, and despair experienced by the Vietnam soldiers in raw, existential terms. In its depiction of the homefront, *The Deer Hunter* established a sense of community that enabled Americans to survive a crisis that nearly tore them apart.

Francis Ford Coppola's *Apocalypse Now* (1979) presents war as a conflict of the soul; the slaughter in Vietnam was depicted as psychological and moral insanity. Technically dazzling, Coppola's film contains realistic battle footage and a famous helicopter attack set to Wagner's "The Ride of the Valkyries." Based in part on Joseph Conrad's *Heart of Darkness, Apocalypse Now* was to be the director's statement about the horror of all wars, but the movie evokes a sense of doom that would be echoed later in *Platoon* (1986), *Full Metal Jacket* (1987), and *Born on the Fourth of July* (1989).

HOLLYWOOD IN THE DOLDRUMS

By the close of the 1960s the movie business was reaching its nadir. Studio executives seemed to have lost touch with their public, as one film company after another reported quarterly losses. Twentieth Century-Fox, for example, lost $65 million in 1969 and $81 million the following year. "Without in any way making excuses for the disappointing performance of some of our pictures," Darryl Zanuck said, "it should be observed that there has been a revolution in public taste which has resulted in the rapid obsolescence of films and story properties which, when originally initiated, represented sound business risks."

With costs escalating, most of the big pictures that were released proved expensive failures. The current emphasis on sex and violence resulted in a loss of the family trade. Even though content in Hollywood's movies matured during the late 1960s, audiences grew tired of cynicism and tragedy, amateurish attempts at social messages, antiestablishment and revisionist statements, the debunking of heroes, and hopeless neurotics on the screen.

The retrenchment in Hollywood meant widespread unemployment for workers in the various film crafts. In March 1970, during the annual hiatus in telefilming, it was reported that 48.8 percent of the industry's total work force was out of a job. Parent companies attempted to hide the devastating returns of their invalid studios through accounting shenanigans, but the majors suffered more than $200 million in losses during 1969 alone. Two years later *Filmmakers Newsletter* stated that "things must now get better since they seem to be at their worst."

By 1973 Hollywood was turning away from the grisly theme of *In Cold Blood* (1967) and the despondency of *They Shoot Horses, Don't They?* (1969) to more escapist entertainment. As the 1960s faded into historical caricature, long hair became less fashionable than "the dry look," protesting was replaced by jogging, heroin was used less frequently than cocaine, and activism as a social ideal gave way to self-realization. Young filmmakers turned their intelligence and technical wizardry to the making of artistic films that were also appealing to general audiences.

Studios continued to rely on series and sequels, since those held the greatest potential for profit without much risk. The James Bond movies, with their lighthearted amorality, set the pace, creating loyal fans that formed a core for successive audiences. Other profitable series included the Pink Panther pictures and the Dirty Harry films. As the decade progressed, the public's interest in moviegoing was rekindled, box office receipts recovered, and the number of feature films released each year increased. Yet of the 199 major films released in 1977, it was calculated that the top six brought in one-third of the year's rentals, the top thirteen accounted for half, and the top twenty-eight were responsible for three-fourths.

DISASTER AND THE OCCULT

For a time in the early 1970s disaster dominated the screen. In January 1971 *Airport* headed the list of box office favorites for the previous year, grossing more than $200 million. Produced by Ross Hunter and featuring a star-studded cast, *Airport* has the look and feel of a big picture from Hollywood's Golden Era. Hunter saw it as "a good old-fashioned *Grand Hotel* of the air." The movie's success led to *Airport 1975* and *Airport '77,* all three dealing with jetliner disasters.

The Poseidon Adventure (1972) followed closely the pattern set by *Airport;* the picture placed a host of stars on a luxury cruise ship that is capsized by a tidal wave. Mindless though it may be, the tale adds up to engrossing entertainment. *The Poseidon Adventure* helped restore the reputation of the big-budget film and paved the way for a sequel, *Beyond the Poseidon Adventure* (1979).

Twentieth Century-Fox and Warner Bros. joined forces for *The Towering Inferno* (1974), which offered a cast of current and former screen stars at a cost of $12.5 million. An idiotic story about a skyscraper that catches on fire the evening of its dedication, *The Towering Inferno* presents gripping pyrotechnics and had movie-goers flocking to the theaters.

Earthquake (1974) cost Universal $7.5 million, had another all-star cast headed by Charlton Heston and Ava Gardner, and was originally released with Sensurround, a gimmick that provided realistic rumbles to thrill theater patrons. *The Hindenburg* (1975) was a less hackneyed disaster epic about the famous 1937 airship explosion that combined newsreel footage of the actual event with material shot by director Robert Wise.

Roman Polanski's *Rosemary's Baby* (1968) launched a cycle of movies that dealt with supernatural terror. Like Alfred Hitchcock, Polanski had long been fascinated with the enigma of violence, but had shown a penchant for presenting fantastic subjects in a realistic manner. "For as far back as I can remember, the line between fantasy and reality has been hopelessly blurred," the Polish director wrote in his autobiography. Influenced by theater of the absurd and surrealism, Polanski's presentation of reality is always somewhat askew. He set off a censorship dispute with a scene in *Rosemary's Baby* where the title character is raped by Satan, a cinematic tour de force in which the director created the look and feel of irrational dreams.

The picture was an overnight sensation, and for a brief time Polanski became Hollywood's golden boy. He was deluged with scripts from major studios, mostly horror stories involving madness and the occult. Ten years after *Rosemary's Baby* was released, forty-five-year-old Polanski fled the United States before he could be sentenced for engaging in sex with a thirteen-year-old girl. Knowing that arrest awaits him, he has not returned.

But the popularity of films dealing with the occult persisted. *The Exorcist,* released late in 1973, was a blockbuster and became one of the top-grossing movies of all time. Directed by William Friedkin, *The Exorcist* deals with the exorcism of demonic spirits from the body of a possessed child. *Film Quarterly* called it "the trash bombshell of 1973, the aesthetic equivalent of being run over by a truck." Although the picture represents an extreme in cinematic cruelty and manipulates the most primitive fears in audiences, it remains a cult favorite.

So does *The Omen* (1976), a sensational horror story about the antichrist residing within a young boy. The movie offers plenty of gore, including a decapitation, but proved a huge moneymaker at the box office and has become a classic of its genre. *Halloween* (1978) cost $320,000 to make and grossed more than $75 million. The thriller about a psychotic murderer had many scares and established a framework for countless *Halloween* clones.

THE MOVIE BRATS

The real achievement of the early 1970s came from a new generation of directors who appeared in Hollywood after the crumbling of the old studio system. Mostly graduates of university film schools, the new breed had been taught to make movies in their own way. Intelligent and independent, these "movie brats," as they became known, were restless under studio bureaucracy and unwilling to sub-scribe to established trends. Their creativity had been honed within the context of a liberal arts education, on both the undergraduate and graduate levels, and they were determined to express them-selves in unique ways. At the forefront of this impressive group were Francis Ford Coppola, Brian DePalma, Martin Scorsese, John Milius, George Lucas, and Steven Spielberg.

Francis Ford Coppola was the first of the six to make a feature film. Coppola entered the University of California at Los Angeles in the fall of 1960; two of his teachers there were Jean Renoir, the great French filmmaster, and Dorothy Arzner, one of old Hollywood's few women directors, both of whom offered him encouragement. Upon graduation, Coppola worked as an assistant to Roger Corman, who eventually gave him a chance to direct his first movie, *Dementia 13*, a low-budget production. The novice director was twenty-two at the time.

An eternal outsider, Coppola's work has been strongly influ-enced by his Italian heritage. Rather than living in Los Angeles and playing the Hollywood game, he chose to make his home in the

Marlon Brando, backed by Robert Duvall, in The Godfather *(1971).*

Napa Valley, later organizing his own production company from a San Francisco base. Coppola's experience directing *Finian's Rainbow* (1968) at Warner Bros. proved an unhappy one. Jack Warner was leaving the studio after forty-five years, and the lot was practically deserted. The young director was expected to work at breakneck speed, had little time to prepare the musical, and by the end of the second week it was clear that *Finian's Rainbow* was in trouble. Although the picture presented Fred Astaire in one of his last dancing roles, it was a financial and critical failure.

Four years later the success of *The Godfather* for Paramount put Coppola at the vanguard of young American filmmakers. A masterpiece of storytelling, *The Godfather* portrays a Mafia organization as an ill-disposed extension of the capitalist system, the American dream turned corrupt. A love of family runs through the film, and many of the country's traditional values are invoked: ambition, diligence, personal mettle, equal opportunity, honor, loyalty. But a gluttony for power is equally pervasive, so that the characters become both villains and heroes. In an era approaching the

Watergate scandal, *The Godfather* seemed to rule out unblemished heroes and success untempered by compromise.

From its opening day the film was a box office phenomenon; for the first few weeks *The Godfather* earned revenue at the rate of $1 million a day. By the end of 1972 Coppola's picture had amassed an estimated gross of $150 million and become the all-time box office champion. Money poured in from soundtrack albums, paperback reprints of the Mario Puzo novel, and *Godfather* games. On Wall Street the price of one share of Gulf + Western stock jumped from $38 to $44; in record time the company was worth $97 million more than before Coppola's movie was released.

The film was nominated for eleven Academy Awards and won the Oscar for best picture of the year. The big-budget philosophy of moviemaking was reinstated, and Coppola was quickly persuaded to sign with Paramount for a sequel. When the studio agreed to let NBC show *The Godfather* on television over two successive nights in 1974, Paramount's fee for the airing was $10 million.

Critics pointed out that Francis Ford Coppola had learned much from Roger Corman. As one observer said, "All the Corman moves are there—a little sex, a little violence, a little social comment." Also Coppola made audiences like his characters, even though they are mafiosi. *The Godfather* helped create a vogue for ethnic actors, as well as new respect for innovative approaches in filming.

In *The Godfather, Part II* (1974), Coppola tried to correct the impression that he intended to romanticize his young Mafia chieftain, Michael Corleone. The sequel grossed $30 million and won seven Academy Awards, including the Oscar for best picture of the year. *The Godfather III* followed in 1990.

Like Francis Ford Coppola, Brian DePalma is Italian American and attended a film school, in this case Columbia University. A great admirer of Alfred Hitchcock, particularly Hitchcock's film *Psycho* (1960), DePalma has been called the contemporary "master of suspense." His films are violent and emotionally charged, often upending conventions and sometimes bordering on pornography. DePalma possesses Hitchcock's exactness, yet understands modern audiences, enjoys playing with them, and hopes to stimulate them. DePalma said:

> I don't believe in letting people off the hook, letting good triumph or basically resolving things, because I think we live in an era in which things are unresolved and terrible events happen and you never forget them.

Carrie (1976) remains his masterpiece, a repellent film in many ways but a gigantic hit. Actress Piper Laurie, who appears in the movie, found DePalma open to all sorts of fresh ideas, operating in a looser fashion than she had heretofore experienced. "He was always putting the camera in strange places," said Laurie, "asking us to try something different. His was a whole new school." DePalma added to his reputation in the horror field with *The Fury* (1978) and *Dressed to Kill* (1980), both of which are bloody but powerful.

Martin Scorsese, another Italian American, graduated from the New York University film school, where he later taught moviemaking. Scorsese grew up in a working-class family and, like Francis Ford Coppola, served his apprenticeship on exploitation pictures with Roger Corman. Corman allowed him to direct *Boxcar Bertha* (1972), but Scorsese's talent did not become recognized until *Mean Streets* caused a stir at the New York Film Festival in 1973.

From the outset Scorsese saw cinema as art and wanted to make films that contained a personal statement. *Taxi Driver,* shot in New York City during the summer of 1975, projects a vision of urban squalor and paranoia, yet is one of the most visually exciting movies of the decade. In the film Travis Bickle, a Vietnam veteran from the Middle West, takes a job as a taxi driver because he cannot sleep at night. Travis, played by Robert DeNiro, is a lonely, isolated man in a city he dislikes. He finds the street life of New York disgusting, while hostile forces blast away inside his thwarted personality. Unable to connect, Travis goes berserk, buys an arsenal of handguns, and shoots up a whorehouse in a climactic bloodbath. He is an angry, tormented man, alienated from a society whose oppression is so anonymous that he knows of no rational way to rebel against it.

After such forceful drama, Scorsese welcomed the prospect of a big-budget Hollywood musical done in the style of the 1940s. *New York, New York* (1977) starred Liza Minnelli and Robert DeNiro, had music and lyrics by Broadway songwriters John Kander and Fred Ebb, but incorporated the director's own ideas of what a serious music drama should be. The result was a noble effort that failed at the box office. Scorsese tried to combine too many disparate elements in a meandering movie that becomes overlong and overly complex. *Raging Bull* (1980), a compelling portrait of a prizefighter whose worst enemy outside the ring is himself, earned an Academy Award for DeNiro. The film is true to life in both characterization and period detail.

John Milius, a graduate of the University of Southern California film school, first won recognition as a screenwriter, producing scripts for *The Life and Times of Judge Roy Bean* and *Jeremiah Johnson* (both 1972). Milius switched to directing with *Dillinger* (1973), which included some of the most realistic gun battles ever filmed. Then he turned to an old-fashioned adventure story, *The Wind and the Lion* (1975). Like the other movie brats, Milius is wary of the corporate structure of the motion picture business and has maintained a degree of aloofness from the conglomerate system. "My pictures are sentimental, idealistic," he said. "I deal with friendships, chivalry, honor, and courage—not just 'guts.'"

George Lucas, another alumnus of the University of Southern California film school, directed his first full-length feature while still in college. Lucas won acclaim for *American Graffiti* (1973), a stunning re-creation of small-town America around 1962, based on his own adolescence in Modesto, California. "The early Sixties were the end of an era," said Lucas. "It hit us all very hard." His film struck home with the post–World War II baby boom generation, and *American Graffiti* became the surprise blockbuster of the year. Made for $750,000, the movie earned more than $21 million.

Lucas wanted to present audiences with positive values. Traditional religion was out of vogue in the 1970s, and the family structure showed signs of weakening. Society seemed to lack any real moral anchor. In *Star Wars* (1977) Lucas gave audiences an epic fantasy that had the struggle between forces of darkness and light as its central theme. Convinced that the Hollywood dream factory needed refurbishing, George Lucas set out to create an overwhelming visual and aural experience. The technical wizardry of the film's special effects was calculated to dazzle and excite. Yet Lucas was determined to do more than merely entertain. He presents the vision of an ideal world in which good triumphs over evil; people accept responsibility and become masters of their fate. *Star Wars* is a futuristic fairy tale, yet its message is religious. A commitment to a higher purpose, friendship, loyalty, hard work, and self-sacrifice are basic to Lucas's faith—resurrected values with a ring of eternal truth.

On May 25, 1977, *Star Wars* was tested in twenty-five theaters across the United States. Immediately there were lines, sometimes eight or nine people deep, extending around the block wherever it was shown. Grauman's Chinese Theater in Los Angeles became a mob scene, with one lane of traffic along Hollywood Boulevard blocked off by police. Within nine days the movie had grossed $3.5 million. It became the most successful picture of all time, earning more than $200 million in film rentals. But Lucas's victory had not

Mark Hamill, Carrie Fisher, and Harrison Ford in Star Wars *(1977).*

come easily. United Artists and Universal had both turned down the project. Finally Alan Ladd, Jr., at Twentieth Century-Fox said yes, with the result that Ladd became the highest-paid executive in Hollywood.

Star Wars proved the continued appeal of the classic American movie; its message aside, the film is a grand adventure with heroic action that could be cheered by all ages. Lucas's fantasy ushered in a new era for the superhit, launched a cycle of expensive science-fiction pictures, and created a set of moral images appropriate for an advanced technological age. The picture was accompanied by a merchandising campaign beyond anything Hollywood had undertaken before. Lucas admitted that he loved toys and had sales in mind from the outset. *Star Wars* products eventually included models, kits, dolls, masks, mugs, glasses, games, records, books, comics, lunch buckets, T-shirts, figurines, and transfers, all prepared after market research and returning infinite profits.

The Empire Strikes Back (1980), the second installment of the *Star Wars* trilogy, continues the positive tone, with good ultimately triumphing over evil. A classic revenge story, *The Empire Strikes Back* offers nearly twice as many special-effects sequences as *Star Wars.* Again audiences were awed, and the sequel proved another gigantic success, as was its successor, *Return of the Jedi,* three years later.

Steven Spielberg, Hollywood's most commercially successful moviemaker, missed the experience of attending a major film school. But Spielberg is steeped in film history and, like George Lucas, has remained a romantic storyteller. Another deeply personal and upbeat moviemaker, Spielberg has emerged as the undisputed superstar among contemporary film directors, although until *Schindler's List* (1993) his success with audiences was far greater than with critics. Basically Spielberg wants to re-create the type of entertainment he remembers from his childhood. "I'm really interested in films from around 1933 to 1954," he said.

Raised in Phoenix, Arizona, Spielberg moved to Los Angeles before he was twenty. In his late teens, he spent hours on the Hollywood movie lots watching masters like Alfred Hitchcock work. He went to work for Universal in 1970, gained experience in television before he directed feature films, and made his first picture, *Sugarland Express* (1974), at age twenty-five. Like Lucas, Spielberg is known for his creative use of technology, and the sheer pace of his movies entices audiences into a suspension of disbelief. For Spielberg good motion picture drama comes when a protagonist loses control of his life, then somehow regains it. "That theme has followed me through my films," he said.

The enormous popularity of *Jaws* (1975) won Spielberg worldwide recognition and began a renaissance for the Hollywood movie industry. The picture, which deals with an enormous white shark that terrorizes a small New England coastal town, became one of the first movies in history to gross more than $100 million. Across the country suburban teenagers cued up outside shopping-center theaters to buy tickets to watch Universal's synthetic shark wreak old-fashioned movie havoc. "What was *Jaws,*" an undisclosed studio executive commented, "but an old Corman monster-from-the-deep flick—plus about $12 million for production and advertising?"

Spielberg's *Close Encounters of the Third Kind* (1977) saved Columbia Pictures at a time when the studio was heavily in debt. Unlike most of the science fiction pictures of earlier decades, which depicted extraterrestrials as monsters bent on destruction, Spielberg's aliens are friendly and desire to communicate with earthly beings. Along with Lucas, Spielberg has restored moral clarity to the American screen and reshaped old-fashioned entertainment for contemporary audiences.

BOGDANOVICH AND ALLEN

Peter Bogdanovich and Woody Allen, although vastly different in their approaches, were also influenced by classic Hollywood filmmakers. Both grew up in New York, but Bogdanovich moved to Los Angeles in 1964 to conquer the movie business. Instead of graduating from a university film department, Bogdanovich worked with Roger Corman, then received a grant from the American Film Institute, enabling him to conduct lengthy interviews with such Hollywood pioneers as John Ford and Allan Dwan, whose traditions he admired.

Bogdanovich came to feel that the most daring innovation might be a return to warmer themes typical of the movies' Golden Age. *The Last Picture Show* (1971), which he purposely shot in black and white, was hailed as a throwback to the days when Hollywood filmmakers put emphasis on clear storytelling and strong character development. *The Last Picture Show* focused on the death of a small Texas town, whose diminishing populace live an aimless existence, bored by the present yet resigned to a hopeless future.

Bogdanovich believed that much was lost with the demise of classic moviemaking during the 1950s. With *The Last Picture Show* and the films that followed, the director attempted to restore to the cinema the beauty and tenderness characteristic of old Hollywood. For two years he enjoyed astounding critical and commercial success. *What's Up, Doc* (1972), starring Barbra Streisand and Ryan O'Neal, was inspired by Howard Hawks's screwball comedy *Bringing Up Baby* (1938), and *Paper Moon* (1973), again in black and white, is reminiscent of the Shirley Temple movies from the Great Depression. But then Bogdanovich experienced a quick decline; *Daisy Miller* (1974); *At Long Last Love* (1975), a Depression-type musical; and *Nickelodeon* (1976) were fiascoes that crippled the director's standing in Hollywood for years. He took a hiatus from moviemaking to rethink his priorities, maintaining later that his problem had been an inability to handle success.

Whereas Peter Bogdanovich's despair came from a loss of the old, Woody Allen's stems from an inability to cope with the present.

An admirer of Charlie Chaplin, Allen created a little man who tries to maintain his sanity in today's complex, ambiguous world. Like Chaplin's little tramp, Allen's central characters are outsiders who try to maintain a standard of ethics in a corrupt, contradictory, and transitory society. His little man's attempt to stay honest sets him apart from the mob that surrounds him. Like Chaplin, Allen mixes comedy and tragedy in his movies, using one to heighten the other. His little man is filled with updated versions of the anxieties that plagued Chaplin's little tramp throughout the 1920s.

Whereas Chaplin had served his apprenticeship in the British musical halls, Woody Allen began performing in the cabarets of Greenwich Village. Allen's humor is more cynical than Chaplin's, but his best work exposes a society that both promises and frustrates the attainment of personal desires. Despite the apparent meaninglessness of life and the jostling he suffers from diverse currents, Allen's little man perseveres with a kind of existential detachment reminiscent of Chaplin's tramp.

Like Chaplin, Woody Allen is an actor, a writer, and a director of films. As a director his greatest critical and commercial success came in 1977 with *Annie Hall,* which won the Academy Award for best picture of the year. An autobiographical love story, which Allen wrote and starred in opposite Diane Keaton, the movie is warm, witty, and exceptionally intelligent. *Interiors* (1978) is an intimate portrait of characters whose lives are ravaged by anxiety and self-doubt; *Manhattan* (1979) is a bittersweet look at a New York comedy writer and his cerebral relationships.

THE QUEST FOR A NEW IDENTITY

The decade and a half following the cheery success of *The Sound of Music* found Hollywood trying to rebuild its shrinking market, while filmmakers meandered their way through a turbulent period in American history when values were shifting dramatically. Movies matured in content during the late 1960s and early 1970s, but lost much of their entertainment quality. Stories became more realistic, characters grew more psychologically complex, and heroes and traditions were debunked as society's attitudes and goals changed rapidly. Screen censorship ended and moviemakers gained unprecedented freedom, allowing them to explore uncharted paths, often without much sense of direction. Although American films became more challenging, they often grew morbid and disturbing rather than making constructive criticism for a society at the crossroads. Audiences became more sophisticated, particularly as a younger generation developed an awareness of film as an art form. But box office receipts dwindled, placing Hollywood in the precarious position of trying to balance substance and amusement at a time when tastes in popular culture were widening tremendously.

Despite increasing sophistication, sentimentality and pure schmaltz never disappeared from the American screen. *Love Story* (1970), a runaway success, gave audiences a much-needed cry and was welcomed by general audiences as a return to wholesome, escapist, if perhaps sappy entertainment. Romantic and sad, the film offers a view of contemporary youth that conservative adults could accept with little anxiety. Likewise, *Summer of '42* (1971) is enticing nostalgia with no pretense at profundity, and *The Goodbye Girl* (1977) is a conventional love story full of warmth and humor.

Roman Polanski's *Chinatown* (1974) harks back to the film noir of the 1940s but presents a vision of America where ideals are destroyed by corporate greed, political deceit, and individual betrayal. The message was one that the contemporary counterculture could respond to enthusiastically, yet the movie's mood and setting returned to the Raymond Chandler mysteries of a previous generation.

As these movies demonstrated, Hollywood was searching for a new identity amid a society torn by ambiguity and conflict, in a decade of transition when consensus was giving way to multiculturalism and the American dream was splintering into factions. While the nation underwent a revolution in manners and morals, Hollywood struggled to redefine itself, both as a business and as a popular art form, willing to try almost anything.

By the late 1960s the traditional western was said to be dead, yet the Italian imports directed by Sergio Leone were notable exceptions. In 1964 Leone's *A Fistful of Dollars,* starring a modestly successful television actor named Clint Eastwood, proved an unexpected hit, and soon "spaghetti western" became a catchphrase. In Leone's imports, which included *The Good, the Bad, and the Ugly* (1968), Eastwood plays an unheroic cowboy, in tune with the counterculture's spirit of revisionism. The director embellished sadism into an acceptable theme and established a cult following. George Roy Hill's *Butch Cassidy and the Sundance Kid* (1969), another huge success, is a whimsical western about the daring exploits of two colorful bandits who flourished around the turn of the century, engagingly played by Paul Newman and Robert Redford. The picture mixes the past with the present, since the duo's historic misadventures are conveyed in a merry contemporary spirit.

But megahits continued to be sporadic and diverse. William Friedkin's *The French Connection* (1971) is a fast-paced thriller, clearly presented, with strong characters and a riveting chase scene. The film launched a wave of police films that included *Dirty Harry* (1971), *Magnum Force* (1973), and *The Enforcer* (1976), which helped make Clint Eastwood a number one box office star. *Serpico* (1973), starring Al Pacino, was different; it was based on a real police detective who became appalled at the corruption within the law-enforcement system and was eventually destroyed by it.

In the counterculture's view the American system had gone berserk, and the honest individual was an endangered species. *One Flew Over the Cuckoo's Nest* became the second highest grossing movie of 1975 and won five Academy Awards, including best picture of the year. *Cuckoo's Nest* deals with a rebel, superbly played by Jack Nicholson, who lands in a prison work farm. Rather than stay there, he fakes insanity and is committed to a madhouse, which antagonizes his rebellious nature all the more. The asylum becomes a microcosm of society, where controls are no less abusive.

Mature filmmakers remained sensitive to potential dangers in American life. *Network* (1976) focuses on the new corrosive, manipulative power of television and points out how reporting is confused with entertainment. *All the President's Men* (1976) deals with the Watergate break-in and political corruption. *The China Syndrome* (1979) bears strong similarities to the nuclear accident on Three Mile Island, yet the film appeared two weeks before the actual event. All three offered forceful warnings yet were dramatically absorbing.

Kramer vs. Kramer, the biggest box office earner of 1979, depicts family problems and changing roles for men and women. In this story of a broken marriage, the failed wife (Meryl Streep) attempts to find herself, whereas her former husband (Dustin Hoffman) struggles to succeed as a homemaker and father.

Mainstream social structure was repeatedly pictured as debased, boring, and stifling, disastrous for a free spirit. Film after film was concerned with the individual trying to establish a personal identity in a mechanized, computerized world demanding conformity. Even *A Man for All Seasons* (1966), based on Robert Bolt's play, took on a contemporary note by pitting Sir Thomas More, a Renaissance man of principle, against an established authority. By the late 1960s, however, swindlers and renegades were more often heroes.

Genial Burt Reynolds played a comical bootlegger in *Smokey and the Bandit* (1977), outracing the sheriff throughout the movie. Reynolds became a superstar with a string of "good ol' boy" parts, much in contrast to the cynicism and toughness that dominated the screen at the time. Although Reynolds's friendly, natural style endeared him to audiences, it was his nude centerfold in the April 1972 issue of *Cosmopolitan* that turned him into a popular culture icon. His bare backside became another example of role reversal, the first time a male centerfold had been featured in a mainstream magazine. Within two days after it appeared on the newsstands, 98 percent of that month's issues had been sold, and the magazine was an immediate collectors' item.

While the content in Hollywood's films deepened in the late 1960s and early 1970s, the industry floundered. The negative mood of its current films became enervating and produced poor box office returns. The nihilistic attitudes of the period offered limited entertainment value, and audiences grew tired of seeing the gross, ugly, downbeat aspects of life paraded before them in images larger than life.

By the mid-1970s many filmmakers realized that contemporary negativism made for less than enthralling screen drama. "The 1960s were very disruptive, very chaotic for the movies," said director Sidney Pollack, who made *The Way We Were* (1973) and *The Electric Horseman* (1979). Although Pollack's own films forcefully attacked the materialistic emphasis within American society, he rejoiced when popular demands in the 1970s began pulling the motion picture industry away from experimentation and radicalism toward a more positive and uplifting point of view.

CONCLUSION

The decade after *The Sound of Music*'s triumph represented a bleak period in Hollywood's history, a time when moviemakers tested new subject matter and floundered, borrowed from new European voices and innovated on their own, matured and regressed, probed the human condition and skated on its periphery. In the face of paradox and despair, the American movie industry struggled to find audiences at the very time when Hollywood's power structure was being reorganized. Few of the old rules seemed to apply, and much of the new had only temporary appeal. Yet even in the darkest years the studios released pictures that stirred the popular imagination and some disturbed the mind.

By the mid-1970s a new breed of Hollywood filmmakers made their appearance, most of them trained in university film schools and the best blessed with talent, technical mastery, and a personalized approach that appealed to audiences. Younger moviegoers rejected the crusading spirit of their older siblings and welcomed such outrageous spoofs as *The Rocky Horror Picture Show* (1975), the disco pulsations of *Saturday Night Fever* (1977), and the mythic heroics of a handsome new *Superman* (1978).

By 1976, America's bicentennial year, general audiences seemed ready for a reaffirmation of traditional values. *Rocky* appeared on the screen, one year after Robert Altman's *Nashville* had predicted the end of the American dream, but Sylvester Stallone's film restores the Horatio Alger hero and celebrates the American success story Alger symbolized. Set in the working-class slums of South Philadelphia, *Rocky* pictures the world of professional boxing and the hard life of the ethnic blue-collar worker, as well as organized crime and media exploitation. Yet the tone of Stallone's film is upbeat and romantic. Against all odds Rocky, a small-time fighter, earns his chance at fame and self-respect. Audiences cheered the gutsy underdog and left the theater emotionally charged. The movie cost $1 million and returned $74 million; it also won the Academy Award for best picture of the year and prompted four sequels.

During the decade prior to *Rocky's* release, American faith had been shaken by a multitude of calamities: the Vietnam War, race riots and campus unrest, the Watergate scandal that resulted in the resignation of an elected president and criminal action against high-ranking government officials, the Arab oil embargo and a recognition that the United States no longer possessed unlimited natural resources, and an unhealthy economy that brought inflation and increased unemployment. Hollywood responded to the crises at hand, exploring the decay of society with a specter of rebellion. Even though movies showed technical gains, much was lost during a prolonged period of reexamination, including the mass audience that movies had enjoyed for nearly half a century. In a heroic rescue, reminiscent of the bravado of old Hollywood, fresh genius arrived in time to save the industry from the deconstructionist posturing that seemed to converge in a series of dead ends. Despite the precarious texture of the years ahead, Hollywood would enjoy a renaissance.

Searchlights announcing a premiere at Grauman's Chinese Theater in Hollywood.

Chapter 5

———

MOVIE PALACES, SHOPPING MALLS, AND MULTIPLEXES

If a society's history is written in its buildings, Hollywood's past and present are reflected in its theaters. The old movie palaces from Hollywood's Golden Age represented elegance and sophistication for their audiences, a splendid combination of art and entertainment. Many of the early palaces, built during the silent era, boasted pipe organs or Mighty Wurlitzers, with grilles set high on the walls flanking the screen. Some of the more lavish theaters resembled Baroque cathedrals, complete with murals on their ceilings and statuary in strategically located niches. Others had entrance lobbies modeled after the Paris Opera or the Hall of Mirrors at Versailles. Grand staircases, crystal chandeliers, draped entryways, and barrel-vaulted halls were common among the larger examples. Several of the movie palaces built during the 1920s and 1930s were patterned after Spanish villas, whereas others were Art Deco or streamlined Moderne in design. The discovery of King Tutankhamen's tomb in 1922 sparked a passion for Egyptian and other exotic motifs.

Since the great movie palaces drew people from all classes, they symbolized material success gone democratic, a tangible expression of the American dream and its riches. Exteriors of theaters were dazzling, but patrons who lined up outside the ticket booths knew that greater wonders awaited them inside. For two hours moviegoers could escape from the troubles of routine lives and find joy and astonishment at prices they could afford. As theater architect Charles Lee said, "The motion picture gave people what was missing from their daily lives: religion, solace, art, and most importantly, a feeling of importance."

The atmosphere surrounding the movie palaces was aimed at helping each patron feel like royalty. An attendant dressed in a splendorous uniform greeted customers at the door, and an attractively lighted candy counter awaited them in the main lobby, along with marble fountains, gilt mirrors, and plush carpets. The familiar sound of a popcorn machine attracted theatergoers' attention, with its familiar smell encouraging them to feel at home. Waiting in the basement of some of the larger theaters was a nursery equipped with a carousel and toys and an attendant to look after restless children. Dragoons of ushers in impeccable uniforms, drilled in efficiency, escorted patrons with downturned flashlights to velvet seats after inquiring about their viewing preference. The management's goal was to create a fantasy world that allowed customers to feel special and part of the theatrical experience.

Movie palaces were strategically located in major cities and towns across America. Most of the new pictures were shown first in downtown theaters, which brought people back to the urban center after dark but lured housewives downtown during the day. Movie palaces adorned with neon lights and brandishing such names as the Tower, the State, the Grand, and the Capital lent a touch of Hollywood glamour to the staid business districts of American cities and towns. New York City had its Roxy, Paramount, Rialto, and Strand; Chicago had the Avalon, the Paradise, and the Oriental; Los Angeles had Grauman's Chinese Theater and Grauman's Egyptian; whereas St. Louis had the Ambassador, and Houston and Dallas each had a Majestic.

Theater row in Dallas began with the Majestic and ended four blocks down Elm Street with the Telenews; in between were the Melba, the Tower, the Palace, the Rialto, and the Capital. But neighborhood theaters were sometimes palaces, too, particularly in the more upscale sections of town. The neighborhood houses usually relied on a solitary tower, most frequently outlined in neon, to announce their presence and suggest to passersby that something monumental awaited them inside. Movies normally played the leading neighborhood theaters, after a clearance period of approximately six weeks, once the downtown run was finished. Gradually films made their way through the maze of lesser theaters, ending as part of a double bill in the less prestigious houses of modest-income areas. As film historian Tino Balio explained, "The merchandising pattern of movies during the thirties and forties was similar to that of other consumer goods: first, the exclusive shops; next, the general department store; and finally, the close-out sales."

Most of the movie palaces in 1945 were owned or controlled by major Hollywood studios or their parent companies. At the end of World War II, Paramount controlled 1,395 theaters, Twentieth Century-Fox 636, Warner Bros. 501, Loew's (the parent company of MGM) 135, and RKO 109. The divorcement decrees issued by the courts shortly after the war meant that studios had to sell off their theater chains. They began by eliminating the weaker houses in small towns, retaining as long as possible their larger first-run theaters. During the 1950s the downtown palaces in major cities—only 20 percent of the nation's theaters—generated the bulk of the motion picture industry's business, while neighborhood theaters were either demolished or turned into churches, automobile repair shops, or some more profitable business.

With Hollywood plagued by what became known as "troubled product," few new theaters were built. Those that were demonstrated simpler, cleaner lines than those constructed during the 1920s and 1930s, as theater architects accepted the "less is more" philosophy of postwar modernism. By the 1950s the gaudy movie palaces of old were losing their flamboyance. A decade later their time had passed, and thousands of once-flourishing theaters closed. Some of the downtown cinemas switched to pornography; others were salvaged by historic preservationists and refurbished for legitimate theater, Broadway musicals, and grand opera.

RETREAT TO THE MALLS

With divestiture in effect, the studios no longer subsidized theater owners for their operating and maintenance expenses. As box office receipts continued to decline, theater managers came to rely more on income from concession stands than on ticket sales for profits. By 1953 movie houses accounted for more than one-fourth of the candy bar sales in the United States, although popcorn was always the best producer of revenue for theater owners, providing nearly half the concession stands' sales. Profits were in the theater lobbies and not in their auditoriums, and theater designers were not slow to recognize the fact.

Instead of providing plush seating and luxurious accommodations inside the theater, architects began to focus on the lobby and its candy counter. As exteriors of theaters grew plainer and interiors ranged from ordinary to drab, the flow of traffic around their concession stands was made more efficient, and its snacks were arranged as enticingly as possible. All amenities that interrupted the candy counter sales or encouraged patrons to linger in the lobby once they had made their purchase were gradually eliminated. Soon it was discovered that several auditoriums could be served by one centrally located concession stand, with several sellers available to accommodate customers. Lobbies in new or reapportioned theaters were expanded, so that they frequently became larger than the auditoriums.

The trend toward theaters subdivided into multiple units began in 1962 with movie houses that contained two or three screens, yet shared the same box office and lobby. The dawning of the multiplex coincided with a sharp decline in yearly ticket sales and the recognition that most of Hollywood's feature films no longer made money. The multiplex concept and the emergence of shopping malls across the country developed simultaneously, since both followed the migration of the middle class into the suburbs. With the deterioration of the urban center, malls were constructed that offered consumers air-conditioned, self-enclosed retail communities and an abundance of free parking. Since movie theaters needed to be convenient to suburban activity, it was logical that they should become part of the one-stop shopping experience.

By 1965 there were 1,500 shopping malls in the United States, 2,500 by 1970, and 22,500 by 1980. Multiscreen movie complexes grew proportionately, named mostly for the shopping centers that housed them or for the number of screens they contained. Gradually the multiplexes in shopping malls became the premier theaters in American cities, while small towns lost their movie houses entirely. Frequently the old neighborhood movie palaces were subdivided, giving patrons a choice of pictures under one roof and theater owners greater flexibility in booking.

The more screens a theater had, the better chance an exhibitor had for booking a popular film. If a blockbuster appeared, the movie could be shown on two or three screens at staggered times, while the management kept the option of cutting back once the film's popularity began to wane. Compared with the old movie palaces, the multiplexes cost far less to operate, yet they offered convenience and efficiency in a relatively clean, safe environment.

Patrons accustomed to the opulence of the old movie palaces complained about the spartan decor of the new multiplexes. Screens were hung in the center of a blank wall, with no stage and no proscenium curtain. The emphasis on functionalism eliminated imaginative lighting and serious attempt at adornment. Seats were hard backed, cushionless, and plastic, and floors were rarely carpeted. Since space was at a premium, screens were often clustered in the basement of multistoried malls, sometimes next to an ice skating rink. Inadequate padding in the walls between screening rooms meant that noise from one tiny auditorium could be heard in the next. Architectural fantasy became a thing of the past, as concession stands emerged as the featured attraction. "Going to the movies," wrote film historian Douglas Gomery, was "reduced to the equivalent of standing in line at the Kmart."

Multiplexes quickly put an end to most people more than thirty-five years old attending the movies with any regularity. Older people objected to concrete floors sticky with soft drinks, too many noisy teenagers, and endless films targeted at adolescent audiences. By the late 1960s teenagers were considered the most reliable moviegoers, and it was widely held in the industry that seventeen-year-olds could determine the success or failure of a picture.

Unlike their elders, teenagers were likely to see movies on impulse. Rather than wait for reviews or word-of-mouth, they often went to pictures as soon as they opened, attracted by big-name stars and influenced by television advertising. During the early 1970s the twelve- to twenty-nine-year-old age group—only 40 percent of the country's total population—accounted for 75 percent of the ticket sales at American movie houses. Hollywood started focusing more than ever on the youth market, providing them with plenty of action-adventure stories and *Friday the 13th* (1980) horror shows, aware that the final verdict on a movie's success would be cast by kids in the suburban shopping malls.

The peak periods for movie attendance fall during the Christmas and summer holidays, although business can be brisk over Easter weekend. The summer season accounts for almost 50 percent of domestic box office income. Studios plan to release their summer blockbusters between the beginning of June and the middle of

August, hoping that the opening weekend will validate the tremendous expense of their big pictures.

Rather than opening a movie on an exclusive run in one theater in each city, and then staggering its availability in the various neighborhood houses, as had been the practice during Hollywood's Golden Era, studios in the 1970s began booking their pictures into as many theaters as possible at the same time. Simultaneous release to several theaters, what came to be known as saturation booking, reduces the advertising cost per theater and takes maximum advantage of the television publicity that accompanies a film's opening. In the summer of 1975 *Jaws* opened in 464 theaters at once during its initial release, setting the pattern that the industry continues to follow.

By opening a picture widely, more revenue is collected early, allowing the studio to regain some of its investment quickly. Since merchandising has become a significant spin-off to filmmaking, a concentration of advertising is essential to related marketing campaigns. When Paramount's *The Great Gatsby* (1974) was released, tie-ins were engineered with a liquor company, a men's sportswear outfit, a chain of beauty salons, and even a new line of cookware. In conjunction with Dino DeLaurentiis's remake of *King Kong* (1976), the makers of Jim Beam concocted a King Kong Kocktail, and 5,000 7-11 stores sold sets of Kong Kong glasses. Such merchandising campaigns need to be synchronized with the promotion of the movie itself, since timing is vital. For expensive pictures with merchandising potential, releasing them shortly before Christmas has obvious advantages besides higher box office returns.

NEW THEATER CHAINS

General Cinema, which had been in the drive-in business earlier, was one of the first corporations to construct twin cinemas and therefore became a pioneer in the concept of multiplexing. Between 1963 and 1970 the company increased its number of screens 198.7 percent, establishing itself as one of the nation's largest theater chains. In 1981 General Cinema owned more screens in the United States than any of its competitors, expanding from 233 screens in 1970 to more than 1,000 in 1984. But the company also invested heavily in soft drink franchises, a related enterprise that brought in 35 percent of its corporate profits.

American Multi-Cinema (AMC) introduced a four-screen theater in 1966 and six screens in 1969. Within a few years AMC theaters housing six to eighteen screens became commonplace—all consistently stark in design, but efficient in handling movie audiences that continued to prove elusive. United Artists Theatre Circuit also appeared during the 1960s as a leader in the building of multiscreen complexes in suburban shopping centers; in the 1970s UA emerged as the nation's largest theater chain.

Many of the former Paramount theaters had been purchased in the 1950s by the American Broadcasting Company (ABC radio and television). In the 1970s ABC, heretofore the lesser of the three major networks, enjoyed greater success in broadcasting and therefore sold its theaters in two stages to one of its former employees, Henry Plitt. For a decade the Plitt theater chain dominated moviegoing in sections of the Sun Belt to the region around Chicago.

During the late 1970s only one of the old theater circuits, Loew's, was still operated by its original successor. By 1959 Loew's no longer was affiliated with Metro-Goldwyn-Mayer, and its number of theaters dropped to fewer than a hundred. By 1978 the company had sold most of its old movie palaces and built a small chain of multiplexes, totaling sixty theaters with 125 screens. Loew's principal focus in the 1970s had shifted to hotels, cigarette manufacturing, and insurance.

The major chains added Dolby sound in 1975, a high-fidelity stereophonic system that delivers clear, lifelike reproduction. Later the better houses added THX sound in an effort to enhance the moviegoing experience. But with all of the theater chains, large and small, concession stands remained the main attraction, since they generated the most dependable profits—60 percent of the total earnings by 1978.

Theater admission prices rose steadily after World War II—from fifty cents in the mid-1950s to $1.00 in the mid-1960s, $2.00 in the mid-1970s, $3.50 in the mid-1980s, and $6.50 to $8.00 in the mid-1990s. Yearly attendance reached a low point in the early 1970s with a total of 17 million; by the end of the decade the figure had climbed back up to 20 million, thanks to better pictures and improved marketing strategies. Movie promotions in the malls became bigger and more sophisticated, while television advertising, particularly for PG- and G-rated films, proved more effective than newspaper layouts and radio spots.

The theater chains that pulled film exhibition out of its doldrums were not the old studio-affiliated circuits, but a new group that had emerged during the age of multiplexes. The multiplex chains functioned with new technology and computer readouts that showed precise demographic results for each picture released. At the top of these companies were United Artists Theater Circuit, General Cinema, American Multi-Cinema, and Plitt Theaters. But these leaders were soon to face competition from a dynamic Toronto-based newcomer that introduced postmodern concepts.

CINEPLEX ODEON

The pattern of multiplexes in the shopping malls would be challenged by Cineplex Odeon, a Canadian company that in April 1979 built a $2 million complex in Toronto housing eighteen auditoriums. Cineplex built theaters containing blocks of up to twenty screens across Canada, then entered the U.S. market in 1982. The Toronto-based company expanded its holdings through mergers and new construction to become the second largest theater chain in North America by the close of the decade.

Cineplex Odeon rejected the drab, closet-sized multiplex units in the malls and built huge complexes of carefully crafted, postmodern picture palaces that offer an array of movie entertainment. The company commissioned paintings and sculpture for its newly constructed theaters and brought elegance and creature comfort back to American moviegoing. Cineplex Odeon's complexes returned to architectural splendor; interiors are ornate yet tasteful, with carpets, interesting lighting, and Art Deco touches. Seats are comfortable and concession areas expansive, illuminated with neon to create a whimsical effect. The company's theaters are generally spotless, maintained by a staff that takes pride in working for the fastest-growing theater chain in the world.

Cineplex Odeon's pleasure palaces are reminiscent of the opulence movie fans experienced during the 1920s and 1930s, but operating costs are kept down by placing ten to twenty auditoriums under one roof. By the end of the 1980s the Canadian company had significantly altered the standards of motion picture exhibition in North America. Going to the movies again became a special experience for audiences, and the number of theater patrons rose by the millions.

Cineplex Odeon startled the film world in August 1985 by purchasing the Plitt Theater chain for $136 million. Cineplex continued to expand rapidly over the next two years, acquiring more theaters faster than at any time in movie history since the 1920s. By the end of 1987 the company owned nearly 500 complexes in twenty states plus the District of Columbia; its total number of screens exceeded 1,600. By 1990 Cineplex Odeon's methods had established a new trend for the industry.

THE STUDIOS' RETURN TO EXHIBITION

The relaxed regulatory environment of the Reagan administration permitted motion picture production companies to reenter the exhibition field. In a renewed atmosphere of laissez-faire toward antitrust laws, the old *Paramount* decrees, which had forbidden Hollywood studios from owning and operating theaters since 1948, were reversed, paving the way in the mid-1980s for a return to producer-distribution-exhibition combines.

MCA revived the trend in 1986 when the company bought 49 percent of Cineplex Odeon. Lew Wasserman, head of Universal Pictures, had become acquainted with Garth Drabinsky, the Canadian lawyer representing Cineplex, during the theater chain's negotiations to build a $10 million complex in the studio's parking lot at Universal City. When Universal Studios Cineplex opened in 1987, the multiplex was a joint venture between the two companies. The eighteen-auditorium, 6,000-seat complex echoed the lavishness of the old movie palaces, complete with clouds and stars on the ceiling of the theater's lobby.

Later in the 1980s Columbia Pictures bought Loew's theater chain, while Paramount Communications in partnership with Time Warner acquired the Mann and Trans-Lux chains. Battles again raged between studio-operated theaters and independents, who were often forced into debt attempting to compete. A sleeper, such as Universal's *Field of Dreams* (1989), could now play in Cineplex Odeon theaters long enough to develop an audience, whereas a non-studio chain would more likely weigh the results of the first week and discard the picture as unprofitable.

By 1989 the six largest theater chains, more than half of which were affiliated with producer-distributors, controlled almost 40 percent of the nation's screens, an increase of 16 percent since 1986.

But the theater business had rediscovered "showbiz," and moviegoing once again was becoming a total experience. New theaters not only were more elegant, they also grew in number. By the close of the 1980s more screens were available in the United States than had existed in the peak year of 1946. Despite sharply increased ticket prices, motion picture attendance continued to rise, including larger numbers of older patrons. In 1993, a record-breaking year, 1.15 billion people attended the movies.

A THRIVING BUSINESS

Going to the movies remains a favorite social activity among young people. In the 1990s seven out of eight admissions still come from patrons under forty, with the bulk of those from teenagers. But in recent years middle-aged baby boomers have rediscovered the movies. Between 1981 and 1992 attendance of people in their forties rose from 6 percent to 16 percent, and the number continued to climb over the next three years. The adolescent population, as a percent of the total, declined during the 1980s, making it advantageous for Hollywood to appeal to more mature audiences.

Frequent moviegoers constitute almost nine-tenths of total admissions, and two-thirds of those have some college education. Audiences tend to be better educated than in the immediate postwar years and reasonably affluent, with the result that Hollywood has responded with more films that appeal to elite audiences. Since segregated movie theaters legally ended in the summer of 1964, with the passage of the civil rights bill, African Americans have constituted an increasing portion of mainstream audiences. Hollywood has addressed the need for more diversified movie fare and expanded its representation of American life to include a growing multiculturalism.

The key to a successful picture still rests in the big city market. The opening weekend of a movie is all important, particularly if the picture is an expensive production. If a film does not attract substantial audiences during the first few days of its release, theater owners as a rule feel they cannot afford to continue showing it. They will turn to another picture and hope for better results. Since stars sell movies, it is vital to the opening week's showing to have a name like Tom Cruise, Mel Gibson, Kevin Costner, or Harrison Ford heading the cast, particularly because teenagers make up a large portion of the initial weekend audience.

Moviegoers lined up for tickets to see Arnold Schwarzenegger in The
Terminator *(1985).*

With success or failure for expensive pictures determined at the
box office during the first few days after their release, bankable stars
can virtually name their own price. Consequently, Arnold
Schwarzenegger was paid $10 million to star in the futuristic *Total
Recall* (1990), and Sylvester Stallone earned more than $20 million
to reprise his role in *Rocky V* (1991). Actresses continue to have less

box office potential, although Julia Roberts, Meg Ryan, and Demi Moore add to a movie's chances for becoming a winner. Since teenagers prefer violent action and flashy special effects, large doses of both are desirable for an impressive opening week's showing, which in part explains why male stars are preferred. Less expensive pictures can open in a few theaters and linger until word-of-mouth establishes them as something worth seeing. With blockbusters, guarantees must be built in, taking the form of bankable stars, presold sequels, and prearranged sales to network and cable television.

Studios are likely to find themselves in the red unless they turn out one or two blockbusters every year. Executives therefore concentrate immense resources on projects that will play the key summer and Christmas dates. Despite the enormous publicity that will likely be given these pictures, a high percentage of them will fail at the box office. Contemporary Hollywood does not enjoy the security of a planned production package the way studios did during the Golden Age. Consequently, market-research departments have become fixtures in Hollywood, and numbers matter more than ever.

Blockbuster movies need the support of other segments of the parent company. Time Warner's *Batman,* for example, was advertised on millions of T-shirts, hats, and place mats, by a cover story in *Time* magazine, in paperbacks from Warner Books, and on Time Warner's cable channel, Home Box Office. Universal's *Back to the Future* movies (1986, 1990, and 1991) were promoted at MCA/Universal's theme park; Disney's *The Little Mermaid* (1990) received wide promotion from Disney theme parks and benefited from a merchandising agreement with McDonald's, as did *Pocahontas* five years later.

Domestic ticket sales at movie theaters in 1974 totalled $1.65 billion; by 1990 receipts had risen to $5.02 billion. In 1994 the number of screens in the United States exceeded 25,000, an increase of more than 14 percent over the past five years. But Hollywood productions have also become the nation's second largest export, surpassed only by military hardware. In 1992 the foreign market for American movies and television shows reached a record high, bringing in $7 billion. Posters advertising Hollywood's motion pictures are common the world over, but especially in Europe and Japan. Around the globe, American movies in 1989 reaped $11.6 billion in revenue.

ANCILLARY MARKETS

Although theater attendance in the United States has improved markedly over recent years, the foreign box office, video sales, and television rentals constitute an even greater market for Hollywood films. The videocassette recorder was introduced for home use in 1975 but did not become a force until the 1980s. VCR sales increased from 30,000 a year in 1976 to 1.4 million in 1981 and over 12.5 million in 1986. By the mid-1980s more than two-thirds of all American households had a videocassette recorder, and the home video market had exploded. Dealers around the country began renting prerecorded videocassettes at a rate of more than 100 million per month, as income from video sales and rentals climbed from $4 billion in 1986 to $11 billion in 1992. Toward the end of the 1980s, prerecorded videos could be rented at convenience stores, gas stations, and supermarkets or purchased through any number of discount houses. Stopping by the video outlet and picking up a selection of weekend movies and assorted snacks soon became a national habit.

At first the home video market was seen by Hollywood executives as a potential threat to theater attendance, but the industry soon began courting the home audience as an auxiliary market. In 1986 more than half the domestic revenue earned by major studios came from videocassette sales and rentals. Warner's blockbuster *Batman,* for instance, grossed $250 million within its first five months of theatrical release; when the picture was released on video, it earned $400 million. In 1990 sales and rentals of videocassettes added $3.37 billion to Hollywood's coffers.

Studios began releasing their feature films on videocassettes within six months after the close of a movie's run in the theaters. By the 1990s home videos had become the second showcase for Hollywood's movies, altering the financial structure of the motion picture industry and changing America's entertainment patterns. Even though videos by no means killed the movie theaters, as many predicted, they did affect second-run motion picture houses, most of which resorted to one dollar admissions to attract audiences.

By the early 1980s pay or cable television had emerged as a formidable ancillary market for Hollywood's features, both old and new. Media tycoon Ted Turner brought classic MGM movies into American homes through his TNT network, launched in October

1988. Home Box Office, a powerful movie channel, invests heavily in pay television rights to new feature films, enough that cable showings have become part of a picture's projected earnings.

Network television remains a significant market for feature films, although proportionately less after 1975 than before. Still, by 1990 television was in more American homes than indoor plumbing, and more than half the nation's homes possessed two or more sets. A network showing of a motion picture can deliver in a single evening a greater audience than any in Hollywood's history, and profits from that source remain substantial. In 1990 rentals of movies to television networks totaled $1.7 billion.

But a film must score well at theater box offices before it can earn big money from subsequent television showings. Since a picture's reputation is made in the theaters, the importance of its theatrical release cannot be overestimated. A major movie in the 1990s will open simultaneously in perhaps 1,000 theaters across the United States. A massive advertising campaign in the press and on television will accompany its release, in an effort to maximize the movie's appeal. If the figures for the opening weekend are high enough, the studio can relax, for executives will flaunt the early success of their product to later distributors.

The typical exhibition pattern currently begins with a first run in the theaters, during which the studio has its initial chance to recoup its investment. A film is generally considered a success at this point if it makes back its cost. The movie's second run will come with its release on videocassette. Its third run will be on cable or pay television, and a fourth run may be on network television. The picture can then be syndicated to local television stations or sold in video outlets at discount prices.

CONCLUSION

The demise of the Golden Age movie palaces coincided with a prolonged decline in domestic theater attendance. Movie theaters during the 1960s followed the middle class out to the suburbs, where land was cheaper, and into the shopping malls that soon became gathering places for teenagers. The shopping center multiplexes that continued to be built in the 1970s emphasized the sale of popcorn, candy, soft drinks, and hotdogs and reduced theater accommodations to the bare essentials. Lobbies were stripped of everything except a concession stand and coin-operated electronic games, both of which brought in dependable revenue. Since television viewing at home had accustomed moviegoers to constant conversation, talking and commotion became a distracting part of the moviegoing experience in the malls.

In the mid-1970s more-entertaining pictures reappeared, and attendance in the suburban movie houses started to increase. The baby boomers who had forsaken the theaters for their television sets began to drift back. Cineplex Odeon demonstrated to a wary movie industry that home video and cable television need not put an end to theater chains. During the 1980s cinema owners and moviegoers joined in realizing what had been lost in the utilitarian approach to theater design. By the 1990s going to the movies no longer was synonymous with going to the mall. As postmodern glamour returned to newly constructed theaters, the public became more devout in its moviegoing, and Hollywood's profits reached unprecedented highs, aided by an expanding foreign market, the advent of videocassettes, and lucrative showings on cable and network television.

JoBeth Williams, Kevin Kline, William Hurt, and Glenn Close in The Big Chill *(1983).*

Chapter 6

RETURN TO ENTERTAINMENT

The 1980s saw self-absorption and veneration of material success become dominant motives for a new generation of American adults. By 1983 the Reagan administration was in its third year, and "yuppies"—the upwardly mobile recent graduates making their mark on the urban business world—had become a frequent term in the American vernacular. That year director Lawrence Kasdan's *The Big Chill* was released, a film that centers on a gathering of once-close friends who attended the University of Michigan together in the 1960s, when campus unrest and political activism were part of the contemporary youth culture. One of their group, Alex, has died, and his former classmates have assembled to attend his funeral. In the years since college the friends have gone their separate ways, achieved a comfortable affluence, and largely abandoned their former ideals.

Their reunion during the weekend of Alex's funeral provides them an opportunity to review their lives since graduation. They gradually acknowledge that they have become too entrenched in their own successes to be deeply disturbed over having sold out to a materialistic order. Alex's death is in part symbolic of the change that has taken place in their lives; his funeral is an occasion for them to bury their former selves. The "big chill" comes when the defectors recognize that their lives have moved in directions they would have thought inconceivable during their activist years. The reunion ends with their coming to terms with the reality of their lives. They accept that not everything they had expected in their idealistic youth is possible and that personal goals have replaced their earlier concerns for society.

The 1980s saw a return of flamboyant business practices in the higher echelons of the financial world that would have been unacceptable to the previous generation. Hollywood's impetuous spending and astronomical returns from successful productions were reflections of new economic trends. The "greed is good" philosophy, which writer-director Oliver Stone graphically portrays in *Wall Street* (1987), came to be seen by champions of "life in the fast lane" (another 1980s cliché) as a streamlined restatement of the American dream. Donald Trump in real estate and Garfield the Cat in cartoons emerged as icons of the decade, both believing that self-interest ultimately is best for the country as a whole. As George Bush observed on the campaign trail during 1988, "The mood of this country has changed from that of *Easy Rider* to that of *Dirty Harry.*"

Hollywood's studios, like other segments of the American economy, sought the big pay-off. They continued to emphasize blockbusters that executives hoped would cushion the losses on a dozen or more other pictures released by their companies that same year. In 1982, for instance, *Rocky III* was responsible for two-thirds of MGM's total movie rentals, earning $65.7 million from the domestic market alone. Although production costs on movies soared from an average of $3 million in 1976 to $20 million in 1988, total box office receipts improved during those years, and credit to finance pictures was readily available. Since only one movie in twenty is likely to become a hit in the theaters, Hollywood aspirants to "the fast lane" suffer from persistent paranoia and panic. Marketing has become increasingly important in the movie industry, yet the adage "You're only as good as your last picture" remains a brutal reality.

Along with economic conservatism, the Reagan era saw a return to homespun values, as dissenting voices from the 1970s grew fainter. Rather than the demythologizing stance characteristic of the previous decade, when serious reappraisal of American institutions and values was in vogue, movies in the 1980s tended toward escapism, aimed at sending audiences out of the theaters with happy endings and good feelings. Cinema, according to film historian Steve Vineberg, became "a logical extension of Reagan's invocation to the American people to stand tall and feel great about our country."

Movies were less critical and tragic, more reverential and trendy in the sentiments they expressed. Instead of fashioning legitimate representations of human experience, the majority of Hollywood's filmmakers seemed dedicated to keeping the real world out of their pictures. Most movies from the Reagan years are slick but cautious, often emotionally synthetic and vacuous, more concerned with huckstering than with extending a popular art form. "With rare exceptions," four-time Academy Award–winner Joseph L. Mankiewicz said in 1982, "today's Hollywood movies are cartoons—rich, yes, and beautifully illustrated, but with no particular depth."

RECOIL TO CONSERVATISM

The Rambo films, which emphasize the physique of actor Sylvester Stallone over content, epitomize the 1980s conservatism. *First Blood* (1982) is flashy but empty, almost a caricature of military destruction and gore. There is little plot, merely a series of violent episodes involving its superhero. John Rambo, trained as a Green Beret to outwit the Viet Cong, is a near-psychopathic loner who dresses like a Native American. With his enormous knife and simple tools, he challenges the superior technology of his enemies. The film proposes that individuals do not have to accept being victimized; they can fight back. *First Blood* appeared at a time when the Reagan administration maintained that the United States had tolerated defeat long enough; the country, Reaganites insisted, should increase its military strength and determine its own destiny in foreign affairs.

The initial Rambo picture proved an enormous success, earning more than $20 million at the box office within two weeks after its release. *Rambo: First Blood,* a no-nonsense sequel, followed in 1985, and *Rambo III* appeared in 1988. Along with Arnold Schwarzenegger, another muscleman whose movies centered on action, Sylvester Stallone emerged as an exaggerated role model for adolescent males during the 1980s. Not only were posters of the bare-chested Stallone sold in abundance, but naysayers could chuckle at a mockup of Ronald Reagan in a similar pose, over a caption that read "Ronbo."

The public's confidence in the American military establishment was in part restored during the period by such revisionist screen celebrations as *An Officer and a Gentleman* (1982) and *Top Gun* (1986). A throwback to the military romances in vogue during

Sylvester Stallone as John Rambo in Rambo: First Blood Part II *(1982).*

World War II, *An Officer and a Gentleman* pairs Richard Gere with Debra Winger and won an Academy Award for black actor Louis Gossett, Jr. *Top Gun,* which stars Tom Cruise, is a glorified view of the contemporary Air Force. As technically sophisticated as it is intellectually shallow, the picture became one of the year's top-grossing films.

The conquest of the corporate world once more came to be viewed by Hollywood as a satisfying route to self-fulfillment. *Working Girl* (1988) finds actress Melanie Griffith achieving success and self-confidence on an upward spiral in Manhattan's financial district. The film, directed by Mike Nichols, grows sentimental and moralistic, but its theme was the credo of the 1980s yuppies.

Rural dramas and films celebrating the community life of small-town America made a comeback. *Places in the Heart* and *The River* (both 1984) are set in the nation's heartland. Their characters are devoted to family, the soil, their community, and Christian virtues. The ritual of grace before dinner returned to Hollywood movies, with family units portrayed as supportive and nurturing, a source of strength rather than an excuse for rebellion.

In *Field of Dreams* (1989) Ray Kinsella (played by Kevin Costner), a former student activist, leaves home after ridiculing his father's ardor for baseball. As a married adult and father himself, Kinsella is haunted by voices and compulsively builds a baseball diamond in the cornfield of his Iowa farm. Before long, his dead father's favorite ball players, headed by Shoeless Joe Jackson, appear to play baseball on Kinsella's field. Ray seeks out his college idol, a black activist writer played by James Earl Jones, and brings him to Iowa. There on Kinsella's baseball diamond, father and son, radical and conservative, black and white resolve their differences in a magical game.

Harmony was clearly a theme in the films of the 1980s. *Back to the Future* (1985), a comic fantasy reminiscent of old Hollywood, centers on a time-traveling teenager, engagingly played by Michael J. Fox. The boy journeys into the past, where he encounters his mother and father when they were teenagers. Much to his surprise he discovers that he and his parents share many of the same anxieties and yearn for a similar peace between their external and inner selves.

Resolution of family conflicts proved a recurring theme during the decade. *Ordinary People* (1980) probed the tenuous nature of a family that seemed to have all the requisites for happiness yet failed to establish loving relationships. *Terms of Endearment* (1983) focuses on the tensions between a mother and daughter, which are eased in the face of crisis and death. *Moonstruck* (1987) is a comedy, warmly romantic, which takes a positive look at love and family life in Brooklyn.

A rash of films appeared about babies; 1987 alone saw the release of *Three Men and a Baby, Raising Arizona,* and *Baby Boom.* During the 1980s the enlightened American male was learning to cope with child rearing, as Michael Keaton showed in *Mr. Mom* (1984) and John Travolta attempted in *Look Who's Talking* (1990).

Movies the entire family could enjoy remained popular throughout the 1980s and continued into the 1990s. *Who Framed Roger Rabbit?* (1989), joyous and giddy, is a combination of cartoon and film noir, adding up to sheer entertainment for children and adults alike. *Home Alone* (1991) is silly and sentimental, yet the comic fantasy of a young boy spending Christmas Eve on his own is difficult to resist. The movie, which cost $18 million, grossed $280 million from domestic rentals and another $200 million from the foreign market. Animation was revived during the early 1990s, in part thanks to computers, and became popular with children and welcomed by adults who had children under age thirteen. *The Little Mermaid* (1990) won praise both for its technical proficiency and its enchanting music, as did *Beauty and the Beast* (1991), which grossed $120 million in domestic rentals alone, and *Aladdin* (1992), with its magic carpet ride and genie with a sense of humor.

THRILLS, SPILLS, AND SPECIAL EFFECTS

Escapist fun in the form of adventure and fast-paced action has long been a Hollywood staple and shows no sign of letup. The 1980s and 1990s saw a number of well-crafted examples. *Romancing the Stone* (1984), starring Michael Douglas and Kathleen Turner, is a romantic comedy-adventure, with a clever script, an attractive cast, and interesting relationships. The movie grossed $75 million and was reprised the next year by *The Jewel of the Nile. Beverly Hills Cop* (1984), which features Eddie Murphy as Axel Foley, a slick-talking, quick-thinking, renegade black police officer, blends pranks with serious encounters with danger. The movie and its sequels proved among the biggest box office attractions within recent years.

Police stories remain high on Hollywood's popularity charts, particularly if they include wild car chases and an abundance of carnage. *Fort Apache, the Bronx* (1981) was a trifle somber for contemporary tastes and offended some factions by depicting an assortment of criminals who are either black or Hispanic. The point of the film, however, is that an entire neighborhood, which happens to be primarily black and Hispanic, is victimized by the rampant crime that persists there.

Lethal Weapon (1987) is a police action-adventure in a more popular mold. The film features two mismatched detectives, one white and one black, who become buddies in the line of duty. Although *Lethal Weapon* contains a great deal of humor, its ultimate strength stems from sensitive character development. Riggs (played by Mel Gibson) grieves for his dead wife and is nearly driven to suicide, whereas Murtaugh (played by Danny Glover) is a staunch family man. The relationship between the two men is galvanized when the black family is threatened with a kidnapping, which prompts the duo into heroic action.

Die Hard (1988), starring Bruce Willis, offers breakneck action, violence, and fun, whereas *The Big Easy* (1987), with Dennis Quaid heading the cast, is reminiscent of the screen's thrillers from the Golden Age. *Jagged Edge* (1985), pairs Glenn Close with Jeff Bridges and is in the tradition of Alfred Hitchcock. Throughout the movie it is impossible to know whether the character played by Bridges is a misunderstood victim or a brutal murderer. As Hitchcock demonstrated earlier, the edge between innocence and evil is sometimes a jagged one. *The Silence of the Lambs* (1991) is a shocking but powerful film, depicting a young FBI trainee on the trail of a psychotic serial killer. The picture was a huge success, both commercially and critically, and won Academy Awards for Jodie Foster and Anthony Hopkins.

Futuristic action movies remained popular during the 1980s, particularly with younger audiences. *Blade Runner* (1982), which finds Harrison Ford in a high-tech film noir, is visually arresting, yet lacks substance. *The Terminator* (1984), a vehicle for Austrian bodybuilder Arnold Schwarzenegger, is another futuristic film noir, depicting a world dominated by dark forces in the year 2029. The Terminator character is the embodiment of evil, yet the cosmos, devastated by nuclear war, contains no counterforce of good. Life holds no deliverance, only a prolonged struggle against machines. Although *The Terminator* contains slambang action, it harbors a philosophical note that added to its impact. The film was a smash hit and led to *Terminator 2: Judgement Day,* the top grosser of 1991. *Total Recall* (1991), another science fiction extravaganza with Schwarzenegger amid amazing visuals, cost $60 million but grossed more than twice that amount in the United States alone.

COURTING THE TEEN MARKET

Movies targeted at teenagers tend to portray adolescents as the ultimate source of sanity and wisdom in a world where adults are superfluous. Fast-paced, gory movies remain favorites within the teen market. *Friday the 13th* (1981) proved such a huge financial success for Paramount that other studios began looking for low-budget, independently produced splatter movies to turn into box office goldmines. *The Slumber Party Massacre* followed in 1982 and *Fright Night* in 1985.

Low comedy combined with special effects and hip patter constitutes another popular genre with teenage audiences, as *Ghostbusters* demonstrated in 1984. *Porky's* (1982), on the other hand, is full of coarse humor and gross gags, causing adolescent film-goers to laugh uproariously and ask for sequels.

Flashdance (1983) mirrored frivolous attitudes of teenagers interested in dancing, fashion, and enjoying a good time. The movie brought nationwide attention to break dancing, a form of sidewalk gymnastics that previously had been restricted to ghetto areas, and made cut-off sweatshirts a national fad among adolescent girls. *Flashdance* has the look of an MTV production, but the picture earned more than $100 million at the box office and millions more from the sale of soundtrack albums. *Footloose,* similar lightweight entertainment, followed in 1984 and, like its predecessor, proved a major commercial success.

Movies based on cartoons and comic strips, which became numerous in the 1980s and 1990s, had the advantage of being largely presold and are frequently enjoyed as much by adults as children and teenagers. *Batman* brought in $450 million in worldwide box office grosses during the summer of 1989, $100 million of which came from its first eleven days on the screen, and the film gave a tremendous boost to the T-shirt industry. Warner agreed to pay actor Jack Nicholson $7 million up front to play the Joker in the movie, in addition to 15 percent of the box office take. In contrast to Steven Spielberg's movies, *Batman* has a dark, brooding feel, enhanced by Danny Elfman's atmospheric score.

Dick Tracy opened in June 1990 to less enthusiastic audiences, despite the presence of Warren Beatty, Madonna, and music by Stephen Sondheim. But the film brought the durable comic strip to life and effectively caricatured vogues of the Great Depression. *The Addams Family,* based on the Charles Addams cartoons and the 1960s television series, became one of the most profitable movies of 1991, grossing more than $110 million. *Teenage Mutant Ninja Turtles,* inspired by another popular comic strip, proved an enormous hit in 1990, despite its lack of stars, and prompted many sequels.

Many black teenagers go to the movies three or four times a month and constitute an audience Hollywood has recognized and now caters to. As a rule, black teenagers prefer their humor raw and uncensored and tend to be suspicious of messages not couched in the language of the streets. *Menace II Society,* a realistic portrayal of a young man trapped in the Watts violence, became a popular film among young urban blacks during the summer of 1993, and violence is often prominent in the films targeted toward African American teenagers. Word-of-mouth is important in determining a picture's success with young black audiences, as well as the beat of the music on the soundtrack. If black teenagers think the music is good, they are likely to see the movie.

Although most pictures aimed at the early teen market border on the imbecilic, older adolescents have grown knowledgeable about films in recent years, and the better educated are capable of appreciating the subtleties in good ones when they come along. *The Karate Kid* (1984), which bears parallels to *Rocky* and shares the same director, had special appeal among sixteen- to twenty-year-olds, although older audiences responded to it as well. An inspirational story of the underdog who wins, *The Karate Kid* takes a fresh look at the martial arts, emphasizing the need for spiritual maturity over physical strength.

Risky Business (1983) cast Tom Cruise as a high school senior who discovers that financial ambition can be as frightening as it is attractive, and the characters in *St. Elmo's Fire* (1985) are apprehensive about themselves, their abilities, and their future in the so-called real world after college. Rob Reiner's *Stand By Me* (1986) offers a touching yet humorous revelation about what it's like to be an adolescent boy, whereas *Dead Poets Society* (1990) is a sensitive portrayal of a boys' prep school in the 1950s, with students who are neither predictable nor ordinary.

LATER DEVELOPMENTS OF THE MOVIE BRATS

The status of successful directors has increased since the "movie brats" first appeared in the late 1960s and early 1970s. Coppola, DePalma, Scorsese, Lucas, and Spielberg have all become powerful figures in the motion picture business. Yet all except Spielberg have shunned Hollywood as an operating base. George Lucas lives quietly but elegantly outside San Francisco, within easy driving distance of Francis Ford Coppola's mansion. Brian DePalma and Martin Scorsese have made New York their home. All five have increased their reputations for technical brilliance and deepened their capacity to enrich audiences with ideas in engaging ways, not always with the desired box office results.

Francis Ford Coppola's career has suffered from turbulence and major setbacks. *The Outsiders* (1983), based on S. E. Hinton's popular youth novel, is a film about adolescence and a reluctance to grow up. The picture is romantic and stylized and came at a time when Coppola felt the need for retrenchment. *The Cotton Club* (1984) is a visually stunning portrait of the Jazz Age, rich in atmosphere and filled with elaborate musical numbers. Its script went through thirty-eight revisions, with *The Cotton Club* costing almost $50 million, at least $22 million more than had been budgeted. When the picture was released, critics were harsh and audiences largely ignored it.

Peggy Sue Got Married (1986) was to be Coppola's comeback project, but the subject seemed an odd choice. A time-travel movie starring Kathleen Turner, *Peggy Sue Got Married* evokes high school life during the 1960s and looks back on the era with more nostalgia than acumen. In November 1989 the director started shooting the third installment of the *Godfather* saga, and his return to prominence followed. Then Coppola reverted to risky, personalized moviemaking again with *Tucker* (1989), the story of a maverick car designer who is eventually forced out of business; its box office appeal was limited.

If Francis Ford Coppola in his middle years failed to capture the public's interest as he had early in his career, Martin Scorsese has persistently gone against the dominant grain, and his films, with rare exceptions, have lacked the optimism and reassurance conducive to big box office grossers. *Raging Bull* (1980) deconstructs the macho cult fostered by Stallone and Schwarzenegger, and *The King of Comedy* (1983) is a disturbing account of an aspiring television star who achieves success after committing a serious crime.

The Color of Money (1986) proved the most commercially successful film in Scorsese's checkered career. A sequel to *The Hustler* (1961), a grim but haunting portrait of pool wizard "Fast" Eddie Felson, *The Color of Money* paired Paul Newman (by then symbolic of old Hollywood) with Tom Cruise (an emblem of the new breed). The picture allowed Scorsese to explore a theme that has remained central to his best work: the existence of offbeat types in urban subcultures. Yet in *The Color of Money* the tone is lighter than in Scorsese's more intensely personal movies.

Two years later the director's *The Last Temptation of Christ*, arguably Hollywood's most controversial film, was released. Protesters gathered outside theaters across the nation to denounce Scorsese's depiction of a confused, uncertain savior. A torrent of debate raced through the media, with objections voiced loudest against the film's candid treatment of sexual intercourse between Jesus and Mary Magdalene. Scorsese argued that his aim was a more human depiction of Christ, but intimidated theater owners in many American cities refused to show the picture.

Scorsese redeemed himself in 1993 with *The Age of Innocence,* a ravishing look at upper middle-class life in New York City during the late nineteenth century. Based on Edith Wharton's novel, the picture has beauty, romance, sensitivity, and maturity, revealing a man torn between two women and contrasting ways of life. Scorsese claimed that his inspiration stemmed from director William Wyler's *The Heiress* (1949), a film classic he had admired as a boy. In *The Age of Innocence* the director succeeded in bringing an era of American history to life in a colorful and relevant way.

With *Blow Out* (1981), Brian DePalma continued working in a vein reminiscent of Alfred Hitchcock. Then he turned to *Scarface,* based on the 1932 movie of that name, with Al Pacino playing the role of the gangster actor Paul Muni had created. DePalma resisted tailoring his films to audiences' demands and objected to sample polls in gauging his movies' success or failure. "It's appalling," he said in 1984, "that 325 people recruited from shopping malls can shake the confidence of professionals who've been working in the industry for decades."

Three years later DePalma directed a film that even mainstream America could love—*The Untouchables,* with Kevin Costner in the role of Eliot Ness. The movie's dense visual texture captures the look of gangster-ridden Chicago during the Prohibition era, while Robert DeNiro plays Al Capone convincingly and Sean Connery delivers an Academy Award–winning performance as a veteran cop gunned down in the line of duty.

Since *Star Wars,* George Lucas has devoted more time to producing than directing motion pictures, working in that capacity on the immensely successful *Raiders of the Lost Ark* (1981). "I wanted to do an adventure that had the same impact and pace as the old serials used to have," said Lucas. The idea of making the hero an archaeologist came from courses in anthropology Lucas had taken at Modesto Junior College. Steven Spielberg, who directed the picture, establishes contact with his audiences in the opening scene, and the relentless, fast-paced action continues throughout the remainder of the film. *Raiders* is exciting, full of allusions to earlier films, yet benefits from strong characterizations. Above all, the movie is technically superb. Spielberg uses his fascination with machines and special effects with dazzling results, yet the director demonstrates his ability to capture the feelings of ordinary people.

Raiders of the Lost Ark grossed more than $112 million during the summer of 1981. Over the next two years enrollment in anthropology courses at major universities rose as much as 28 percent. *Indiana Jones and the Temple of Doom* (1984), the sequel to *Raiders*, continued the excitement, yet cost $30 million, almost twice what *Raiders* had cost. "Same crew, same number of shooting days, everything the same," George Lucas said. "That's the inflation between those two pictures." The budget Lucas presented to Paramount in 1989 for *Indiana Jones and the Last Crusade*, the third segment of the trilogy, was for $44 million; like its two predecessors, it returned more than $100 million.

In between the Indiana Jones movies, Spielberg directed *E.T.: The Extra-Terrestrial* (1982), which was considered his masterpiece for more than a decade. *E. T.* drew upon the inner lives of children, their anxieties as well as their capacity for fantasy. The film depicts an extra-terrestrial visitor, stranded on Earth when his spaceship leaves without him, who is befriended by a young boy. The alien is loving and wise and quickly wins the hearts of audiences, regardless of age. Always an unabashed sentimentalist, Spielberg was able to melt the hearts of postwar generations steeped in cynicism. *E.T.* became the all-time box office champion, grossing more than $300 million.

The Color Purple (1985) seemed like a departure for the director, since its story is far from the realm of fantasy and high adventure Spielberg had mastered. Based on black feminist writer Alice Walker's novel, *The Color Purple* deals with the efforts of three black women to transform their oppressive, often brutal world into a happy one. Spielberg captures the poignancy and emotional beauty of Walker's prize-winning book and drew powerful performances from Whoopi Goldberg and Oprah Winfrey, prompting major careers for both.

With *Empire of the Sun* (1987) Spielberg returned to telling a story through the eyes of a child. The movie begins in Shanghai early in December 1941, with the Japanese army dug in nearby. A boy grows from innocence to awareness under the fierce conditions of war, suffering the loss of his parents. Steven Spielberg evokes the pain and the wonder of the boy's coming of age, amid turmoil that is visually exciting.

Always (1990) is Spielberg's reworking of the 1943 classic *A Guy Named Joe*, a bathetic wartime romance the director had enjoyed as a child. *Jurassic Park* (1993), with astonishing special effects, suspense, and nonstop action, topped *E.T.* as the all-time top box office moneymaker, taking in a gross of $705 million and setting attendance records in Japan, Great Britain, Hong Kong, and other nations.

Although Spielberg's popularity with the public became undisputed, he had been dismissed by many critics as mawkish and lightweight. The director was repeatedly ignored when awards were handed out. *Schindler's List* (1993) changed that, earning Spielberg the Academy Award for best director of the year, in addition to winning six other Oscars in various categories, including best picture. *Schindler's List* stands as Spielberg's cinematic masterpiece, a powerful journey through the Nazi holocaust. The black-and-white film balances devastating episodes of death and brutality with human dignity and personal heroics. *Schindler's List* was a personal film for Spielberg, yet one that holds universal appeal, earning $96 million during its run in the theaters.

OLIVER STONE: RELEVANCE AND SUBJECTIVITY

Director Oliver Stone emerged during the 1980s as an undisputed talent, one that has repeatedly looked back on the dark side of the 1960s and probed recent history from a personal point of view. Stone graduated in 1971 from the New York University film school, where he took courses taught by Martin Scorsese. A twice-decorated veteran of the Vietnam War, Stone won the Academy Award for best director of 1986 with *Platoon,* which also won the best picture award. Based on Stone's own experiences as a Marine, *Platoon* depicts the ghastliness of war; its action assaults the viewer with unrelenting force. Yet in the end the filmmaker concludes that the warriors' enemy has really been themselves, since their own humanity is at stake.

Salvador (1986) takes a radical look at American foreign policy in Central America. A brutal film, *Salvador* is filled with images of butchery. Stone consistently leans toward a naked attack, whatever his subject. In *Wall Street* (1988) he explores the contemporary world of high finance and securities trading. Made at a time when insider-trading scandals were much in the news, *Wall Street* offers a critical view of life in the fast lane. Gordon Gekko, the predatory character played in the film by Michael Douglas, is a modern buccaneer who scorns his more established competitors within the corporate hierarchy. Rather than the slow, patient investment pattern that built the country, Gekko's avarice and coercive power exemplify the contamination that Oliver Stone feels the capitalist system has undergone. The director said:

> My main reason for making *Wall Street* was to take a look at the 1980s era in terms of Yuppies living in urban centers. It reflects a reality wherein money has become the sex of the eighties. Net worth equals self-worth. And these protagonists represent a valueless system.

Stone returned to the Vietnam War in *Born on the Fourth of July* (1989). Based on Ron Kovic's autobiographical book detailing a patriotic boy's agonies in the Asian war and the permanent injuries he suffered there, *Born on the Fourth of July* goes to the core of the Vietnam tragedy. Stone depicts the confusion and horrors of the battlefield, as well as the physical, psychic, and moral wounds suffered there by American service personnel. Nor does the director ignore the division and turmoil the war created at home. "Coming home," Stone said, "was a second war." After searching his soul for meaning in the face of ruin and discord, Kovic aspired to a political career and became an outspoken proponent of Vietnam Veterans Against the War.

In *The Doors* (1991), Oliver Stone chronicles with amazing fidelity the rise, decline, and death of Jim Morrison, the sensitive, intellectual, self-indulgent, and self-destructive rock icon of the 1960s. But the most controversial of Stone's films to date is *JFK* (1991), which takes a conspiratorial view of the assassination of John F. Kennedy. The director mixes newsreel footage with material he filmed in Dallas, recreating the mood of the event with haunting accuracy. Although some viewers found Stone's explanation plausible, many historians were outraged at what they considered his irresponsibility in mingling fact with hearsay.

SOCIAL COMMENT AND HISTORICAL REVISION

Mature filmmakers have always felt a need to do more than simply entertain, but some, like Oliver Stone, establish a consistent pattern of social comment. Recent filmmakers have dealt honestly with controversial issues, sometimes launching frontal attacks on national policy and established institutions. The challenge for commercial filmmakers is to make a significant statement without relinquishing their role as commercial artists.

In *Missing* (1982), for example, director Constantin Costa-Gavras recounts the unsettling story of covert American involvement in the politics of Chile. *Missing* was one of several films in the 1980s that dealt with conditions in the Third World, but its appeal at the box office was assured by the presence of Jack Lemmon and Sissy Spacek in leading roles. *Silkwood* (1983), directed by Mike Nichols, details the growing activism of Karen Silkwood, a worker in the Kerr-McGee plutonium plant in Oklahoma who grew concerned about the safety standards there. Meryl Streep plays the title role, while singer-actress Cher delivers a convincing portrayal of Karen's lesbian friend, Dolly Pellicker. *Silkwood* is gloomy drama, yet its director and stars make the movie powerful for mature audiences.

Broadcast News (1987), directed by James L. Brooks, probes the ethics of television journalism, yet softens its message by including a love story. *Mississippi Burning* (1989), on the other hand, is held together by suspense. Set in 1964, the film chronicles the search for three young civil rights workers who have disappeared from a small town in Mississippi. When FBI agents arrive to investigate, they meet bigotry and racial hatred at every turn.

Filmmakers frequently reexamine history and, like historians, view the past through values of their own time. Hector Babenco's *Ironweed* (1987), based on the novel by William Kennedy, pictures the 1930s not as the "good old days," but as a dark period filled with personal anguish. Warren Beatty's *Reds* (1981) is based on the life of leftist writer John Reed and Reed's relationship with Louise Bryant. Not primarily concerned with the Russian Revolution, *Reds* portrays radical dissent in the pre–World War I years among bohemians living in Greenwich Village—such as literary figures Floyd Dell, Edna St. Vincent Millay, and Max Eastman—who opposed the war, rejected middle-class values, and came to sympathize with the Russian revolutionaries. *Glory* (1990) is an eloquent, heartrending epic about the first black infantry regiment in the American Civil War. The movie combines spectacle, action, and drama, yet makes statements about race relations that stand in sharp contrast to the attitudes conveyed by *Gone with the Wind* and other Civil War pictures produced during Hollywood's classic era.

Although the western movie was said to be dead during the late 1960s and 1970s, the genre showed signs of recovery in the 1980s, yet with an updated point of view. Recent interpretations of frontier history have made a significant impact on the scholarship on the West, and motion pictures followed similar paths to the new Western history. Michael Cimino's *Heaven's Gate* (1981), credited with being the biggest fiasco in film history from a commercial stand-point, is an epic centered around the Johnson County War. Critics lambasted the movie, yet Cimino makes a strong statement consistent with contemporary historical writing. *Heaven's Gate* attempts to illustrate the suspicion of foreigners on the frontier and explores in laborious detail the underside of American capitalism.

After the disaster of *Heaven's Gate,* westerns seemed all but finished. In 1985 *Silverado* and *Pale Rider* gave signs of reversing the trend. Four years later *Young Guns,* a retelling of the Lincoln County War, captured the attention of the youth market. Emilio Estevez portrays Billy the Kid in a picture that is brutal, honest, funny, and consistent with contemporary attitudes. Clint Eastwood's *Unforgiven* (1992), a realistic portrait of an aging ex-gunfighter drawn back into his former occupation to avenge an attack on a frontier prostitute, made an even stronger impact on adults and serious critics.

The huge success of *Dances with Wolves* (1991) did most to bring the western back into vogue. The movie is grand enough to cause audiences to long for the vanished frontier, yet contemporary enough to mirror acceptance of multiculturalism. *Dances with Wolves* depicts the life of the Plains Indians with sensitivity, using subtitles to convey dialogue. The film's director, Kevin Costner, plays Lieutenant John Dunbar, a man who goes to the frontier by choice, gains respect for Native American cultures, and discovers himself in the process.

ATTENTION TO MINORITIES

The limited view of American life that Hollywood projected during its heyday has been greatly expanded since the Civil Rights Act of 1964. Jewish actors who in an earlier age would likely have altered their names to fit a mainstream stereotype now join African Americans, Hispanics, Asians, and Native Americans in celebrating ethnic diversity. Lou Diamond Phillips and Rodney A. Grant have emerged in recent years as popular Native American actors, whereas Eddie Murphy, Whoopi Goldberg (the first black woman to win an Academy Award since Hattie McDaniel in 1939), Denzel Washington (another Oscar winner), Morgan Freeman (yet another), Danny Glover, Lou Gossett, Jr., Richard Pryor, Gregory Hines, and James Earl Jones head a growing list of significant black actors and actresses, all with images far different from that advanced by Sidney Poitier three decades before.

The 1980s and 1990s saw the emergence of a new generation of African American directors who moved from the fringes of independent production into the mainstream of commercial moviemaking. Spike Lee stands among the leaders. A graduate of the New York University film school, Lee won critical laurels with his first feature film, *She's Gotta Have It* (1986). With one exception his cast was composed entirely of blacks, although the director wrote the screenplay about issues not exclusively linked to racial identity. *Malcolm X,* Lee's film about the boisterous civil rights leader of the 1960s, earned acclaim in 1992 and established its director as a mainstream moviemaker.

John Singleton, a black filmmaker who directed his own screenplay entitled *Boyz N the Hood* (1991), at age twenty-three became the youngest director ever to be nominated for Academy Awards—for best director and best picture of the year. African American director Bill Duke's *A Rage in Harlem* (1991) centers on crime and sexuality in New York's black ghetto during the 1950s, winning Duke critical attention. Other noteworthy black directors include Charles Burnett, Mario Van Peebles, and Robert Townsend.

By the end of 1991 at least a dozen features directed by African Americans had been released to mainstream audiences during that year. Spike Lee's success and the popularity of rap music contributed to the increased visibility of black filmmakers. Market research during the early 1990s revealed that whereas African Americans represented 12 percent of the country's population, they accounted for approximately 25 percent of the money spent in the United States on entertainment, mostly moviegoing and sports.

Women directors also have become more numerous in recent Hollywood. During the Golden Age there were few women behind the camera except in design, screenwriting, and film editing. Of the 7,332 features made in Hollywood between 1939 and 1979, only fourteen were directed by women. Dorothy Arzner stood virtually alone in the Directors Guild, joined later by Ida Lupino. In 1990 women directed twenty-three of the 406 feature films made that year under contracts authorized by the Directors Guild of America.

Both the Directors Guild and the Writers Guild in Hollywood have sought to equalize hiring practices in their respective fields. In 1983 the Directors Guild filed discrimination suits against Warner Bros. and Columbia, but women filmmakers still claim that studio executives are reluctant to trust them with big action and special effects pictures. Yet during the 1980s and 1990s female directors in the American movie industry became more than token, as an increasing number of women filmmakers began sustaining coherent careers.

Joan Micklin Silver made her mark as a feature director with such independent productions as *Hester Street* (1975) and *Between the Lines* (1977). Martha Coolidge earned an early reputation with *Valley Girl* (1982), a Romeo and Juliet story in which love transcends the distance and social boundaries between West Los Angeles and the San Fernando Valley. Coolidge went on to direct *Rambling Rose* (1991), *Lost in Yonkers* (1993), and *Angie* (1994), specializing in personal stories.

Amy Jones won attention with *Love Letters* (1984), Susan Seidelman with *Making Mr. Right* (1987), Randa Haines with *Children of a Lesser God* (1986), and Kathryn Bigelow with *Point Break* (1991). Penny Marshall enjoyed major success with *Big* (1989) and *A League of Their Own* (1992), and Barbra Streisand scored as a director with *Prince of Tides* (1991). Yet women filmmakers have suffered their share of failures; *Ishtar* (1987), an offbeat comedy directed by Elaine May, was destroyed by reviewers and quickly withdrawn from the theaters, despite an energetic marketing campaign. *Ishtar*'s $45 million budget was the largest awarded any movie undertaken by a woman to date, but not even the combination of Warren Beatty and Dustin Hoffman in the cast could rescue the picture from public apathy.

The depiction of women on the screen has experienced significant shifts in recent productions. Sydney Pollack's *Tootsie* (1982) cast Dustin Hoffman as a struggling actor who masquerades as a woman to find work. The experience of cross-dressing not only causes Hoffman's character to understand women better, but also produces startling insights into his own personality. *Mystic Pizza* (1989) is a coming-of-age story for three young women in Mystic, Connecticut, and explores their need for female bonding.

Thelma and Louise (1991) starts out as a female buddy movie, as two Arkansas women take to the road looking for fun and relaxation. Along the way they experience sexual exploitation, an attempted rape, murder, and theft. They grow more assertive as their journey progresses and come to know themselves in ways that suggest they can never go back to their old lives. *Thelma and Louise* remains one of the few movies in recent decades to focus on women. Although some critics accused the film of "male bashing," feminists retorted that the characters played by Susan Sarandon and Geena Davis merely learned to behave more like men.

Pretty Woman (1990) became a favorite with audiences and earned $82 million in domestic rentals, although feminists attacked its Cinderella-like theme. An attractive Hollywood prostitute (Julia Roberts) and a visiting businessman (Richard Gere) fall in love in the rags-to-riches romance, with him introducing her to culture and sophistication and her showing him the pleasure of living.

Screen attitudes toward homosexuals have changed since the sensationalized *Cruising* (1980) portrayed sadomasochistic sex and a psychopathic killer who mutilates gay victims with a bread knife. The central character in *Making Love* (1982) is a handsome, rich, married doctor who comes to terms with his homosexuality, divorces his understanding wife, and establishes a lasting relationship with another man. In *Victor/Victoria* (1982) a woman impersonates a man; although the film makes statements about gender differences, its humor defuses subject matter that might otherwise prove threatening. *Deathtrap* (1982) mixes mystery and comedy and pairs Michael Caine and Christopher Reeve as homosexual lovers, seen in a screen kiss. The lovers have staged a murder in order to kill the actual victim, who suffers from a weak heart and thereby dies of natural causes from shock.

Far more sensitive is *Kiss of the Spider Woman* (1985). Directed by Hector Babenco, the film casts William Hurt (in an Academy Award–winning performance) and Raul Julia as prisoners in a South American jail. Molina, the Hurt character, is a flamboyant homosexual serving a prison sentence for molesting a minor. Valentin, the Julia character, is a political prisoner and is straight. Fantasy provides Molina an escape from the drab reality of his life. Underlying his flamboyance is deep despair, for he has suffered a life of humiliation. Placed together in the same cell, Valentin is at first hostile toward Molina, but they slowly establish a strong relationship, which affects them both. Molina's love for Valentin becomes his source of strength; he no longer allows himself to be humiliated. *Kiss of the Spider Woman* is a forceful and moving film, which was later turned into a long-running Broadway musical. "Here are two characters who start from opposite poles and end up loving each other," said William Hurt, "and through their love for each other they find greater self-respect."

Torch Song Trilogy (1989), based on a play by Harvey Fierstein, is another treatment of gays' gaining self-acceptance and a resolution not to be victimized. *Longtime Companion* (1991) and *The Band Plays On* (1994) both deal with the AIDS epidemic, which decimated the arts.

Curiously perhaps, the impact of AIDS resulted in a revival of vampire pictures, among them *Vampires in Havana* (1988) and *Interview with the Vampire* (1994). In *Vamp* (1987) Grace Jones is a singles-bar performer whose one-night stands awake the next morning to find themselves suffering from a strange malady. *The Lost Boys* (1988) casts Kiefer Sutherland as the leader of an unruly teenage gang who dupes victims into drinking blood that turns them into vampires.

The aged have been treated with sensitivity in recent Hollywood films and in a number of cases with genuine insight. To Universal's surprise, *On Golden Pond* (1981) proved the box office smash of the season. The picture won Academy Awards for both Henry Fonda and Katharine Hepburn and was popular with old and young alike. *A Trip to Bountiful* (1985), based on Horton Foote's original teleplay, is quietly eloquent and deeply touching, containing an emotional wholeness seldom found in commercial movies. Set in the early 1950s, *A Trip to Bountiful* casts Geraldine Page as Carrie Watts, an aging mother who lives with her married son yet longs to visit her girlhood home one last time. Carrie's need becomes an obsession, but Page (in an Oscar-winning performance) never allows her characterization to become overly sentimental.

Cocoon (1985) is a geriatric comedy directed by former child actor Ron Howard, who captures the sadness of growing old in contemporary America. Howard manages to balance humor and compassion in an original and winning combination, and *Cocoon* won an Academy Award for veteran actor Don Ameche. *Driving Miss Daisy* (1990), based on an off-Broadway play, blends humor, charm, and tenderness in its depiction of a Southern octogenarian's reluctant acceptance of her black chauffeur. In the title role Jessica Tandy became the oldest recipient of the Oscar for best actress, and Morgan Freeman turned in a performance of exceptional warmth and dignity as the chauffeur. Producer Richard Zanuck had to fight to convince Warner executives to permit him to make the movie, which cost $8 million and earned $50 million.

SEX, VIOLENCE, NUDITY, AND PROFANITY

Staunch conservatives have persistently maintained that Hollywood has a predilection for vulgar, nihilistic content. Michael Medved contends in his vehement book *Hollywood vs. America* (1992) that the movie colony has contempt for middle-class morality and in recent years has delighted in assailing traditional norms. "Tens of millions of Americans now see the entertainment industry as an all-powerful enemy," Medved wrote, "an alien force that assaults our most cherished values and corrupts our children."

Many current films do offend the sensibilities of more conventional moviegoers with nudity, graphic violence, explicit language, and simulated sex. Many complain about the gore and sadism of contemporary movies, their ugliness, their lack of good taste, and their tendency to focus on the degraded aspects of human nature. Others find no need to show incest, degeneracy, bestiality, urination, and similarly questionable scenes in motion pictures, while diehards even call for a return to censorship.

Body Heat (1981), a contemporary film noir starring William Hurt and Kathleen Turner, created much controversy upon its release. The film is erotic, contains extensive nudity, steamy sexual imagery, and exceedingly frank dialogue, which many found unnecessary. *Blue Velvet* (1986), with its vivid depiction of abnormal sexual practices, provoked lively debate, particularly among feminist circles. Brilliant but disturbing, *Blue Velvet* exhibits sadomasochistic sex games with jarring ferocity, which caused the film to be one of the most condemned of its era.

Fatal Attraction (1987), a hysterical thriller featuring Michael Douglas and Glenn Close, traverses a world of promiscuity and adultery. The film borrows visual images from a number of classic horror movies, especially Hitchcock's *Psycho* (1960), and includes scenes of appalling violence. *Fatal Attraction* carries strongly antifeminist undercurrents, but the film became the third highest grossing picture of 1987, generating more than $70 million from its run in the theaters. *Basic Instinct* (1992), another thriller calculated for big box office success, is even more sexually adventuresome and created in actress Sharon Stone a femme fatale of the most predatory variety. Although some viewers dismissed the movie as smut, *Basic Instinct* proved a smash hit in the number of tickets sold.

DISCOVERING THE AUSTRALIAN CINEMA

The 1970s constituted an exciting decade for the budding film industry in Australia. Even though movies were often made there on minuscule budgets, a talented group of Australian filmmakers won recognition early in the decade for their experimental approach. They honed their skills, so that the period from 1975 to 1982 proved even more fertile for the Australian cinema, both in terms of quality and the number of pictures produced. American critics discovered the Australian moviemakers during the late 1970s and early 1980s, and some of the best talent from down under was lured to the United States—stars and directors, as well as film technicians.

Peter Weir, a professed loner who came to Hollywood with an art-house reputation, emerged as one of Australia's finest directors. *Gallipoli* (1981) and *The Year of Living Dangerously* (1983), both of which starred Mel Gibson, introduced Weir to American audiences. *Witness* (1985) and *Dead Poets Society* (1989) followed, earning Weir a large American following. In *Witness* the director proves effective in capturing the sense of community within the Amish world of Pennsylvania. In a movie rich in atmosphere Weir contrasts the simple Amish traditions with those of mainstream America, yet holds his film together with riveting suspense.

Another Australian director, George Miller, won attention in the United States with *Mad Max* (1979) and *The Man from Snowy River* (1982); Bruce Beresford established his reputation in Hollywood with *Tender Mercies* (1982), *Crimes of the Heart* (1986), and *Driving Miss Daisy* (1989), all set in provincial America. *Tender Mercies,* a modest film made on a small budget, is an honest depiction of a country singer's battle to find fulfillment and self-worth, with an outstanding performance by Robert Duvall. *Crimes of the Heart,* based on Beth Henley's Pulitzer Prize–winning play, combines humor with solid characterizations.

Among the Australian actors, Mel Gibson has achieved superstardom in Hollywood, earning a minimum of $10 million per movie since the success of *Lethal Weapon* (1987). Paul Hogan scored with American audiences in *Crocodile Dundee* (1986), a pleasant mixture of lightweight comedy and serious adventure. Paramount distributed the movie, earning substantial profits both from the initial film and its popular sequel.

The advantages for Australian moviemakers remaining in Hollywood are numerous: greater exposure, larger budgets, and bigger financial rewards. Dean Semler, who won an Academy Award for his outstanding photography in *Dances with Wolves,* would earn far more money working in the United States than he could by staying in Australia, and the artistic horizons are also broader in Hollywood.

MORE ACTORS THAN STARS

Most current actors and actresses dislike having undue emphasis placed on their status as celebrities, preferring to think of themselves as serious professionals whose craft happens to be acting. Certainly the larger-than-life image of stardom is not what it was during Hollywood's golden years. Actors and actresses continue to be revered by the public, and those considered "bankable" in the industry are stars by virtue of their economic potential. Stars sell tickets and earn millions of dollars on each picture, yet their standing is precarious; a failure or two in succession can topple them. In 1982 Richard Gere ranked among Hollywood's most sought after leading men. The failure of *The Cotton Club* (1984) and *King David* (1985), however, which cost nearly $30 million and earned only $5 million, threatened to destroy the actor's career. It took *Pretty Woman* (1990) to put Gere back on top.

Many of Hollywood's current stars feel comfortable shuttling back and forth between movies and the stage. Despite her enormous success in films, Glenn Close was not hailed as a superstar until her recent success in Los Angeles and New York with Andrew Lloyd Webber's musical adaptation of *Sunset Boulevard* (1994). Christopher Reeve, best known as the big screen's most recent Superman, performed the Count in Beaumarchais's *The Marriage of Figaro* (1985) on Broadway and saw no conflict between the two approaches. Kathleen Turner, at the height of her popularity in motion pictures, took time out to appear in a revival of Tennessee Williams's *Cat on a Hot Tin Roof* (1990) in New York, although she insisted on a limited run. Kevin Kline, Jeremy Irons, and Amy Irving all feel comfortable in both media.

A number of the screen's current actors established themselves first on television: Burt Reynolds, John Travolta, Michael J. Fox, Eddie Murphy, Robin Williams, and Bruce Willis, among others. Teenage idols often begin as movie personalities, then develop into solid performers, as Tom Cruise, Patrick Swayze, Emilio Estevez, Rob Lowe, Matt Dillon, and Sean Penn exemplify.

Meryl Streep and Jessica Lange seemed rivals for the best parts for actresses a few years ago, but Jodie Foster and Emma Thompson dominated the field a few years later, even though Julia Roberts was considered Hollywood's hottest female star in terms of box office. Foster became newsworthy in 1981 when President Ronald Reagan came close to assassination. Gunman John Hinckley, who shot

Reagan, claimed he was obsessed with the young actress and wanted to gain her attention.

Whereas ethnic heroes abounded in the 1970s, the Reagan years saw a return to white Anglo-Saxon leading men, as Harrison Ford, William Hurt, Kevin Costner, and Christopher Reeve illustrate. Only a handful of stars are considered bankable enough to open a movie, yet even they frequently fail to attract the desired audiences. Kevin Costner proved a disappointment in *Wyatt Earp* (1994), as did Julia Roberts and Nick Nolte in *I Love Trouble* (1994). The critically lambasted *Cocktail* (1988), on the other hand, made $80 million thanks mainly to the presence of Tom Cruise.

Fans still read about their favorite actors and actresses in the tabloids and delight in reports of their romantic entanglements. Some observers are still convinced that Hollywood is the Babylon it has been accused of being since the Fatty Arbuckle arrest in the 1920s. Moralists today are shocked when prominent entertainers proudly bear children out of wedlock, as Goldie Hawn and Kurt Russell, Susan Sarandon and Tim Robbins, Jessica Lange and Sam Shepard, Farrah Fawcett and Ryan O'Neal, and Mia Farrow and Woody Allen have done. Yet less critical fans point to the devoutly Catholic Mel Gibson, married with six children, as proof that old-fashioned virtues can survive even in Tinseltown.

CONCLUSION

The market for Hollywood movies is booming, not only in the United States but all over the world, with attendance records broken almost every year. Domestic box office returns by the 1990s, however, accounted for only 20 percent of a film's total profits, whereas video sales and video rentals had become the major source of revenue for movies. In 1990 consumers in North America spent $9 billion to view videocassettes at home. The growth of the foreign market is also a vital factor in continued profits for Hollywood's product, and film executives have recently been adept at opening up outlets in Eastern Europe: Russia, Poland, Hungary, the Czech Republic, Slovakia, Rumania, and Bulgaria.

People in small towns demonstrate different tastes in movies than people living in large cities, and word-of-mouth is more important outside metropolitan areas. Small-town moviegoers prefer action pictures and comedies over love stories and do not generally like sexually explicit material. Regional and local differences are also reflected in entertainment tastes. The military residents around Jacksonville, North Carolina, for instance, preferred *Rambo* over *Sleepless in Seattle* (1993). Southern moviegoers were lukewarm about Robert Redford's scenic *A River Runs Through It* (1992), whereas the movie was an enormous success in Montana and elsewhere in the country.

Sequels remain assured moneymakers, since audiences hope to repeat the experience they enjoyed with the original movie. They do not want the second picture to be unduly different from the first, yet neither do they want to be bored with a reprise that is too similar. Disappointments are frequent; *Sister Act* (1992), with Whoopi Goldberg masquerading as a nun, was a comedy hard to resist (even nuns liked it), but *Sister Act II* (1994) proved a tepid replay.

Films in the 1990s open simultaneously at between 750 to 1,500 screens across the country in an effort to maximize the all-important response during the initial weekend. Although box office records are consistently shattered, domestic movie attendance has actually declined in percentage of the overall population. The number of middle age and senior citizens patronizing movie theaters has increased during recent years, but only 8 percent of adults over forty attended films regularly in 1992.

Tastes in entertainment continue to shift with the times. In the 1990s Hollywood producers showed an increased awareness of environmental issues, at least as an incidental part of plots. They gave evidence of backing away from the previous decade's slasher and sexploitation pictures in favor of more family-oriented entertainment. The proportion of R-rated movies rose from 39 percent to 61 percent in the twenty years after 1974, yet recent data indicates that G- and PG-rated films earn bigger income in the theaters.

Although more features are made outside Hollywood than in earlier decades, California in 1990 still hosted two-thirds of all American movie locations, with New York ranking second, followed by Florida, Texas, Arizona, and Washington State. Texas and other states offer the advantages of cheaper labor and fewer union regulations, but cost-conscious producers have found similar benefits available in Canada. Still, the average cost for a studio production in the early 1990s ranged between $27 and 30 million.

With the economic pressures resulting from ballooning costs, several studio heads indicated in 1991 that fewer high-budget movies and more modest-budget projects would be forthcoming. During the summer of 1994 plans for big-budget films were falling apart throughout

Hollywood, with some projects disappearing altogether. The budget on the 11th-century action movie *Crusade,* planned for Arnold Schwarzenegger, had soared to more than $100 million. Big stars were voicing concern over giant projects with unpolished scripts, fearful that a weak showing in an expensive picture would damage their careers. Meanwhile, small pictures like *Fresh* and *Clerks* (1994) were making their way onto the Top Twenty charts of weekly box office winners.

A new breed of independent production company has appeared, sufficiently capitalized to make movies without the aid of studio financing. Three of the five pictures that grossed more than $100 million in 1991 were made by independent companies and simply distributed by the major studios; *Terminator 2: Judgement Day* was made by Carolco, *Robin Hood: Prince of Thieves* by Morgan Creek, and *City Slickers* by Castle Rock. Yet even Carolco Pictures, producer of the year's top hit, was forced to cut production and lay off a quarter of its employees as part of a December 1991 retrenchment.

Nothing seems certain in the motion picture business, except perhaps an obsession with new technology and special effects. Even during the 1980s there were filmmakers who swam against the conservative tide, and the decade produced a number of memorable pictures and outstanding performances. *Frances* (1982) cast Jessica Lange as Frances Farmer, a left-wing actress who did not fit the Hollywood mold and was crushed during the 1940s.

Despite market research, surprises at the box office continue. MGM/UA's *Rain Man* (1989), with Dustin Hoffman playing an autistic savant and Tom Cruise as his avaricious brother, became Metro's biggest hit since *Gone with the Wind,* a genuine blockbuster that earned $100 million within its first nine weeks in the theaters. "The only thing the picture had going for it," studio executive Peter Bart said, "was that it was superbly directed and performed. And it rang true." *The Four Seasons* (1981), a mature examination of friendship, proved a bigger commercial success than studio executives had anticipated, as did *Hoosiers* (1986), a modest movie about small-town high school basketball.

Although special effects seem to have become the crux of recent Hollywood's output, award-winning movies were made during the 1980s from serious books (*Ragtime, Sophie's Choice, A Passage to India, Out of Africa*) and plays (*Amadeus, Children of a Lesser God, 84 Charing Cross Road*), all of which illustrate that substance was not forgotten during the vacuous Reagan years. Broadway musicals fared less well on the screen; critics roasted *Annie* (1982), *The Best Little*

Whorehouse in Texas (1982), and *A Chorus Line* (1985), despite their successes on the stage. Bob Fosse's autobiographical *All That Jazz* (1980), one of the few original movie musicals in recent years, proved far better and benefitted from fully drawn characterizations.

Old-timers maintain that part of the uncertainty in the present movie business stems from placing too many novices in positions of leadership. In 1980 almost a third of all feature films were in the hands of first-time directors. Veteran actors insist that most newcomers are unsure of themselves and add to the cost of a production by wasting time. Others argue that studios have become overly dependent on computerized marketing reports and follow what appear to be safe routes rather than fresher approaches. Many blame the motion picture industry's all-or-nothing attitude, its impatience, and the fact that films are not allowed enough time to build audiences. Still others say that society has become too jaded to accept screen heroes, that American life is now seen through the eyes of the least common denominator, and that merchandising has replaced creativity in all areas.

The 1990s brought hope for a greater mix of movies, an increasing number of which offered adult themes yet still proved entertaining and original. Film appreciation courses plus pithy television commentary from such critics as Gene Siskel and Roger Ebert have helped shape more sophisticated audiences. Current movie patrons are capable of responding favorably to a warm family movie like *Mrs. Doubtfire* (1993), in which Robin Williams resorts to cross-dressing as a housekeeper to spend time with his ex-wife and children. Yet many can also admire a psychologically complex drama such as *The Piano* (1993) and appreciate its fine performances and photography. For today's mature audiences, spectacles need to offer more than eye appeal, as the success of *The Last of the Mohicans* (1992) illustrates. Films made from best-selling novels are expected to live up to their literary reputations; failure to do so, as the movie version of *The Bonfire of the Vanities* (1991) demonstrated, will bring censure from a discerning public as well as professional critics. A growing segment of current movie audiences expects more depth from feature films than what they find on television. They are astute enough to appreciate well-crafted story lines, intelligent acting, and the work of designers, composers, and editors that enhance the cinematic experience. On the whole, current movie audiences are more visually literate than earlier viewers, know more about how to read a film, and are sensitive to the subtleties of the filmmaker's art.

*Vivian Vance, Lucille Ball, Desi Arnaz, and William Frawley
(clockwise from top) on the set of* I Love Lucy.

Chapter 7

THE SMALL SCREEN

As Americans moved to the suburbs, the television antenna soon became symbolic of changes in the nation's entertainment pattern. Beginning in February 1950 *Your Show of Shows* (1950-1954), a ninety-minute variety series, grew into a Saturday night ritual with those families electronically advanced enough to own a television set. The show, which starred Sid Caesar and Imogene Coca, had the markings of the theatrical revues that producer Max Liebman had staged earlier in the Catskill Mountains with Caesar and Coca. Limited though the number of television sets were in 1950, *Your Show of Shows* became so popular in the New York City area that people rushed home early from dining out on Saturday evenings to watch the program, and taxicab drivers noted a drop in receipts during the hour and a half the show was on the air.

Liebman's two stars specialized in comedy, but Coca was also a talented singer and dancer, and Caesar played the saxophone and was a wizard at monologues and pantomime. Carl Reiner and Howard Morris headed the supporting players on the show, with singers including Marguerite Piazza and Robert Merrill from opera and Bill Hayes from Broadway contributing their talents. The Billy Williams Quartet were among the jazz musicians, and there were weekly production numbers involving the entire company. Mel Tolkin and Lucille Kallen, who wrote most of the material for the show, were supplemented by such exceptional comedy writers as Larry Gelbart, Mel Brooks, Neil Simon, and Woody Allen.

Television in 1950 was still basically a metropolitan phenomenon. The shows emanating from New York were mainly conversions of successful radio programs, controlled by sponsors and advertising agencies. Until production moved to Hollywood, television, according to writer-producer Roy Huggins, was simply "radio with pictures." *Your Show of Shows* proved to be more than that; it preserved a dying gasp of a cultural heritage that dated back to vaudeville, burlesque, and the theatrical revue.

After several weeks on the air, Imogene Coca felt that she was running out of material for the show. She went to producer Max Liebman and suggested that she and Sid Caesar perform "Slowly I Turn," a classic burlesque sketch. Caesar was reluctant, insisting that the routine was tired from repeated use, but Coca informed her costar that burlesque comedian Rags Ragland had given her his version of the sketch. "I've done it," she told Caesar, "and it works." The two performed the sketch that week on *Your Show of Shows,* and it was a tremendous success. Over the next four years, Coca said, "The writers must have rewritten 'Slowly I Turn' thirty times."

Since *Your Show of Shows* offered a variety of entertainment, each program included marvelous musical numbers, with great singing and brilliant dancing. Soprano Marguerite Piazza sang Madame Butterfly's death scene, and Coca performed a satire on *Afternoon of a Faun,* using the Nijinsky choreography. "We always used the regular choreography of whatever ballet we did," the comedienne recalled. "We only changed bits and pieces, but the basic choreography was always the original."

The show was staged before a large theater audience, and performers directed their work toward the spectators in the house rather than to the television cameras. "It was up to the cameraman to find us," Imogene Coca said. "There was no teleprompter to look at; there were no cue-cards. We played a sketch the exact way we would play it on the stage." Sketches were worked out in careful detail, sometimes requiring lengthy discussions about what the characters would wear, since they fell within a specific income bracket. "We all worked on the same theory," said Coca, "which was that true comedy is based on truth. If there isn't a basis of truth, there's no comedy. Then we'd take the truth and extend it."

Censorship in early television was rigid, for advertising agencies feared a loss of sponsors, and sponsors worried about losing buyers should they allow questionable programming to enter American homes. The word "pregnant," for instance, could not be used on the air; when a science class on the weekly sitcom *Mr. Peepers* (1952–1955) was slated to see the birth of a calf, sponsors objected, and the scene was eliminated. In addition, the McCarthy investigation of political subversives made advertisers wary of any content that might be construed as controversial. Producers were ever mindful that they were entering the average American's living room, and the family's orientation in the early 1950s was likely to be conservative. Caution must be exercised, since children had access to television screens. Programming was therefore safe and family oriented. "Television," playwright Paddy Chayefsky harshly declared, "is democracy at its ugliest." Certainly throughout the 1950s the medium portrayed American life in images that were wholesome, optimistic, and congratulatory.

THE SHIFT FROM NEW YORK TO HOLLYWOOD

Although most of the early television programs were broadcast from New York, Hollywood entered the field in the late 1940s, led by independent producers and a few Poverty Row studios. In 1948 Jerry Fairbanks, a producer of short subjects at Paramount for many years, independently produced *Public Prosecutor* for NBC, the first filmed series on network television. The show starred John Howard and had a budget of $8,800 per episode, but it was discontinued before the season was over.

Ziv Television Programs began production in Hollywood late 1949 with *The Cisco Kid* (1950–1956), the first of the company's weekly series. Ziv specialized in action shows with male heroes, such as *Dangerous Assignment* (1951–1952) and *Boston Blackie* (1951–1953). Actor William Boyd, who starred as Hopalong Cassidy in more than sixty movies between 1935 and 1948, acquired the television rights to the Cassidy films and edited them into segments suitable for television. *Hopalong Cassidy* (1949–1952) proved so popular as a weekly series that Boyd made an additional fifty-two episodes expressly for home viewing.

Hal Roach Studios came to television production as an established Poverty Row movie company and made an early impact. Roach produced such situation comedies as *My Little Margie* (1952–1955), which featured actress Gale Storm, and crime dramas like *Racket Squad* (1950-1953), a bargain-basement series but among the first of its kind. Most of Hollywood's initial television programming originated from producers who were content with small profits and had little stake in the big studio system of filmmaking.

Disney Studios entered the television field in December 1950. Later *Disneyland* (1954-1958) proved ABC's most successful weekly series and caused Hollywood's larger studios to reconsider the potential of television production. In October 1954, with the home audience expanded to include 56 percent of the nation's population, Columbia Pictures began producing episodic television programs through its Screen Gems subsidiary, starting with *The Adventures of Rin Tin Tin* (1954-1959) and *Father Knows Best* (1954-1963).

In 1955 Warner Bros. became the first of the major studios to enter the television field, scoring an initial success with *Cheyenne* (1955-1963), an hour-long western series featuring Clint Walker as Cheyenne Bodie, the archetypal frontier hero. Before then, the studio's production head, Jack L. Warner, refused to allow a video set to be shown in any Warner Bros. movie. Yet by 1955 he accepted the new realities of Hollywood and became convinced that his company's future lay in small screen entertainment. Warner created a television department at his studio, placing it under the direction of his son-in-law, William Orr.

Warner instructed Orr to hold production expenditures to $50,000 per episode. To cut costs, *Cheyenne's* producer, Roy Huggins, relied heavily on stock footage from the Warner Bros. vault. "I could build quite interesting western shows," said Huggins, "by using shots from their vast film library." The studio constructed a western town on the backlot for the series; very little of the show was filmed on location. Huggins said:

> We didn't have the money for that. I had already concluded that the approach to television should be the same as making motion pictures, only in a slightly abbreviated form. But the story should look to the audience like a movie story.

Warner Bros. used television to continue the basic production method the studio had employed during its Golden Era. The new medium allowed the company to sign exclusive contracts with actors, producers, and technicians; rebuild production departments; maintain an administrative staff; and keep activity on the lot humming. Clint Walker became the first television star for Warner Bros., while studio executives secured their jobs with a steady supply of telefilms.

In January 1959 Warner Bros. had no theatrical motion pictures before the cameras. Other major studios had also cut back on the production of feature films and soon began testing the rewards of television production. Twentieth Century-Fox and Metro-Goldwyn-Mayer also launched television series in 1955, although neither was as successful in the medium as Warner Bros. But within a matter of months Hollywood would become the major supplier of the networks' prime-time programming. Once filmed television dominated the field, it was evident that the Hollywood studios possessed the equipment, personnel, and know-how to assume a position of leadership.

Most Hollywood producers made the transition from movies to television without fanfare, since meager budgets and rapid-pace production schedules afforded little glory to early television work. Episodic series quickly became the medium's primary format. By the end of 1957 more than one hundred filmed television series were on the air or in production, with virtually all of them Hollywood products.

The networks enlisted the studios in part as a means of toppling the sponsors' control over production. In the early 1950s sponsors owned programs and exercised tight supervision over their content. Eager to wrest control from the agencies, the networks welcomed the energetic role assumed by Hollywood's major studios, since their well-defined method of operation reduced the power of the advertising agencies without the networks' having to assume the financial burden of program production.

THE PLACID FIFTIES

The sitcom, borrowed from radio, soon became television's most dependably popular form of entertainment. Although live dramas, variety shows, and musicals continued to be aired from New York during the late 1950s, the networks quickly discovered the financial benefits offered by filmed series, since they could be repeated in syndication time and again. Sitcoms have been viewed by critics through the decades as anathema to meaningful programming, yet they serve as a window onto contemporary society—never starkly realistic, but tinted images within a defined range. Media historian Robert Sklar maintained:

> Television programs certainly don't 'reflect' American society in any precise sense, but to be popular they do need to express, in their various conventional stylized ways, some of the real feelings and concerns of their audience.

Most sitcoms are filmed exclusively indoors on studio sets. They tend to be friendly, intimate, comforting, creating a feeling of warmth and security. Sitcoms during the 1950s expressed the ideals of America's corporate culture and emphasized consensus. Disagreement was usually the result of poor communication; no real conflict existed between opposing factions. Harmony was established through compromise rather than adhering to individual principles. Families were seen as idealized social units, models of decorum.

The Adventures of Ozzie and Harriet (1952–1966) set the pace for a string of suburban family shows, depicting a harmonious Neverland inhabited by a smiling, self-satisfied, upper-middle-class white couple and their two teenage sons. The United States had emerged from World War II the richest nation in the world, and suburban America basked in the economic boom of the Cold War. Veterans who had fought in the war came home eager to buy a house, start a family, and grill burgers in their backyard. Ozzie Nelson helped them smile at their recoil from macho heroics and sanctioned the comfort of their new lifestyle.

Ozzie, a former bandleader in real life, seemed to do little more on the family's television series than hang around the house, read the newspaper, and make folksy comments. Neither money nor work was ever mentioned. At a time when suburban fathers were often absent, since men frequently commuted some distance to work, the constant presence of Ozzie Nelson at home was a comforting reminder of cozier times, offering wish fulfillment to a society in transition. Harriet Nelson, Ozzie's former band vocalist and actual wife, came across on the television show as a perfect spouse and mother. David Nelson was the wholesome older brother, whereas Rick, with boy-next-door good looks, soon became a teenage heartthrob of the 1950s. When Rick began singing on the show, he seemed like a tame version of Elvis Presley, but no threat to accepted mores.

Plots on *Ozzie and Harriet* never contained real conflict; the characters simply provoked and teased one another. Bland though its content might be, the series projected the fantasy of a typical American family, living in an affluent suburban neighborhood and solving its domestic problems by consensus. Sponsors wanted their shows to present ideal images that made viewers feel good about themselves and eager to buy their way into a corner of the American dream.

Father Knows Best arrived on television after five years on radio, reiterating what 1950s sponsors suggested correct family behavior should be. Jim Anderson, played by Robert Young, earned the money, bought the house, set most of his family's rules, and refereed their disputes. His wife Margaret, played by Jane Wyatt, was witty, ornamental, and socially adept. She not only kept a neat house but reinforced her husband's authority when their children erred, sometimes convincing him to soften his stand.

A host of imitations followed. *Leave It to Beaver* (1957-1963) continued the theme of idealized family relationships. The doctor's wife that actress Donna Reed played on *The Donna Reed Show* (1958-1966) was so flawless and prim that critics remarked that the series should be called *The Madonna Reed Show.*

Exceptional for its time was *The Life of Riley,* which had a long span on radio and came to television twice—first (1949-1950) with the then little-known Jackie Gleason in the title role and again (1953-1958) with film star William Bendix. The show was unusual in that it centered on a blue-collar husband and father who frequently found life exasperating. "We did the show very cheaply," said Rosemary DeCamp, who played Riley's wife in both television versions. "They didn't make the scripts over at first; we simply used the old radio scripts and shot them in five days." The series won an Emmy Award in 1950, but the sponsor canceled the show the next day. "The agency said the sponsor didn't want art," DeCamp maintained; "it wanted something the boys could watch in bars having a drink."

But the sitcom to have the greatest impact was unquestionably *I Love Lucy* (1951-1957), the most consistently popular series in television history. The show captured the national mood of the 1950s like no other. It came at a time when Americans had put the Depression and global war behind them and were ready to return to normal living, which for women of that era meant domesticity. Lucy Ricardo was a housewife who submitted to her husband's commands because she thought that was what she was supposed to do, yet she rebels against him consistently. Lucy embodied female energy with no meaningful outlet—no career, no children at first, no power, and a minimum of housework. She was childlike but seldom stupid, coming up with improbable schemes and determined to break into show business.

Domestic harmony was frequently threatened when Lucy developed desires that ran counter to the welfare of the other characters on the show. Eventually she had to put aside her selfish ambitions and surrender to the wisdom of the group. "No one, we found out, must ever be angry with Lucy," said Lucille Ball, who created the part with her writers. "She must be tolerated like a child, because if someone got angry at her, the audience stopped laughing. Phony anger was all right, but not real anger."

Ball and her husband Desi Arnaz founded Desilu, telefilm's fastest-rising independent production company, and insisted that *I Love Lucy* be filmed in Hollywood. More than any other, the show demonstrated the advantages of film in television programming and made Hollywood a permanent force in sitcom production. With television becoming a dominant part of major studios' output, Desi Arnaz and Lucille Ball bought the old RKO lot, where she had once been under contract, turned Desilu into a thriving operation, and pioneered production techniques that are still in use today.

Rather than relying on canned laughter, which Ball thought sounded phony, she performed *Lucy* before a studio audience, arguing that a live audience would enhance the show's spontaneity. Ball and Arnaz hired cinematographer Karl Freund, who was ready to retire from feature films, and with his expertise devised the three-camera technique of telefilming. With three cameras running at the same time, a long-shot, a medium-shot, and a close-up could be photographed during a single performance, then blended together to make a cohesive film. Marks were arranged on the floor, and through earphones a camera coordinator instructed the three operators when to move right or left, forward or backward, to achieve the best picture.

During the first year of the series, Desilu produced thirty-nine *I Love Lucy* episodes, then tapered off to thirty-six and gradually less. Philip Morris, a cigarette company, sponsored the show and put up the money, exercising strict control over its content. "The advertising agency would make comments about the script," writers Madelyn Davis and Bob Carroll said in a joint interview. "We had trouble with Philip Morris; we couldn't use the word 'lucky,' since Lucky Strike was the name of another cigarette company."

Lucille Ball became "the first lady of television" and a master at situation comedy, working in close harmony with her cohort Vivian Vance, who played Lucy's neighbor Ethel Mertz in the series. "Vivian and I learned what would pay off," Ball said later, "how to approach a scene, how to get light and shade, how not to give everything at the beginning of a long block of comedy, and then how to time it all." Veteran character actor William Frawley, who played Ethel's husband Fred, never liked the scripts and seldom understood why his lines were funny, yet his character became a television classic. Desi Arnaz played

Lucy's husband Ricky and also supervised most of the business aspects of their company, freeing Ball to concentrate on the series itself.

Despite its madcap humor, *I Love Lucy* contained enough reality to make for memorable comedy. Believability was the essential ingredient, Lucille Ball maintained. "I had to believe in the situation, no matter how unbelievable it was," she said. "If I could believe that I could ski off a roof, then that scene would work."

By mid-decade *I Love Lucy* was earning more than $1 million a year from reruns. With *Lucy*'s success producers and networks hurriedly produced scores of filmed sitcoms using the Desilu system of production. The fall of 1952 brought seventeen new entries into the field, more than doubling the number of situation comedies on the air. The next year saw fifteen more, and 1954 brought another nineteen. Almost all of them were filmed in Hollywood.

Desilu expanded its operation with *Our Miss Brooks* (1952-1956) and *December Bride* (1954-1959). In the first, Eve Arden played Connie Brooks, a brassy, wisecracking high school English teacher who was eager to marry. Much of the show revolved around Connie's attempts to snare a shy biology teacher, Philip Boynton, and outwit her blustery principal, Osgood Conklin. *December Bride* focused on a widow, played by character actress Spring Byington, who lived with her married daughter and son-in-law. Most of the episodes dealt with the wacky troubles women caused for the men in their lives. The series was directed by Frederick DeCordova, later producer of *The Tonight Show,* who had been a successful B picturemaker. DeCordova said:

> *December Bride* was a great ensemble show. I had Spring Byington in the cast; Verna Felton, who played Spring's friend Hilda; Frances Rafferty, who had been a young leading lady in films at Metro; and Harry Morgan, who later appeared with such success on *M*A*S*H.* That basic group was a joy to work with.

Other series made an effort to address the changes that were taking place in American life. In *The Real McCoys* (1957-1963), television's first successful rural sitcom, Grandpappy Amos (played by three-time Academy Award–winning character actor Walter Brennan) longed for his backwoods past, was stubbornly wedded to his old ways, and ridiculed everything new and different.

The liberal writers of *Lassie* (1954-1971) wanted to make social statements that the show's sponsor rejected. When an exchange student appeared in the series, the writers wanted him to be black, but the sponsor rejected the idea. "We had a little trouble making him Oriental," said Jan Clayton, who played the mother on the original show. Nor would the sponsor allow the boy on the series to grow up. "That's the number one problem with television," Clayton said. "They get a formula, and when it works, they aren't going to change one little bit."

Lassie was aired on Sunday nights, when most families were at home together. Jan Clayton maintained:

> People could stand sentiment more in those days, bald, raw sentiment, which we were certainly guilty of. When I was in Vietnam, I discovered what an incredible inroad *Lassie* had made in the American home. The boys saw me as their second mother. Those in hospitals didn't want pretty young girls seeing them in that condition. They were comfortable with me and wanted to talk about the dog.

By 1957 family comedy series had been joined by a torrent of filmed action shows. *Dragnet* (1951-1959) was one of the early filmed crime shows, followed by *Richard Diamond, Private Detective* (1957-1960), *Peter Gunn* (1958-1961), and *Naked City* (1958-1963). The Warner Bros. production *77 Sunset Strip* (1958-1964) combined action with humor and was considered a paradigm of hipness in the late 1950s. The series featured Efrem Zimbalist, Jr., as a private detective and teen idol Edd Byrnes as Kookie, a parking lot attendant given to incessant hair combing.

Desilu again innovated by bringing motion picture techniques into *The Untouchables* (1959-1963), a series about gangsters and violence in Chicago during the early 1930s, with Robert Stack in the role of Eliot Ness. Stack said:

> We used lots of extras, lots of cars, and lots of special effects, things that had not been used in television production before. Doing those things for the small screen, with its limited frame of reference, was quite difficult.

The Untouchables was an expensive series for its time. An entire city was built for the show on the old Selznick lot in Culver City. "They would redress the buildings for every third or fourth episode," Robert Stack said. "We shot night after night till two or three or four in the morning." Initially Stack played Ness as a man in terrific turmoil, who exploded in unexpected moments:

> That made him mysterious and made the guy work. But it also required good writing. The writers began losing that quality during

the second year, and the third year it became a copy of a copy. The fourth year it didn't work at all.

Stack won an Emmy for his performance in *The Untouchables,* but coming from feature films as he did, the actor harbored a measure of contempt for television awards. "I used to make fun of the Emmy," Stack confessed later, "calling it The World's Biggest Midget. A lot of us who had a background in motion pictures felt that way."

For increasing numbers of performers, the only work available was in television. Anne Jeffreys and her husband Robert Sterling starred in the *Topper* series (1953-1955) after spending their formative years in movies. Jeffreys said:

It was hard, grueling work. Each half hour show had a three-day schedule. We shot two episodes a week, and in those days we worked six days a week. We would shoot until Wednesday midnight, hoping to finish one segment. Then we would start again early Thursday morning and work until Saturday midnight. On Sundays we collapsed, because at four o'clock on Monday we were back on the set. The wardrobe women were run ragged shopping. But it got so we didn't even have to read the next script; we knew the characters and what their reactions would be. So the show became easy that way.

Raymond Burr and Barbara Hale, both of whom were veterans of feature films, enjoyed lengthy careers on *Perry Mason* (1957-1966, plus periodic specials later). Hale said:

We shot those hour-long episodes just like a motion picture. It was a six-day shoot, and we worked until eight or ten at night. All of us tried very hard to keep a fresh approach, not just "phone our performance in," as those of us in the business say.

Dick Powell, David Niven, Charles Boyer, and Ida Lupino—all established movie stars—formed Four Star Films in 1952, which by the end of the decade had become one of the largest suppliers of filmed television programming. The company started with *Four Star Playhouse* (1952-1956), then expanded into sitcoms and other shows. *Mr. Adams and Eve* (1957-1958), a comedy starring Lupino and her current spouse, Howard Duff, was a more sophisticated husband and wife series than was typical of the 1950s. "We were a little ahead of our time," director Frederick DeCordova said. Writer Sol Saks spent sufficient time with the show's stars to incorporate some of their foibles and actual domestic happenstances into his scripts. "All of the exteriors were filmed at our house in Brentwood," said Duff, "so the show had a somewhat realistic flavor."

Warner's success with *Cheyenne* prompted that studio and others to introduce a barrage of westerns in 1957. At that time westerns were a popular genre that enjoyed a loyal following and were almost an assured success. *Maverick* (1957–1962), starring James Garner, was a frontier series with humor, but not a comedy. Maverick was a more complicated character than Cheyenne Bodie, capable of deflating the clichés of moral guardians. Maverick gambled for a living and was not unduly concerned with the troubles of others. Ultimately his basic decency surfaced, but he was far from pure and did not welcome the role of paladin.

Altogether, 1957 saw fifteen new westerns appear on prime-time television. *Sugarfoot* (1957–1961) and *Colt 45* (1957–1960) were also produced at Warner Bros.; the studio's *Lawman* (1958–1962), starring John Russell, followed the next year. Already on the network were *Death Valley Days* (1952–1970), *The Life and Legend of Wyatt Earp* (1955–1961), *Have Gun Will Travel* (1957–1963), and *Tales of Wells Fargo* (1957–1962); *Bonanza* (1959–1973) would become a top-rated western series for seven consecutive seasons. Michael Landon, who appeared on *Bonanza* as Little Joe Cartwright, claimed the show was popular because it gave "people sitting at home a sense of security in the old-fashioned values."

But the most successful of all television westerns was *Gunsmoke* (1955–1975), the first of the so-called adult westerns. For twenty years James Arness played Marshal Matt Dillon, Dodge City's tough lawman, with Amanda Blake as Kitty, owner of Dodge's Long Branch saloon. Milburn Stone, the character actor featured as Doc Adams on the show, said:

> *Gunsmoke* went on the air at ten o'clock in the East because of that subliminal idea that Matt and Kitty were carrying on upstairs in the Long Branch, which was true. Kitty got to be owner of the Long Branch because she'd hustled a bit. Then she fell in love with this big beautiful guy who was winning the West all by himself. That was the way we all felt about it. Kitty walked the slenderest tightrope in television—hooker tough and schoolteacher sweet.

Gunsmoke's creators aimed for a semi-documentary look, and the series was remarkably realistic for its time. In the first episode, for instance, Matt Dillon lost a gunfight; he was by no means an inescapable hero. Future movie director Sam Peckinpah wrote some of the scripts, and Andrew McLaglen, who later worked on feature films with John Wayne, directed ninety-five of *Gunsmoke's* episodes. McLaglen said:

> That series was a tremendous training ground. We shot the half-hour shows in three days. We'd leave the studio at 6:30 or 7:00 in the morning and be out on location from dawn until sunset. At the studio we'd sometimes work late into the night.

But while *Mr. Adams and Eve, Gunsmoke,* and a few other series aimed for reality, most television programs in the 1950s perpetuated the old stereotypes. *My Little Margie, A Date with Judy* (1951-1953), *My Friend Irma* (1952-1955), and *Private Secretary* (1953-1954) all dealt with attractive but dizzy women. *Love That Bob* (1955-1959) found actor Bob Cummings as an unmarried fashion photographer whose life is an endless parade of busty, beautiful models. Cummings cast his affable womanizer in the image of Hugh Hefner's popular *Playboy* magazine, seen at the time as almost a bachelor's handbook. *Amos 'n' Andy* (1951-1953), based on the radio program that originated in 1928, reinforced many of the prejudiced views white Americans held toward blacks. *Amos 'n' Andy's* central characters, although played on television by African Americans, drew on stereotypes from the old minstrel shows and portrayed blacks as lazy, conniving, and dishonest. Eventually the series brought enough pressure from civil rights groups that CBS withdrew it from syndication.

By the close of the decade all of Hollywood's studios were engaged in the making of telefilms. Budgets for television shows grew larger, while production techniques became more sophisticated. Sitcoms were filmed mainly along the lines established at Desilu. *It's Always Jan* (1955-1956), for example, was photographed before a live audience with the three-camera technique. "We spent time on lighting," said Janis Paige, the show's star. "We rehearsed onstage with the camera." Action shows were shot much like B movies—fast, inexpensively, and with compromises. Cowboy star Gene Autry said:

> I made ninety-one half-hour television films, and they weren't shot much different than the regular western pictures I'd made at Republic and Columbia. We went by the clock. We had to knock the television shows out in three days, whereas in pictures I was used to fourteen days on each one.

The firm control over content still exercised by sponsors brought complaints from writers, directors, and performers. On a show sponsored by Procter and Gamble, writers Madelyn Davis and Bob Carroll could not have their characters sing "Joy to the World," because "Joy," a popular dishwashing liquid, wasn't a Procter and Gamble product. Soon after writer Everett Greenbaum arrived in Hollywood to work on *The George Gobel Show* (1954–1960), he wrote a joke in which a grandfather said to his young grandson, "Drink your milk." When the boy wanted to know why, his grand-dad explained, "It's good for your teeth." The boy asked, "Well, why do you keep your teeth in water at night?" The show's sponsor insisted that the line be changed to "Condensed milk is good for your teeth," since that was their product. Greenbaum argued that the altered line made no sense; he refused to make the change and was fired.

The frantic pace of television production demanded regimented procedures, which the Hollywood studios had already worked out and could revise to accommodate the new medium's requirements. "Television production is even more of a sausage machine than films," said veteran actor Gale Gordon. "You are fighting deadlines that were set eight or ten weeks in advance." In the early years the annual cycle for network series consisted of thirty-nine episodes, thirteen of which would be repeated during the summer. "Time is the frightful element," said actor-director Joseph Pevney. "But even with the compromises you have to make, you can do some good work."

THE TURBULENT SIXTIES

By the 1960s the movie industry was coming to terms with television. Paramount, which had made little effort to compete in the television market during the 1950s, increased its output in the field and soon became a leader. With 140 million television sets abroad in 1968—almost twice as many as in the United States—more than 100 countries had become markets for American telefilms. Most of the ideas for network series originated on the West Coast, sometimes as many as 800 proposals in a single year. At some studios television executives were promoted into top positions, although the power of determining program content shifted from the sponsors to the networks, the strongest of which was CBS.

Even though the 1960s saw racial tensions, urban riots, student protests, and marines landing in Vietnam, the American public seemed to want escapist entertainment in its home viewing. Television producers relied heavily on family comedies and action shows, imitating earlier successes time after time. Sitcoms remained among the most popular: *The Flintstones* (1960-1966), the first animated series for prime-time; *Mister Ed* (1961-1966), about a talking horse; *Hazel* (1961-1966), based on a cartoon character; *Gilligan's Island* (1964-1967), about a motley group stranded on a Pacific island; and *The Munsters* (1964-1966), which depicted a family of misfits who resembled the Frankenstein monster and vampires, yet were thoroughly lovable.

Commercials, also produced in Hollywood, often suggested the magic powers of cleansers and detergents, but a number of sitcom heroes and heroines also possessed occult powers. Teenagers and preteens had become fascinated with science fiction, monsters, and secret weapons, and television capitalized on their obsession. In *I Dream of Jeannie* (1965-1970) the title character was a genie out of a bottle found by an American astronaut when he splashed down near a tropical island. *My Favorite Martian* (1963-1966) pictured an extraterrestrial whose spaceship crashed on Earth and who moved in with the reporter who had witnessed his landing. *Bewitched* (1964-1972) focused on a witch married to a mortal, who tried to curb her supernatural tendencies.

Route 66 (1960-1964) was an hour-long adventure series centered on two young men driving around the country in a 1960 Corvette. The show was filmed on location throughout the United States on a budget of slightly less than $100,000 per episode. Actor George Maharis said of the character he played on the series:

> I *was* Buzz. I had done a lot of those crazy things the scripts called for, and directors would let me do pretty much what I thought was right for my character. The marvelous thing about the show was that we were out on the road almost all year.

Daktari (1966-1969), an African adventure series, was filmed mainly in California, although a crew went to Africa for a month or more to shoot background footage, which was then matched with what was shot closer to Hollywood. Telefilms demonstrated an increased interest in foreign settings, real and imaginary, as the public's awareness of the world scene expanded. *The Man Called X*

(1956–1957), for instance, gave the impression that it was based on incidents from the files of the Central Intelligence Agency.

International intrigue and spy shows were highly popular, as CIA activities in various coups in Latin America and Southeast Asia were discussed by the media. Each episode of *The Man from U.N.C.L.E.* (1964–1968) depicted clandestine warfare against coalitions of foreign enemies. The show, which starred Robert Vaughn, possessed charm and sophistication and cast its casual heroes against melodramatic action. *Mission: Impossible* (1966–1973) focused on the exploits of a governmental agency that undertook hazardous and intricate espionage assignments carried out in utmost secret.

Although the war in Vietnam inspired no television series in the 1960s, an outburst of military sitcoms appeared about more popular wars. *McHale's Navy* (1962–1966) was set on a South Pacific island during World War II, and *Hogan's Heroes* (1964–1971) took place in a Nazi prisoner-of-war camp. The pivotal character of *Gomer Pyle, U.S.M.C.* (1964–1969) was a naive gas pump attendant from Mayberry, North Carolina, who joined the Marines, serving a five-year enlistment as a private. All three shows were played for laughs rather than adventure.

The 1960s saw a deluge of medical shows: *Dr. Kildare* (1961–1966), *Ben Casey* (1961–1966), and *The Nurses* (1962–1965) prepared the way for *Medical Center* (1969–1976) and *Marcus Welby, M.D.* (1969–1976). Westerns remained in vogue: *The Gunslinger* (1961–1962), *The Virginian* (1962–1970), *The Big Valley* (1965–1969), and *The High Chaparral* (1967–1971).

Yet curiously enough for a decade of social unrest, the highest-rated series on television was *The Beverly Hillbillies* (1962–1971), a slapstick comedy full of rural clichés. Blasted by critics for exploiting stereotypes, the show told the story of a backwoods family who suddenly became extraordinarily wealthy when oil was discovered on their property. The clan moved to sophisticated Beverly Hills where they were courted by the local bank president but failed to fit in. Granny, played by Irene Ryan, was a cultural reactionary, unwilling to change her habits, her tastes, or her superstitions to accommodate her new surroundings. The mountaineers continued to drink corn liquor, keep "critters" in their lavish house, drive an old flatbed truck, and remained impervious to the ridicule of city dwellers they encountered. For nine years the series flourished during a period in American history when society was torn by indignation, protest, and violence.

Writer Paul Henning, who created the show, came from a farm outside Independence, Missouri, and could remember his mother making lye soap in the backyard, much as Granny did on *The Beverly Hillbillies*. As a boy Henning saw vaudeville at the Main Street Theatre in Kansas City and particularly enjoyed the Weaver Brothers and Elviry, a hillbilly act then popular throughout the Southwest. "I've always been a fan of rural humor," said Henning. "A country boy going to the big city and outsmarting the city slickers was a basic theme of the old Toby shows," which had played in provincial American theaters. "I was amazed when *The Beverly Hillbillies* proved to be successful in such countries as Japan, Holland, Mexico, and Australia. But each country has its hillbillies, even if they don't call them that."

The show proved so popular with audiences that a spin-off, *Petticoat Junction* (1963–1970), was launched the following season, soon joined by *Green Acres* (1965–1971). The latter reversed the plot by depicting a wealthy couple who left the big city to live in the hinterland. Paul Henning said:

> I learned early that the characters are the important thing in television. A successful movie can have characters that the audience wouldn't want to meet again. But in television you're hopeful that people will become interested and begin to care about your characters and will welcome them back the following week and the week after that.

The gap between the emerging realities of American life and the sweetened images presented on television had become a chasm. Nowhere was the gulf any clearer than in the view of family life advanced by situation comedies. *The Brady Bunch* (1969–1974) was a synthesis of bourgeois ideals, picturing bland but attractive parents and their half dozen fetching children, carefully arranged in age and disposition to entice maximum preteen interest. The Brady children were created as role models for America's youth. When Marcia, the oldest Brady daughter, changed her hairdo, she affected female grooming habits of entire junior high schools. Florence Henderson, who played the mother on the show, also was a fashion plate. "People laughed at all my different hairdos and my skirt length going up and down," said Henderson. "But the producers wanted me to keep up with the times."

Since ratings were all important in determining the life of a show, writers, producers, and directors were sensitive to details the public liked or found fascinating, repeating them frequently. "The audience wanted to see all nine of us together in one scene," said Ann B. Davis, who played the Brady's maid, Alice. "Almost every episode the director would say, 'Get ready for the tight nine shot,' and we'd all bunch together for a closeup. That was always fun and interesting."

My Three Sons (1960–1972) recounted the mild struggles of a widowed aeronautical engineer, played by veteran film star Fred MacMurray, to raise three boys, aided by his cranky father-in-law. The problems posed on the show were never serious, and *My Three Sons,* despite cast changes, became second to *Ozzie and Harriet* as network television's longest-running sitcom.

By contrast, *The Doris Day Show* (1968–1973), starring the vivacious singer and film star, weathered four formats during its five seasons. Day said:

> CBS kept making changes. I had children, I didn't have children. I was on a farm, then I wasn't on the farm. It's very difficult to keep a series fresh and keep finding marvelous ideas, but there were too many changes on our show. The network was pressured and insecure and didn't know what to do. Our ratings were terrific until football; then everything went down the drain.

With so much concern for top ratings, the networks were reluctant to try programming that was radically different. Lucille Ball's second series, *The Lucy Show* (1962–1968), cast the comedienne as a working widow with two children to support, a more realistic format than *I Love Lucy* had offered. But Ball was again paired with familiar sidekick Vivian Vance, and proven formulas were employed to assure the series' popularity. "Lucille knew that if I got soaked with water or a seltzer bottle the show would be a success," said Gale Gordon, who played Lucy's cantankerous boss. They used that gag week after week.

By 1965 ABC's programming head, Tom Moore, said, "All the shows began to look alike. *77 Sunset Strip* looked like *Surfside 6* (1960–1962), *Surfside 6* like *Hawaiian Eye* (1959–1963). We wore out our source of supply." Surveys showed that relatively few teenagers watched television; most of them preferred more exciting activities outside the home. Prime-time viewers consisted mainly of younger children, their parents, and the elderly, all of whom appeared to prefer conservative shows that posed little challenge to conventional values.

But some attempts at innovation were seen in the television programs of the 1960s. *The Fugitive* (1963–1967), an adventure series starring David Janssen, found Dr. Richard Kimble wrongly convicted of killing his wife and sentenced to death. Kimble escaped while being transported to prison and spent the next four years searching for a man he had seen running from his house the night his wife was murdered. His search was complicated by the fact that he was relentlessly pursued by police officer Philip Gerard. Here was an original concept, but not one the networks and sponsors immediately welcomed. "*The Fugitive* was an idea that offended everybody," said Roy Huggins, who created the show. The series was clearly ahead of its time, although it became popular and in 1993 was made into a successful movie with Harrison Ford in the lead.

Star Trek (1966-1969) offered optimistic morality plays for an increasingly troubled decade, but the series did contain television's first interracial kiss. *The Outcasts* (1968-1969) was an hour-long western about two bounty hunters, one black and one white. The black man was a former slave; the white man a former slave owner. The two became coworkers, yet their relationship remained abrasive. They were never at peace with one another and never truly accepted each other as a friend, although they developed mutual respect. Don Murray, who played the white character, said:

> At the time the Black Panthers were in the newspapers every day, and a lot of people were afraid of the violence in the black movement and were not ready to invite an angry black man with a gun into their living room. I thought the show made an important enough social statement to try to make it work.

Critically the series did work, but its ratings hovered around the middle, not sufficient to overcome the controversy the show created. "Even though *The Outcasts* only lasted for a year," Murray said, "I consider it probably the most important year of my career."

Julia (1968-1971) proved a pioneering series, since it centered around a black heroine, yet was masterfully inoffensive. Diahann Carroll played Julia Baker, a nurse whose husband had been killed in Vietnam. She lived with her young son, Corey, in a lifestyle consistent with standards set by middle-class whites. *Julia's* producer, Hal Kanter, said:

> Because the show was adventurous, nobody knew quite how to handle the situation. I think we made possible all the black shows that followed by proving that white audiences would accept blacks into their homes. We presented for the first time to young black children an image with which they could identify. Corey Baker became a role model for many young blacks.

Bill Cosby, who had earlier costarred with Robert Culp in the adventure series *I Spy* (1965-1968), returned to television in *The Bill Cosby Show* (1969-1971), playing a high school gym teacher. Cosby emerged as the most successful black star on the air and would reappear in the 1980s in the highest-rated situation comedy in network programming.

The revue format of the early 1950s returned with *The Carol Burnett Show* (1967-1978), and prime-time soap opera made its appearance with *Peyton Place* (1964-1969). Based on Grace Metalious's best-selling novel, which had been made into a feature film in 1957, *Peyton Place* was initially telecast twice a week, but showed such singular ratings that the series was expanded to three times a week during its second season. The show starred Dorothy Malone, Mia Farrow, and Ryan O'Neal and returned in a daytime format in 1972.

The first made-for-television movie appeared on NBC in 1964, a joint production between the network and Universal. Full-length films made expressly for television approximated the production values of pictures distributed to the theaters, but were shot faster and produced on smaller budgets. The arrival of made-for-television movies had far-reaching consequences for the Hollywood studios, since all three networks turned to them during the second half of the 1960s. In the 1971-1972 season, features made specifically for home viewing became commonplace, outnumbering theatrical movies in network programming.

By 1968 the single-sponsor shows had almost vanished; no longer could any one sponsor afford an entire program. *The Brady Bunch* had twelve different sponsors; *The Big Valley,* an hour-long series, had twenty-six. The multiplicity of advertisers further encouraged the homogenizing effect. Control over content now rested with the networks, which clung to fixed formulas. The social turbulence of the 1960s was reflected only in oblique ways and then with caution. Costs for half-hour sitcoms had risen to approximately $80,000. An hour-long action series would be budgeted at twice that amount. *The Virginian,* a ninety-minute show, cost $275,000 per episode. The networks' decisions were based on ratings, since the agencies and their clients were keeping a close tally. The stakes were high; low ratings caused heads to roll, both at the networks and at the studios. Fortunes rose and fell, but there was always tension. For the first time in 1968 the operating revenue for network television reached $1 billion.

Feature filmmakers complained that American television was as much a verbal medium as it was visual and yearned for a more artistic approach. "The basic problem in raising the calibre of television series is not a matter of budgets or shooting schedules," Roy Huggins said in 1969. "It's talent. There simply isn't enough of it to fit today's needs." The demand for sufficient programming to fill television's requirements was insatiable. Huggins said:

> The mass audience resists the new, the innovative, the provoca-
> tive, the disturbing, the controversial, the subtle. That audience
> has demonstrated that it wants continuing characters, preferably
> ones that are lovable.

THE INNOVATIVE SEVENTIES

The 1970s brought inflation and recession, the worst economic slow-down since the Great Depression. The boom that followed World War II seemed over, and the American dream as displayed in the suburbs appeared to be slipping from the grasp of the average worker. The sanitized vision of American life projected by *Ozzie and Harriet* and *Father Knows Best* no longer seemed relevant. The yokel comedies and escapist fare that had captured a mass audience in the 1960s looked dated and were soon replaced by socially significant shows with urban settings. More people from the workplace were portrayed on prime-time television, as well as more minorities, more senior citizens, and more working women. Provocative dialogue and innovative plot situations became characteristic of the sitcoms of the early 1970s, as the tone of television programming changed drastically.

Demographics played a decisive part in the shift. Previous audiences had consisted largely of retired, preteen, and rural viewers; during the 1970s advertisers preferred to concentrate on the city population between the ages of eighteen and thirty-four and those with the greatest buying power. Profits for the networks had declined alarmingly, since Congress had recently banned cigarette commercials on television, a tremendous source of revenue, and programmers were open to innovative suggestions.

Producer Norman Lear did the most to alter the face of network broadcasting. Lear's shows tore away the gentility of former decades and introduced a social realism that came to dominate sitcoms over the years ahead. "Norman Lear didn't want just laughs," director Paul Bogart said; "he wanted substance." The producer denied that situation comedies must be superficial and lend support to the status quo. His series brought a more authentic treatment of blacks to television, confronted generational conflict, and dealt with relevant issues rang-

Jean Stapleton and Carroll O'Connor in All in the Family.

ing from liberal politics and economic uncertainty to abortion and homosexuality. The families depicted on his shows not only loved one another, they disagreed and fought among themselves, as families actually do. Media historian Robert Sklar wrote:

> There's a lot of anger and aggression in Lear's comedies, a lot of shock humor on racial, ethnic, and sexual themes—all against the grain of America's pieties and taboos—but the moral equation is always carefully balanced.

Lear introduced his brand of social commentary with *All in the Family* (1971–1979), although the series also contained a deep strain of sentimentality. Archie Bunker, the show's pivotal figure, was a bigoted, reactionary foreman living in Queens, New York. Lovable yet unprepared to accept the changes in the contemporary world, Archie, played by Carroll O'Connor, mouthed politically incorrect remarks with words that heretofore had been taboo on prime-time television, such as hebe, spic, polack, mick, spade, and fag. By daring to suggest that America's ideal of assimilation and consensus was not working, *All in the Family* altered the tenor of the nation's popular culture.

The show was successful in part because it could be viewed on different levels. Liberals, intellectuals, and alienated youth could rejoice in having their beliefs confirmed, while conservatives discovered a new hero in Archie. Those in between found support for their anxieties and confusion over the domestic conflict represented. Gloria and Mike, Archie's daughter and son-in-law who live with the Bunkers, were outspoken champions of a liberal, multiethnic point of view that seemed to be Lear's own. Edith, Archie's adoring wife (played by Jean Stapleton), was patient, tolerant, and even tempered, able to cope with a changing world far better than her husband.

Adapted from a British television show called *Till Death Us Do Part*, *All in the Family* arrived in 1971 as a midseason replacement that CBS aired with trepidation. After a slow beginning the series became the top-rated network show for five consecutive seasons. Janis Paige, who was a guest star in two episodes, felt that the interplay between Edith and Archie explained much of *All in the Family's* phenomenal success. "Her innocence and reasonableness was in such contrast to his high emotions and bigotry," said Paige. "And yet you understood why she loved him, and you knew why he loved her."

The series' working-class setting was unusual for television in the early 1970s, but many viewers could identify with Archie when he suffered the indignities of an erratic economy—layoffs, rising prices, and other obstacles previously considered too real for situation comedy. Some shared his opinions so thoroughly that they plastered "Archie Bunker for President" signs on their car bumpers. Others rushed up to Betty Garrett, who played Archie's neighbor and persistent foil, threw their arms around the actress as she did her shopping, and said, "You give Archie hell, Betty. Just give him hell."

The show was videotaped in front of a live audience. Paul Bogart, who directed more than a hundred episodes of *All in the Family*, said:

> I would encourage the actors to go for the dark moment, the serious straight moment. If we could invent a moment where we had the audience laughing and then hit them with something that moved them, we knew we'd hit gold. Those characters were so strong that we could do a show simply about feelings. Feelings aren't often dealt with on television; television deals with jokes and situations.

Normally episodes were photographed a scene at a time. After each one the crew would take a break, and the audience would applaud. The actors would temporarily drop out of character, then they would move on to the next scene. Before taping an episode in which Edith was almost raped, Bogart said to Norman Lear, "This show is so full of tension that I do not want the audience to relax. I'd like to do it straight through." Lear agreed, adding an extra camera to make certain that everything needed got photographed. "It worked like a charm," Bogart remembered. "At the end of the play, where Edith eluded her attacker and got away from him, the audience went berserk—screamed and shouted and stamped on the bleachers."

When *All in the Family* ended in 1979, Archie and Edith's living-room chairs were donated to the Smithsonian Institution. The chairs had become television icons by then. The show had not only broken new ground, it also helped change the direction of situation comedy.

Maude (1972–1978) and *The Jeffersons* (1975–1985) were direct spin-offs. Maude Findlay was Edith Bunker's liberated, combative cousin who was on her fourth marriage. With feminism pervasive in the mass culture of the 1970s, *Maude* led the way on prime-time television. While Maude was a well-to-do matron living in suburban Westchester, she got pregnant and had an abortion. She went through menopause. She saw a psychiatrist and had a face-lift. Her husband suffered a nervous breakdown and was revealed to be an alcoholic. Maude and her psychiatrist toyed with the notion of spouse-swapping, but ended up not going to bed together. That episode made headlines even before it was broadcast, creating much talk and controversy. Traditionalists were appeased when the psychiatrist confessed that his sexual adventures were actually a mask to disguise his crumbling marriage.

The Jeffersons were the Bunkers' black neighbors, who moved from Queens to Manhattan's East Side. Their series perpetuated comic stereotypes and dealt heavily with male chauvinism, both asserting it and putting it down. But the Jeffersons' upstairs neighbors, Tom and Helen Willis, were the first interracial couple to appear as regular characters in an American sitcom.

Maude's black maid, Florida Evans, became the focal point of *Good Times* (1974–1979), a program about lower-class blacks living in a ghetto housing project. Although Florida's family struggled to make ends meet, their values were essentially middle class. They bickered among themselves, showed love and anger, could be petty and selfish as well as generous and sensitive, yet recognized that race was a factor in their lives.

Sanford and Son (1972-1977), another Lear comedy about an African American family, cast Redd Foxx as cantankerous Fred Sanford, a widowed junkyard owner living in Watts. Fred was a black Archie Bunker—provincial, racist, trapped in a shabby socioeconomic environment and suspicious of the white world outside. His son Lamont on the other hand was eager to prepare himself for a job that would enable him to rise above the color line. The show acknowledged that there were people who lived on a poverty level and were at odds with the American consensus.

Lear's *One Day at a Time* (1975-1984) featured Bonnie Franklin as Ann Romano, the first divorced single parent in American sitcom history. Ann, a feisty woman in her forties with two teenage daughters to support, was forced to return to work after her marriage failed. Having led a conventional, steadfast life for seventeen years, Ann suddenly found herself struggling to guide her children through their rebellious years. The rules she had lived by no longer applied, yet Ann was wise enough to learn from her daughters.

By 1975 Norman Lear stood as the indisputable sovereign of prime-time television with seven sitcoms on the air. His was a pattern to emulate, and ethnic comedies became common. *Chico and the Man* (1974-1978) was set in the barrio of East Los Angeles and starred Freddie Prinze as a Mexican American mechanic. His boss, played by Jack Albertson, was a lonely, hard-drinking white man, hostile to a neighborhood that had come to be dominated by Chicanos. The happy-go-lucky Chico not only outsmarted his boss in business deals, but also gradually helped the old man to mollify his bigotry.

In *Diff'rent Strokes* (1978-1986) a white millionaire adopted two black ghetto children, one of whom was undersized Gary Coleman, who won most of the laughs on the show. *Harris and Company* (1979), on the other hand, was a dramatic series about blacks, starring Bernie Casey. *Harris and Company*'s executive producer, Stanley Robertson, emerged as one of the few African Americans in television to hold a top management position. Robertson had risen from a page at the NBC studio in Burbank to become the network's vice president in charge of motion pictures for television.

Several series during the later 1970s presented the workplace as a family unit, supervised by a benevolent father figure. *Barney Miller* (1975-1982) was an unusual cop show in that it focused on the day-to-day problems faced by a big-city police department. Captain Barney Miller, played by Hal Linden, presided over a culturally diverse staff, each with personal eccentricities, whose jobs bound them together as they coped with the thieves, streetwalkers, perverts, political activists, lunatics, and complainers thrust on them by the outside world. Although the show maintained a light touch, it treated social issues in a realistic way. "I think we're doing a tremendous disservice to the American people," said Danny Arnold, the show's writer-producer, "if we keep telling them that life is *The Brady Bunch.* "

Taxi (1978–1983) portrayed another family of workers, in this case employees of a New York City taxi garage. Amid the grease and sweat of a blue-collar setting, there was a similar bonding against outside lunacy to that seen on *Barney Miller.* The sitcom added Italians and a Slav to its family unit, but no Arabs or Asians. Yet the nation's growing ethnic diversity had gained a foothold in American popular culture.

A totally different workplace was established on *The Mary Tyler Moore Show* (1970–1977). Mary Richards was an unmarried career woman, somewhere in her thirties, working in a television newsroom in Minneapolis and not desperate to find a husband. The series grew in popularity over its seven years to become perhaps the most respected sitcom of its time. The show presented a positive and independent image of the life and professional aspirations of a contemporary American woman and her associates. Jay Sandrich, who directed more than two-thirds of the episodes, brought movement, pace, and subtlety to the show, which like *All in the Family* was videotaped before a live audience. "Audiences bring an unknown element," Sandrich explained. "An audience forces actors into things that wouldn't happen on a silent sound stage."

Alice (1976–1985) told the story of a New Jersey widow, played by Linda Lavin, who heads for California with her twelve-year-old son and ends up working as a waitress in a roadside diner in Phoenix, Arizona. Like other successful sitcoms, the show's popularity depended in part on its supporting characters. Flo was Alice's brassy, man-hungry coworker, while Vera was a mousy scatterbrain. All three battled but pampered Mel, the diner's short-tempered owner, yet the show's strength lay in interpersonal relationships.

The early 1970s saw an escalation of American troops in Vietnam, and the public was reminded night after night on the evening news of the war's horrendous numbers of casualties. *M*A*S*H* (1972–1983) reached a vast public with its antiwar message, but also became recognized as perhaps the most literate series on television. Based on the 1970 movie and set in the Korean War, the comedy focused on an army medical unit that joked while they worked over the maimed bodies of wounded service personnel. Its humor was dark yet grew out of genuine concerns of the military: sex, loneliness, bureaucracy, drugs, homosexuality, venereal disease, crime. Larry Gelbart, the show's writer, said:

> It would have seemed a terrible disservice to everybody's sensibilities to make another *Hogan's Heroes* or *McHale's Navy*. We had to take into account the fact that people were getting killed. We began to see the potential for mixing tragedy and comedy.

Although *M*A*S*H* made a strong statement, it referred to the past and its liberal bias rarely became offensive. What won the show a loyal following was its ensemble comedy and the escape it offered from current sexual politics. *M*A*S*H* glorified male bonding; its denizens (particularly in the beginning) were relentless in their pursuit of women and sexual favors. When they encountered Major Houlihan, an attractive but austere army nurse, they nicknamed her Hot Lips and taunted her endlessly.

The series offered a lighthearted surface combined with complex but likeable characters, skillful performances, and a dignity in handling sensitive yet meaningful material. Gelbart said:

> What gave the show its integrity was the underlying theme of the wastefulness of war. Some weeks we were very political, but everyone could agree that war is dehumanizing. The only objections the network raised came over lines or words that were considered sacrilegious or too sexual in their connotation. The original censor's note from CBS did urge us to stay away from the operating room; they thought that would be too serious and bloody.

Despite the impact of Norman Lear's progressive sitcoms, banality and sentimentality never disappeared from the prime-time programming of the 1970s. *The Partridge Family* (1970-1974) made no pretense at social comment, but was a popular show particularly among younger viewers. "It was a light little family comedy with bubblegum music," said Shirley Jones, the series' star. "It was honest and fun, and the cast was good. A lot of those stories came right out of my own home."

The Waltons (1972-1981) took place in rural Virginia during the Great Depression, but pictured the era as a time of warmth and close family ties. With current unemployment figures assuming alarming proportions, audiences were prepared for a weekly program about hard times, a direction that would have appalled sponsors a few years earlier.

Toward the end of the decade, series dealing with reality and conflict were submerged in another wave of upbeat domestic programs and action shows. After years of national division, viewers seemed eager to return to themes of harmony and escapism. *Little House on the Prairie* (1974-1982), which starred Michael Landon, reaffirmed traditional family values and became the highest-rated series on television. *Barnaby Jones* (1973-1980), a detective show, found Buddy Ebsen fresh from *The Beverly Hillbillies* playing a soft-spoken, milk-drinking private eye. *Starsky and Hutch* (1975-1979) brought more violence to television than viewers were accustomed to, and *Soap* (1977-1981) introduced raunchier dialogue.

Ostensibly a soap opera, *Soap* was a loud and wacky comedy about a rich family, headed by a philandering husband and a sexy older woman. Nearly every episode involved sex, flirtation, adultery, and innuendo. *Soap,* which featured Billy Crystal in the lead, was too full of mockery to be taken seriously, although the disco generation could construe the show's obsession with hedonism as the morality of the moment.

More mainstream was *Happy Days* (1974-1984), with its comfortable suburban setting and appealing depiction of middle-class life during the 1950s. The fascinating element was the Fonz, the show's ultimate hero, who came from a working-class background and was the envy of his high school peers. Fonzie, played by Henry Winkler, had no nuclear family, but appeared to know how to handle women. Just the snap of his fingers and he had any girl he wanted on the back of his motorcycle. The Fonz not only was cool, he also seemed to have more fun than people with more money.

Laverne and Shirley (1976-1983) was a spin-off of *Happy Days* and equally mindless. Again set in the 1950s, Laverne and Shirley centered on two working-class women employed by a Milwaukee brewery to put caps on beer bottles. Like *Happy Days* it was a product of the unit at Paramount Television headed by Garry Marshall. Nostalgic and youth oriented, the shows replaced the topical comedies of Norman Lear as pacesetters in the sitcom field.

Marshall once more illustrated that he had his hand on the pulse of mass audiences during the late 1970s when *Mork and Mindy* (1978-1982) proved an instantaneous hit. Mork was from the planet Ork and had been sent to Earth to observe the natives there. Much of the show's humor stemmed from a contrast between Earth people and Orkans. Mork, played by Robin Williams, was thoroughly congenial, taking everything in his stride and with a smile. Nobody human could be so agreeable in the face of adversity. *Mork and Mindy* used special effects to create a magical atmosphere and propelled Robin Williams into major stardom in feature films.

By the decade's close, rebellion and relevance had been eclipsed by sentimentality and conservatism on network television. The national mood appeared to have grown apathetic, while popular culture doted on the trivial. The young people on *Three's Company* (1977–1984) demonstrated an apolitical hipness, but lacked any suggestion of depth. Although sexual references abounded in the series, all were innuendo. Jack Tripper, played by John Ritter, moved in as a roommate of two attractive female friends—one sensible and cute, the other a zany sexpot. Jack frequently hoped otherwise, but neither girl had any sexual interest in him. They placated their nosy landlord by telling him that Jack was gay. Despite its verbal suggestiveness, *Three's Company* revolved around slapstick and pure escapism.

Daytime soap operas rely more heavily on sexual fantasy. During the 1970s an increasing number of women left home to join the work force, with the result that the demographics of soap-opera audiences changed. More college students, including a significant number of males, began watching such enduring afternoon favorites as *The Guiding Light* (1952–), *As the World Turns* (1956–), *General Hospital* (1963–), *All My Children* (1970–), and *The Young and the Restless* (1973–). Soaps enable viewers to become caught up in the daily lives of other people without getting involved in a threatening way—appealing in a culture that suffers from extensive loneliness. Yet the social context projected by the daytime serials remains highly artificial.

Dallas (1978–1991) not only established the soap opera format on prime-time television, but also brought ruthless economics, leveraged buyouts, and arbitrage to home-screen viewing. J. R. Ewing, played by Larry Hagman, was the cold, calculating, immoral head of the Texas-based Ewing Oil empire. The tycoon emerged as an unfeeling monster, the American dream gone awry, driven by sexual passions and an unquenchable greed for money and power. *Dallas* emerged as television's number one show not only in the United States, but also in Great Britain and elsewhere. The lifestyle it portrayed was absurdly unrealistic, yet seemed fascinating and perhaps even desirable to mass audiences. Flaunting wealth, infidelities, and outrageous behavior, the series grew into a Friday night obsession around the world. When J. R. Ewing was shot at the end of the 1979–1980 season, bumper stickers, badges, and professional gamblers spent the summer asking, "Who shot J. R.?" Suspense mounted as *Dallas* achieved top ratings during the fall months.

As theatrical features became less important to network programming, the number of made-for-television movies and dramatic miniseries increased. In 1974 only 118 theatrical films were shown during prime-time hours, compared with 130 new made-for-television movies. *Brian's Song* (1971) in particular marked the coming of age of made-for-television films. One-third of the nation's households were estimated to have turned on ABC to watch this story of a football player who died of cancer. Such classics as *David Copperfield* (1970), *Jane Eyre* (1971), and *Kidnapped* (1972) were photographed on location with top-notch casts and a seasoned director specifically for home viewing. *Love among the Ruins* (1975) was made for television on a substantial budget, with superstars Katharine Hepburn and Laurence Olivier heading the cast and veteran filmmaker George Cukor directing. By the end of the decade made-for-television motion pictures had become a staple, and big stars, established directors, and top writers agreed to work on tighter schedules.

The miniseries format appeared during the 1970s, often presenting entire novels over several evenings. *Rich Man, Poor Man* (1975) began the trend; *Holocaust* (1978) convinced the industry that the enlarged format could produce impressive ratings. *Wheels* (1978), based on Arthur Hailey's best-selling book about the automobile industry, starred Rock Hudson and Lee Remick. The ten-hour series, filmed in six weeks, was aired with much fanfare over five consecutive nights. "Ten hours is the equivalent of five movies," Rock Hudson pointed out. "But a miniseries is a good idea because an actor can take a role and expose many facets of that character."

Roots (1977), a miniseries based on Alex Haley's book, drew the largest audience in television history, an estimated 130 million viewers, for its concluding segment. Shown on eight nights, the twelve-hour drama began in West Africa, followed a black family through the degradations of slavery in America, and continued from generation to generation up to the present. Leslie Uggams, who played Kizzy in the series, said:

> *Roots* was an exceptional experience. The cast had been filming for five weeks before I got there, but when I walked on the set, I could feel something special in the air. There was such care taken on the project that we put our hearts and souls into it.

Roots went on to triumph in international syndication.

By the 1970s American television shows were seen around the globe, a vital factor in creating an international culture. Although the number of crime shows had diminished during the last half of the decade, *Police Woman* (1974–1978) remained a popular series. Angie Dickinson played an attractive divorcee on the show who worked as an undercover officer, with Earl Holliman as Sundance, her frequent companion. During its first year *Police Woman* was aired in fifty countries. Holliman later made a trip to Europe and was greeted wherever he went like an old friend:

> I went to Greece and spent six weeks. I started walking up the gangplank of this ship, and a Greek sailor happened to be ahead of me. He turned around, saw me, and went, 'Bang, bang.' He was excited because he was seeing Sundance.

Betty Garrett, who had been a star on stage and screen before her career in television, said:

> It's a phenomenal kind of attitude the public has toward television performers. They really think of us as intimate friends and approach us in a familiar way. They don't do that with movie stars; they're a little bit in awe of movie stars. But it's a different attitude toward television personalities. People stand two feet away from me and point at me and talk about me to my face. I think it's because they're used to seeing us in their homes.

Without question television ranked among the most powerful forces in American life, obliterating the line between reality and fantasy. As one by one time-honored newspapers and magazines collapsed, television displaced the press as the dominant means of public information, commingling news and entertainment. The small screen, which in dramatic terms represented a miniaturization process, made a prime impact on the public's conscience as a pervasive arbiter of current events—selecting, weighing, and evaluating issues of importance.

THE SOMNAMBULISTIC EIGHTIES

Whereas the late 1960s and early 1970s constituted a period of upheaval, during which established rules were broken and accepted standards were reversed, the 1980s saw a swing to conservatism. Ronald Reagan insisted that the time had come for Americans to feel good about themselves again. Like television, with its fleeting glimpses and emphasis on simplicity, Reagan offered a short-term approach to national well-being, vended largely on his personal charisma and ability to use the media. Historian Haynes Johnson declared:

> In the eighties, Ronald Reagan and television fitted into American society like a plug into a socket. Together they produced a parade of pleasing images that glowed in more and more living rooms and affected the country like little that had gone before.

The surface of American life was changing at a rate that many citizens found alarming. Advertisements for cigarettes were no longer acceptable on television, but commercials for vaginal suppositories were. What had once been good taste suddenly seemed old-fashioned. ABC, which had merged with United Paramount Theatres, rose to the top of prime-time ratings during the middle 1970s, but by the decade's end cable television had won an enthusiastic following and would soon challenge the dominance of the three major networks. New kinds of entertainment began to invade the American home, while an older generation voiced concern over the amount of skin, perversity, sex, and violence that was on display during family viewing hours.

MTV, or music television, emerged from Warner in 1981 as one of the worst offenders of conservative taste. Sex, drugs, homoeroticism, and violence proliferate in MTV's synthesis of music and images. Within three years MTV had earned an audience of 24.2 million. Targeted primarily at teenagers who had grown up with television and rock music, the cable channel became a symbol of the new youth culture. "The bursts of rock music fitted easily with the psyche of a young America," Haynes Johnson wrote. "Presented in three-to-five-minute videos were elements that fulfilled a need for fantasy and escape."

Parents and traditionalists were often scandalized by what they saw on MTV, which some held as proof that decadence had indeed taken over the airwaves. But others were equally disturbed by the excesses to which America's fascination with fame and fortune were portrayed on the networks.

Dallas had created a vogue for shows that centered on the glamorous exploits of American royalty. *Dynasty* (1981–1989), which revolved around Blake Carrington, his present wife Krystle, and his first wife Alexis, detailed the family's amoral accumulation of wealth, lavish spending, opulent lifestyle, and endless intrigue. *Falcon Crest* (1981–1990), set in the northern California wine country, focused on the Channing family, whose matriarch, Angela, was as ruthless as *Dallas's* J. R. Ewing. The part was played by Academy Award-winning actress Jane Wyman, who happened to be Reagan's first wife.

During the 1980s a materialistic society appeared to have turned its curiosity about the rich and powerful into an obsession. Yet television programming still offered its share of handsome heroes who righted wrongs and captured hearts with charm and nonchalance: Tom Selleck on *Magnum, P. I.* (1980-1988) and David Hasselhoff on *Knight Rider* (1982-1986) are two examples. Veteran actress Angela Lansbury proved a wise and enduring sleuth on *Murder, She Wrote* (1984-), and *Cagney and Lacey* (1982-1988), about two women detectives, became the first police show in television history to attract a predominantly female audience.

Hill Street Blues (1981-1987), *St. Elsewhere* (1982-1988), *Miami Vice* (1984-1989), and *L. A. Law* (1986-1994) were all critically acclaimed, hour-long dramas that won an educated following during the 1980s. *Hill Street Blues* was a police series that presented its harried, emotionally complex cops as driven to the brink by the turmoil of modern inner-city life. The series became famous for its ensemble acting and eventually won twenty-six Emmy Awards. *St. Elsewhere* pictured a large hospital in Boston, whose doctors had their shortcomings and failures in treating patients, yet dealt with problems that other hospitals chose to ignore. *Miami Vice,* another police drama, was among the first series to be broadcast in stereo and became noted for its stylistic innovations—complex camera angles, artful editing, and adept fusion of music and image. It had a budget of $1.5 million per episode, emphasized production values over content, and elevated Don Johnson into major stardom. *L. A. Law* showed the legal process in a far more realistic manner than *Perry Mason* ever did, presenting cases that involved such current issues as AIDS, computer break-ins, divorce settlements, dating services, and endorsements. "I liked *L. A. Law* because it was slick," said Tom Moore, who directed several of the episodes. "But you couldn't really tell my contribution because they all ended up looking the same."

Consistency of style ranked among the basic concerns of television producers, who wanted solid direction on a series without destroying the established texture. *Twin Peaks* (1990-1991), like *L. A. Law,* was a show that attracted directors of quality. Among the sitcoms, *The Golden Girls* (1985-1992) initially benefited from the direction of Jay Sandrich, but the show also reflected the aging of the country's population. *Golden Girls* pictured three women over fifty and a sharp-tongued octogenarian who found financial and emotional security by sharing a house in a retirement area in Florida.

Other sitcoms of the 1980s dealt with women in the workplace. Four female decorators given to waspish remarks and innuendo opened their own business in *Designing Women* (1986–1993) and hired a black assistant. Well-written, the series became an instant success. *Murphy Brown* (1988–) casts Candice Bergen as a single television newscaster who is past forty and an alumna of the Betty Ford Clinic. When Murphy Brown decided to have a child out of wedlock in the fall of 1991, the show became an issue in the 1992 presidential campaign when Vice President Dan Quayle argued that the sitcom was indicative of the wrong-headed thinking of his liberal opponents.

In *Who's the Boss?* (1984–1992) sex roles were reversed. Tony Danza played a widowed former baseball player with an eleven-year-old daughter to support and a desire for a college education. He answered an ad for a live-in housekeeper placed by Angela, a divorced advertising executive, and moved into her house. Tony, a macho guy from a blue-collar Italian background, found himself faced with adapting to a feminine role as an employee of the liberated Angela, although she remained deferential enough never to seriously threaten his manly authority. Tony's daughter and Angela's eight-year-old son quickly functioned as brother and sister, while Mona, Angela's divorced mother and a lecherous geriatric, provided moments of sexual titillation.

Roseanne (1988–) reflects the times by following the life of a contemporary housewife who is a far cry from Harriet Nelson, Margaret Anderson, or even Lucy Ricardo. Roseanne, played by the abrasive comedienne Roseanne Barr, is a domineering, overweight, white mother who lives in a working-class neighborhood and suffers from a precarious economy. She and her less-than-perfect family are given to vulgarity and redneck shrieking, yet the series maintains a top rating.

Most of the sitcom families of the 1980s crossed ethnic lines. Perhaps the biggest throwback to the sanitized series of the 1950s was the black family depicted on *The Cosby Show* (1984–1993), since they enjoyed both affluence and family love. Dad was a doctor, mom was a lawyer, and their children dressed in designer clothes. *The Cosby Show* continued into the next decade as the most consistently watched half-hour series on network television. *Family Ties* (1984–1988) presented a current generation of yuppy-minded

Bill Cosby, Carl Payne, and Malcolm-Jamal Warner (left to right) in an episode of The Cosby Show, *1986.*

white children, whose parents were graduates of the 1960s and sometimes balked at their newer point of view.

The sitcom remained the most resilient genre on prime-time television, with seldom less than a half-dozen shows in the top-rated ten. Costs by the 1980s had increased to such a degree that the average television series consisted of only about twenty-two new episodes each season, a shrinkage that signaled a loss of revenue for program producers. A screen actors' strike in 1980 and a writers' strike in 1988 both related to the question of residual rights, since telefilms' actors and writers contributed to shows that were repeated on the air and earned continuing profits.

By the 1980s the motion picture business was indistinguishable from the television industry, both in the making of series and full-length movies for home viewing. *The Winds of War* (1983), a miniseries presented on six successive evenings for a total of eighteen hours, cost nearly $40 million and starred Robert Mitchum and Ali MacGraw, both established actors in feature films. *Lonesome Dove* (1988), based on Larry McMurtry's award-winning western novel, was budgeted at $20 million, shot on location, and boasted a cast headed by Robert Duvall, Tommy Lee Jones, and Anjelica Huston. Both films were later released on videocassette.

Although made-for-television movies frequently concentrated on family and domestic issues, they occasionally ventured into such exotic and sensational subjects as male strippers. As the decade progressed, television movies began to concentrate more on social issues—the homeless, missing children, teenage suicide, union activism, toxic waste, drug addiction, child abuse, incest, battered women, and continued racism. Since their characters and situations do not enter the American home week after week, television movies can deal with controversial material with less likelihood of losing an audience, since movies are aired during a single evening.

Most made-for-television productions are produced by independent companies and then sold or rented to the networks or cable channels. Frequently they have been judged by filmmakers as an arena in which to learn one's craft before moving on to feature films. Television has figured as a training ground for a number of top directors, including several women, although the medium remains largely in the hands of producers. "The producer has the ultimate control," director Tom Moore maintained, "since they're the ones who have developed the concept."

INTO THE NINETIES

By 1990 television advertising revenue had increased to $26.3 billion annually. The domestic and foreign market for television show reruns alone was estimated at $5.5 billion a year. Yet the networks were in a state of flux, threatened by competition from the cable channels. In 1994 ratings for each of the three networks were up, whereas those for nine of the top ten cable channels either fell or remained constant. The Arts and Entertainment channel was the only one to grow. Even though the broadcast networks reached virtually every home in America, cable was available in only about 63 percent.

At the end of 1995 a revolution faced television production, involving the manner in which shows were made and sold. Federal regulations separating the production of television shows from their distribution had gone into effect in 1970, when the networks were at the height of their power. At that time the government intended to prevent a monopoly by allowing the Hollywood studios to dominate television production for the next twenty-five years. The studios rented shows they made to the networks; once a network had broadcast the show twice, the rights reverted to the studio, which was then free to sell the show as reruns to local television stations. But by November 1995 federal restrictions were phased out, so that the networks became free to create and produce their own shows. No longer were they obligated to rely on Hollywood's studios. Money earned from reruns went to the network producing the show rather than to Paramount or Warner as had been the case in the past.

Hollywood again found itself on the verge of pandemonium, since its studios confronted the possibility of being locked out of television production or of having their role sharply reduced. Consequently the major entertainment companies—Time Warner, Ted Turner, Walt Disney, and others—began merger talks with the three major networks, and Twentieth Century-Fox and Viacom, which owns Paramount, launched their own broadcast networks.

Fox built a viewership of minorities with its African American shows. Blacks prefer ethnic sitcoms that depict their lifestyle and culture, and since the networks had created few Hispanic comedies, Latinos turned to the black shows. Although Fox's *Beverly Hills, 90210* (1990-) and *Melrose Place* (1992-) rank relatively low in the overall ratings, both score high with Hispanics. *Beverly Hills, 90210* treats social issues confronting American teenagers in the 1990s such as drug and alcohol abuse, safe sex, date rape, and suicide, but has become internationally popular, especially in Latin American countries.

Offbeat topics could be seen regularly on prime-time television during the early 1990s. *Northern Exposure* (1990-1995) was set in modern Alaska and had among its characters a new age disc jockey, a female bush pilot, a pair of gay lovers, and a bar owner and mayor whose wife was forty years his junior. *Gabriel's Fire* (1990-1992) cast James Earl Jones as a Chicago cop who prevented the killing of a mother and child by shooting his white partner and was sent to prison. *Life Goes On* (1989-1992) dramatized the AIDS crisis with penetrating effectiveness; *NYPD Blue* (1993-) contains a sprinkling of salty language and deals with alcoholic despair and a female detective who has been forced to commit multiple murders. Because of its adult content some affiliate stations refuse to air the program despite its late hour. In 1994 *NYPD Blue* received twenty-six Emmy nominations, a record for any show.

CONCLUSION

Live television production in New York tended to be an extension of radio and drew heavily from vaudeville, burlesque, and the Broadway stage. When filmed shows proved to have greater advantages, production shifted to Hollywood, where the studios possessed the facilities, personnel, and system needed for making episodic telefilms. The image of American life projected by television in the 1950s and early 1960s was essentially a continuation of the innocence and glamour that Hollywood had offered during the golden age of motion pictures. Not until the 1970s did television sitcoms address serious social issues or attempt to portray society in realistic terms. Crime shows, dramas, soap operas, and adventure series tended to emphasize the bizarre, degenerate, sensational aspects of life with a moralistic attitude demanded by sponsors and deemed suitable for home viewing.

As late as 1980, television's concept of America, according to Robert Sklar, was:

> the America you used to see in the old tabloid yellow press and in the poverty-row exploitation movies and the carnival sideshows at county fairgrounds, an America of freakishness and sensations treated with solemn import, an America of prurience and violence nicely coated with sanctimony.

Surveys made during the 1980s indicated that the primary watchers of television sitcoms were children and young teenagers, although their parents frequently joined them. Most television programs were therefore targeted at a thirteen-year-old mentality, with occasional inserts of greater maturity. Television prevails as the most popular form of mass culture, reflecting tastes, shaping opinions, and creating celebrities, both in the entertainment field and in the political arena. Bruce Willis moved quickly from the costar of *Moonlighting* (1981–1989) to stardom in theatrical movies; *Cheers* (1982–1993) did the same for Ted Danson. Television has compelled politicians to perform more like actors, a trend solidified by Ronald Reagan, a former movie star.

Made-for-television movies have come to play a vital role in both network and cable programming. Barry Diller, who became an executive at ABC in the early 1970s, received credit for bolstering that network's ratings in large part through the introduction of the television movie format. More made-for-television movies were filmed on location, subjects became more adult and challenging, and directors and stars began to look upon them as not much different from theatrical features.

Corporate mergers within recent decades have produced conglomerates in which various media have become increasingly interwoven. Hollywood, once the motion picture capital, now ranks as the leading center for television production, movies, the popular music business, and related merchandising. Rather than diminishing, Hollywood's impact has grown, reaching around the globe through multiple images—a predominant force in the standardization of world culture.

Adolescents passing time on the once glamorous Sunset Strip, 1966.

Chapter 8

HOLLYWOOD'S ENDURING MYSTIQUE

In popular thinking, Hollywood represents more than the geographical name of a place; it is a reference to the American movie industry as a whole. With the growth of television and the number of Los Angeles-based record labels and talent agencies, Hollywood comes close to becoming a synonym for show business in the United States. But it is also an emblem representing wealth, fame, sex, and power—the most alluring manifestations of the American dream. The name "Hollywood" has become almost a trademark for glamour around the world, attracting millions of starstruck tourists to Los Angeles annually. Most come from the American heartland, but nearly as many are dream seekers from other continents. Untold numbers of vagrants, drifters, and young runaways also make their way to the city each year—some hoping for stardom, more seeking excitement or an easy handout in a town where tinsel is thought to be gold.

In terms of sophistication, visual splendor, technology, and lavish production values, Hollywood's films cannot be matched. A new elegance has returned to moviegoing with recently built complexes that offer cappuccino bars, pizza parlors, lobby game rooms, and spacious theaters boasting handsome decor and comfortable seats. With the arrival of videocassettes and cable channels, movies for home viewing are in demand. Another generation has become familiar with classic films, sometimes in colorized versions of the old black-and-white pictures, which purists argue destroy the original composition and artistic intention of cinematographers and directors.

Outside the United States, the demand for Hollywood's product is greater than ever. Entertainment has become the nation's second largest export. In Japan the home video market doubled during the late 1980s, while in Europe the launching of additional television stations, the building of new theaters, and the expanding market for videocassettes have added hundreds of millions of dollars to the profits of major American companies and their parent corporations.

Yet the entertainment industry is a complicated, capricious business, in which periodic cutbacks are inevitable. Motion picture companies became cautious about extravagant spending on oversized productions in 1994, and Time Warner Cable cut its capital spending by $100 million. Veterans in the business insist that hard work and tenacity, if not blind obsession, are essential to a lasting career, and most argue that political savvy within the trade is as important as talent.

But fans watch the Oscar ceremonies on television each spring and have their belief in Hollywood as the glamour capital confirmed. They pour into Los Angeles during vacations eager to smell the orange blossoms, ogle the famous, dine at trendy restaurants, and have their fantasies come true. They board tour buses and catch occasional glimpses of Hollywood's fabled past. They drive through Bel-Air and Beverly Hills, note the mansions with iron gates, security systems, and private guards and come away with their romantic notions substantiated. They see movie crews filming on streets lined with red-tiled bungalows or high-rise apartments, and their excitement mounts. For fans who stroll down avenues of palm trees, amid seemingly endless luxury and sunshine, Hollywood indeed appears to be a wonderland equal to its reputation.

In truth, the wealthy of Los Angeles consume as conspicuously as anywhere else in the world. The mansions of Beverly Hills rival European palaces, and that exclusive section does house more famous residents and the densest concentration of wealth of any community of its size anywhere. Hollywood's elite dress in designer clothes, drive to work in Mercedes Benzes and Porsches, and attend swank parties where the rich mingle with the beautiful and the celebrated. They breakfast at the Polo Lounge in the refurbished Beverly Hills Hotel, lunch at Le Dome, and occasionally eat dinner at Spago's

The famous Beverly Hills Hotel, temporary residence of innumerable Hollywood stars and home of the Polo Lounge.

or the Bistro. Some return to their fortresslike castles, walled off from public view, and perhaps even engage in the hyperactive sex recounted in lore. Money, glamour, and power do converge in a select few.

For most Hollywood workers, however, even the highly successful, the sheen is less splendid. They live well rather than opulently, work long hours, and come home exhausted. They enjoy their coterie of friends and strive to do right by their children. They are workers in a craft that borders on art, attempting to earn a comfortable living in a tough profession.

Young hopefuls awaiting their chance lead lives of anticipation; they often wait tables or work nights as valet parking attendants. Some grow discouraged and return home; others stay on and find work in another field; still others fail to recognize defeat until it is too late, with results ranging from sad to tragic. A few realize their dream, only to discover that they must fight to keep it.

From the outside, the Hollywood mystique has lost little of its luster. If today's film stars are overshadowed by rock and television personalities, there is still enough glitter in movies to quicken the public's fancy. Letters pour in from all over the world, many requesting autographed pictures of a favorite star. "I am amazed by fans waiting outside theaters, restaurants, hotels—sometimes for hours," said veteran movie actor Kirk Douglas. "They all have a need to fill some void in their life. We all have fantasies."

THE REALITY: URBAN BLIGHT

Even though Los Angeles maintains the image of Tinseltown, its reality is far more somber. The majority of the city's polyglot population are people of color who are poor and needy. An estimated seventy-five languages are spoken in its school system, and more immigrants move into the city every year. In 1991 Los Angeles was 44 percent Hispanic and approximately 12 percent Asian. The city has a growing colony of homeless and is plagued with environmental problems. Its working class despairs over the lack of decent-paying jobs, while gangs and crime terrorize areas of greatest distress. In 1992 Los Angeles was again rocked by race riots. Along Sunset Boulevard prostitutes motion to men in passing cars, and male hustlers, many of them underage, do the same along a stretch of Santa Monica Boulevard. In recent years even collegiate Westwood has seen an influx of panhandlers, and the overall economy has grown so bad that Los Angeles has been described as "the ultimate area of Darwinian capitalism."

Hollywood itself has become a cesspool, teaming with vagrants, crime, and mental illness. Rapes, robberies, and assaults occur there regularly, and around eighty people a year kill themselves. Hollywood Boulevard's once stylish Art Deco buildings have been defaced by graffiti, and moochers and drug dealers prowl the street's Walk of Fame. The names of entertainers celebrated in terrazzo and brass stars are covered with trash, with the homeless sleeping in nearby alcoves of tacky tourist traps. The feted intersection of Hollywood and Vine has been a sleazy corner for decades, more the territory of rival gangs than movie stars.

Since the mid-1980s a $900 million redevelopment plan has been discussed for Hollywood, which would subsidize new office buildings, upscale restaurants, and theaters along the decayed corridors off the area's major boulevards, but the plan has been hampered by prolonged recession. Meanwhile, rootlessness and destitution persist. The median income for Hollywood's households is a mere $18,445 a year. During the decade between 1984 and 1994, the area's white population declined from 50 percent to 30 percent. The recent inflow of immigrants has brought legions of small merchants and impoverished service workers from the Third World. Since inexpensive rental housing is available in Hollywood, newcomers flock to its cheap apartments and dilapidated bungalows. In the early 1990s eight out of ten Hollywood residents were renters. East Hollywood has become known as Thai Town, for the Thai culture is much in evidence there. But so is unwavering poverty.

A PRECARIOUS BUSINESS

If the city's ills seem incurable, the movie industry itself has lost much of its luster. "There's not much stardust left anymore," said dancer Dan Dailey shortly before his death in 1978. Most of the remaining Golden Age stars agree that behind a mask of luxury and confidence, Hollywood is gripped by doubts, fears, and colossal insecurities.

The number of people who succeed in the business is far less than 1 percent. Yet the only thing Hollywood seems to trust is success, and the frantic urge to excel ensures ferocious competition. People define themselves by success or failure. Since the movies are a youth-oriented industry, looking young becomes essential, even among those who do not work before the camera. Narcissism infects most of the community, so that cosmetic surgery has almost become a rite of passage. The entertainment business is so self-absorbed that its trade papers—the *Hollywood Reporter* and *Daily Variety*—are its most frequent sources of printed news, whereas intelligent reporting of world events goes unnoticed.

The capacity to earn money remains the primary yardstick of quality, and even established stars are measured by their latest box office returns. No one can feel confident when failure and rejection lay just under the mirage of success. Actresses know that once they reach a certain age the first question their agent will be asked, when he or she submits her name for parts, is "What does she look like these days?"

Life for studio executives is no easier. Within three years after the *Heaven's Gate* debacle, the management of every major motion picture company in Hollywood except one had changed. Not one studio production head in 1985 was where he was three and a half years before. Since then the turnover has been even faster, making continuity and development almost impossible.

Drugs, particularly cocaine, have become an epidemic in Hollywood. Tony Curtis claimed that by 1974 cocaine could be bought on most movie sets, usually through the wardrobe department. Drug use has not only become accepted, it is also considered chic in certain circles. Careers of habitual users have been ruined, and tragedies all too frequent. Comedian John Belushi died from a combined injection of heroin and cocaine in a room at the famed Chateau Marmont on Sunset Boulevard. River Phoenix, the promising young actor whose performance in *Running on Empty* (1988) earned him an Academy Award nomination at age seventeen, died of a drug overdose outside a Los Angeles nightclub. Although Phoenix remained close to his family and selected projects of substance and quality, in the end his career became another example of a wasted talent in a callous business.

Freddie Prinze, the Puerto Rican comedian who found fame at nineteen on television's *Chico and the Man,* committed suicide in a fashionable apartment on Wilshire Boulevard. Prinze's rise to stardom was so rapid that he often had difficulty accepting success. Full of insecurities, he resorted to Quaaludes and other drugs. When police investigators arrived on the scene of his death, they found a note reading, "I can't go on."

Handsome Rob Lowe's career went into a death spin when the young actor was caught videotaping his drunken sexual escapades with two women in an Atlanta hotel room during the 1988 Democratic National Convention. The tape became an instant classic on late-night cable, but the scandal put a halt to Lowe's rise as a Hollywood heartthrob.

Rather than destroying the movie capital's charisma, periodic scandal seems to feed the public's interest. Weekly tabloids report in lurid detail messy divorces, illicit affairs, drug busts, and rumors too hot or unfounded to find their way into the more legitimate press. The sordid events occurring in Hollywood often receive more attention than those happening elsewhere, magnified by overexposure and gossip.

In 1977 director Roman Polanski was arrested on charges of having drugged and raped a thirteen-year-old girl in actor Jack Nicholson's house on Mulholland Drive. Polanski admitted that he had sexual intercourse with the girl but was angry about the accusation of rape.

Eight years before, Polanski's girlfriend, actress Sharon Tate, the child she was carrying, hairdresser Jay Sebring, and three others were slaughtered in a Bel-Air mansion by followers of Charles Manson. The bloodbath, more shocking than most fiction, startled Hollywood and eventually found its way into a national best-seller and a made-for-television movie.

In 1980 Peter Bogdanovich's lover, *Playboy* magazine centerfold Dorothy Stratten, was murdered shortly before the director's film starring her, *They All Laughed* (1981), was scheduled for release. Rock Hudson's death from AIDS in 1985 made headlines on front pages around the world and was followed by prolonged discussions of his sexual orientation. The accusation that Michael Jackson was guilty of child molestation often found its way into print, as did Woody Allen's affair with his stepdaughter and Hollywood madam Heidi Fleiss's list of star and mogul clients.

Yet for the general public the sparkle of movieland seems to remain untarnished. Anyone who has visited a movie set knows how boring the work really is, and the costume trailers and lighting tripods necessary for outdoor filming are anything but glamorous. Yet tourists thrill at the sight of a movie crew and hope for a glance at some recognizable star. Celebrity hounds continue to pour into Hollywood, where they snap up James Dean posters and Marilyn Monroe coffee mugs and find their way to Kevin Costner's house with the aid of a $7 map purchased on a corner of Sunset Boulevard.

Entertainment celebrities come and go at a faster and faster rate, as media exposure builds them up for an almost inevitable kill. The public hungers for stars and demands a rotation of its superstars, welcoming them as bigger than life before watching them fall. Critic Richard Schickel observed that in contemporary America one is either a celebrity or nothing. That might be true in business, politics, sports, even in academe, but it definitely is true in the entertainment field. Yet the shelf life of celebrities in modern society is brief. Few people talk about or care to understand the sacrifices and frustrations, not to mention the pain, in the struggle for superstardom. "It's hard to make friends in Hollywood," Kirk Douglas said. "It's a cruel, unhappy town, and success is even more difficult to handle than failure."

But even though other areas of southern California's economy have retrenched, the entertainment business has stayed resilient. Real estate in Los Angeles sank during the late 1980s, the aerospace industry declined, and retail chains collapsed. The movie, television, and recording industries, on the other hand, continued to chart new heights.

LESS A PLACE THAN A CONCEPT

Even during their Golden Era most of the movie studios were in Culver City, Century City, Burbank, or other sections of the San Fernando Valley rather than in Hollywood. In recent decades the movie business has decentralized even more. Most films are shot on location, and lower costs often lure production companies to Arizona, Texas, Florida, or, more recently, Canada.

Increasingly, major stars and top directors live away from Los Angeles. Dustin Hoffman prefers New York, whereas Robert Redford spends most of his time in Utah. John Travolta lives in Santa Barbara, but also has houses in Florida and Maine. "I can't take Hollywood," said Travolta. "That's a place for lawyers and agents." Director Brian DePalma agrees. "Never, never live in Hollywood," DePalma said. "I hate this insulated universe where film is the most important thing."

Many industry workers find Hollywood an intellectual vacuum, far less stimulating and creative than they think the business ought to be. Some object to the industry's tendency to cling to people with proven records and its unwillingness to take risks. They object to projects being judged on their marketing potential and bemoan the increased use of computers and market research. Many fault the emphasis on star power and the bureaucratic channels imposed by conglomerate takeovers. Their solution is to live and, whenever possible, work elsewhere, leaving Hollywood to the attorneys, the agencies, and the corporate offices.

THE BLURRED LINE BETWEEN REALITY AND FANTASY

The media, particularly television, has become so pervasive in our lives that it is sometimes difficult to separate images from actual events. Television invades the average American home approximately thirty hours a week, with the result that the medium has become one of the most potent forces in our lives. "The consequence," according to Ian Mitroff and Warren Bennis, "is that TV not only defines what is reality, but much more importantly and disturbingly, TV obliterates the very distinction, the very line, between reality and unreality."

In the decades since World War II, the reality of the outside world has grown increasingly complex. To avoid coping with these complexities, a significant portion of the population has retreated into unreality, making it a primary mode of reference. Mitroff and Bennis in their book *The Unreality Industry* (1989) argue that this penchant has become virtually psychopathic and that "the deliberate creation of unreality" is one of the pivotal social forces shaping our lives.

Rather than dealing with problems honestly, directly, and intelligently, society has become adept at substituting unrealities, which give individuals the illusion of control. The distinction between the real and the unreal has become vague if not meaningless. "Unreality is big business," Mitroff and Bennis maintain. "It is manufactured and sold on a gigantic scale." Beyond question, television has insinuated itself throughout world culture to such a degree that viewers place themselves inside small screen images. "If anything, unreality is the new reality," Mitroff and Bennis conclude.

Important aspects of contemporary life have been reduced to entertainment—politics, religion, education, sports, even the reporting of news. Everything needs to be packaged in ten-second sound bites to hold the public's attention. In the process the trivial gets mistaken for the serious.

Television's soap operas provide viewers with the illusion of intimacy, whereas talk shows appear to represent raw reality, since participants appear to confess their darkest secrets. MTV has invented its own world, explicitly dream oriented. Time and space on music videos are fragmented; grotesqueness becomes the norm; sets, costumes, and colors are exaggerated; and male and female figures transform themselves back and forth with such fluidity that a distinction is almost nonexistent.

Television's reporting of news has become another form of entertainment, since ratings are as important to newscasters as they are to prime-time sitcoms. Accurate coverage of the day's events is therefore secondary to capturing a mass audience. Politicians plan their public acts for maximum impact through media coverage. Yet care must be taken that television viewers not see too much of their leaders, since overexposure would cause them to lose their aura and might reduce their stature as important figures. Political careers have been made and ruined by controlled coverage.

The rise of Ronald Reagan from movie star to president of the United States is a dramatic example of the power of movies and television and indicates how the line between entertainment and politics has become blurred. Reagan brought to the White House a personal charm that years before had won him a contract at Warner Bros.

Indeed he failed at times to differentiate between movies and actual events. During a televised talk in which he spoke of the need to revive heroism, Reagan cried when he cited a Korean War incident during which an airman sacrificed his life for his companions. Reporters pointed out later that the president had referred to a totally fictitious scene in the movie *The Bridges at Toko-Ri* (1954).

In his 1980 campaign Reagan insisted that the United States must get American hostages back from Iran at any cost. It was later discovered that he had inadvertently quoted from John Wayne's dialogue in *The Searchers* (1956), a John Ford western in which Wayne endeavors to free a female captive from the Comanche.

If Hollywood's celebrities look to politicians for validation and respect, politicians seem no less disposed to use celluloid examples to support their positions on current affairs. House Speaker Newt Gingrich, a confessed movie buff, suggested in early 1995 that striking baseball players and team owners might break their six-month deadlock by studying the 1989 movie *Field of Dreams*. Gingrich had created a controversy earlier when he proposed that Hillary Rodham Clinton watch the 1938 Hollywood classic *Boys Town* before dismissing his proposal that welfare reform include placing more children in orphanages.

Entertainment by its very nature requires simplification. "If a person can tell me the idea in twenty-five words or less, it's going to make a pretty good movie," said Steven Spielberg. "I like ideas, especially movie ideas, that you can hold in your hand." Spielberg is a master at the art of motion pictures, but reality is a more complex matter. As the world grows more convoluted, astute analysis becomes increasingly essential. Entertainment, even in its richest forms, is no substitute for intelligence and candor in grappling with contemporary issues, yet it has become difficult to separate the real from the unreal.

EXAMPLE: THE O. J. SIMPSON CASE

On the evening of Friday, June 17, 1994, two-thirds of America's households turned on their television sets to watch a white Ford Bronco glide along the Los Angeles freeway system. O. J. Simpson, All-American football player turned sportscaster and movie star, had bolted in the vehicle rather than face arrest as a first-degree murder suspect in the death of his wife, Nicole, and her friend Ron Goldman.

Simpson had been missing all afternoon; police had been dispatched to watch the Mexican border and airports and train stations throughout southern California. At 5:25 p.m. Simpson and his longtime friend Al Cowlings were spotted in Cowlings's white Bronco, driving down Interstate 5. Soon squad cars three deep were following the fleeing Bronco, spread across the width of the five-lane freeway, with police and news helicopters hovering overhead.

As television cameras followed the caravan, the number of viewers at home continued to swell. Around 7:00 p.m. the police received a call from Cowlings's cellular telephone, stating that Simpson, who was sitting in the Bronco's back seat, had a gun to his head and would pull the trigger if anybody tried to stop the car or block the highway. By then the manhunt had turned into a parade route. Crowds of fans, recognizing the direction of the Bronco's path, raced to the highway, filling its overpasses and cheering on the fugitive. By the time the Bronco entered the San Diego Freeway from Interstate 91, spectators lined the thoroughfare, screaming "Run, O. J.! Run!" People began putting lawnchairs up on the edge of the freeway, waiting for the show to pass. Some held signs reading "Go, O. J., Go," while others waved, honked horns, and yelled encouragement. Most motorists along the road pulled over to the side and got out of their cars to watch the procession pass. Already the chase had become one of the most dramatic moments in television history.

Cowlings assured police from his car phone that all Simpson wanted was to see his mother. Meanwhile Special Weapons and Tactics Teams were being readied for an emergency. A twenty-five person SWAT team was sent to Simpson's Brentwood home in unmarked cars. Some hid in the shrubbery and behind palm trees that lined the streets around the Simpson mansion, and snipers were positioned on nearby roofs. Police efforts in the neighborhood were hampered by a growing crowd that awaited Simpson after hearing on television that the former sports figure planned to return home.

The Bronco turned onto Sunset Boulevard and headed west into Brentwood. By the time Cowlings pulled into Simpson's cobblestone driveway off Rockingham Drive, a mob was there shoving to get a better look, and others tried to climb the walls around his house. "We love the Juice," some yelled, seemingly unmindful that the legendary ball player was at that moment a fugitive from justice. With cameras from all three networks and CNN trained on Cowlings's white Bronco for live coverage, viewers throughout most of the world stayed glued, unsure whether they were watching a made-for-television action movie or a real-life drama. As evening shadows grew longer around Simpson's stately house, millions waited in suspense, not knowing if they were going to witness the former gridiron hero's death or his surrender into police custody. The wait seemed interminable, as friend called friend, causing the television audience to grow to Superbowl proportions.

Finally as darkness approached, the dramatic manhunt ended when a distraught O. J. Simpson lowered the revolver and climbed out of the Bronco, clutching a rosary in his hand. He tottered up the short walkway to his front door and apologized to police who awaited him inside. He was soon loaded into a squad car, placed between two detectives, and driven in a motorcade to police head-quarters, where around 10:00 p.m. he was booked on two counts of murder. He was then placed in a cell under a twenty-four-hour suicide watch.

The spectacle seemed more fantasy than reality. Fans cheered Simpson as he fled down the freeways as if he were again the powerful running back headed toward the goal line in a championship playoff. The chase and his ultimate capture offered the drama and excitement of a Hollywood adventure yarn. Its star, the most famous professional football player of his generation, was a handsome, affable Heisman Trophy winner who first won fame playing for the University of Southern California Trojans. He went on to professional glory with the Buffalo Bills and the San Francisco Forty-Niners, broke athletic records, and was inducted into the Football Hall of Fame. He had also become a successful sports anchor on television; an actor in such movies as *The Dirty Dozen* (1967), *The Towering Inferno* (1974), and *The Cassandra Crossing* (1977); and a familiar spokesman for Hertz rental cars. Intelligent, poised, and articulate, the extroverted Simpson moved through his various careers with dignity and grace, surrounded by beautiful women. A multimillionaire at the time of his arrest, the star seemed to accept his celebrity with ease and humility. He wore expensive tailored clothes, yet was an avid worker with youth programs and had become an idol for millions of underprivileged children. Although he was an African American icon, Simpson seemed to transcend the issue of race. Unlike Jim Brown, who had enjoyed similar fame during the late 1960s and early 1970s but had become identified with the Black Power movement, O. J. Simpson represented congeniality. He was

Mr. Nice Guy, a black man who had reached the top in white America and established himself as a genuine American hero, a star in three arenas—sports, television, and movies.

The sight of this legend, so admired by all races, wearing handcuffs and pictured in mug shots, shocked the nation and the world. No longer would O. J. Simpson's fame be restricted to sports and entertainment; he had entered the annals of crime as well. The real seemed unreal. Few knew of his personal problems—that he was sometimes lonely and bored, that he slipped easily into depression, that he was possessive and jealous, that he had been physically abusive to his wife on numerous occasions. Those were complexities inconsistent with his dashing, genial image. "I really enjoy being liked," said Simpson. "I loved it when kids stopped me for autographs. I loved it when people recognized me on the street." Both the public and the media loved Simpson's banter and public disposition and treated him as a Hollywood-style superstar.

Then came the report that Simpson's ex-wife, along with a younger male friend, had been murdered outside her condominium on Bundy Drive in fashionable Brentwood. Nicole Brown Simpson, a thirty-five-year-old blond beauty, had married Simpson in 1985, after living with him for nearly seven years. They had two children, and O. J. had two others by his previous marriage. Simpson proved a violent husband, and domestic quarrels frequently brought police to their home and resulted in 911 calls later. Yet when the battered Nicole filed for divorce, Simpson was unhappy. Following their separation in 1992, he became despondent and obsessive, occasionally threatening his former wife and stalking her.

On the night of Sunday, June 12, 1994, Nicole Brown Simpson died of multiple stab wounds. Ronald Goldman, the other murder victim, was a twenty-five-year-old waiter and part-time model who had been seen squiring Nicole around town. Goldman, too, had been stabbed repeatedly following an apparent struggle. Both bodies were discovered sprawled on the tiled walkway beside the gate to Nicole's townhouse. Approximately an hour after the slayings, O. J. Simpson was on a plane bound for Chicago. Told of his ex-wife's death the next morning, he returned to Los Angeles and attended Nicole's funeral the next Thursday. By then television crews had erected platforms outside his home, and people everywhere were forming opinions about his guilt or innocence.

Even before his arrest Simpson's case had become a media circus. Rockingham Drive, a normally quiet street, was suddenly lined with television trucks in the blocks around Simpson's house. As neighbors complained, the public began snapping up every available morsel of information, clamoring for more. In the weeks after his arrest, otherwise sophisticated people drove by his home in a steady stream just to have a look. Nicole's house on Bundy Drive became the talk of Los Angeles, even among movie people.

Simpson was formally charged with first degree murder but pleaded not guilty. His trial became a televised serial, made all the more exciting because it involved a multimedia star and took place in the vicinity of Hollywood. Guilty or innocent, Simpson became a victim of his own celebrity. His case resulted in the trial of the century, about which everybody had an opinion. The president's state-of-the-union message was eclipsed by an evening report on the O. J. Simpson trial, and nightly seminars on the subject were held in bars around the globe.

Meanwhile street-corner entrepreneurs lined their pockets. Everything from T-shirts to hastily written books were merchandised in vast quantities. A limited edition of three hundred football cards, signed and dated by O. J. Simpson from his jail cell, sold for $850 each. An autograph he gave on the day of the slayings brought $4,000 at an auction the following November. An Andy Warhol portrait of Simpson, finished in 1978, sold for $34,500 on an otherwise average day at Sotheby's.

While the mania continued, five stories of camera scaffolding were constructed outside the Hall of Justice in downtown Los Angeles. Media hordes from around the world flocked to the city to chronicle a saga filled with sensationalism and stardust. "This is bigger than any event we've ever had, including the World Cup," said Howard Fine, a board member of the Los Angeles Radio and Television News Association. "Haiti [with its political turmoil and human suffering] is what people need to know about, but O. J. Simpson is what they want to know about."

By the time Simpson's trial began, the aggressive coverage raised fundamental questions about legal and ethical procedures, but the public, almost numb to the actual events involved, had its nightly entertainment. A folk hero stood at the center of a melodrama that for a time dwarfed all other news. The fact that a man, rather than a legend, was on trial for a double murder—actual slayings, not celluloid concoctions—seemed lost in a veil of trivialized realities. Yet such is the power of Hollywood's images.

CONCLUSION

In the decades since the end of World War II, Hollywood has survived a political purge, the breakup of the big studio system, and the advent of a new medium that usurped the mass audience movies had come to enjoy since the dawn of the century. After a period of adjustment, motion picture studios embraced television, incorporating the networks' needs into their patterns of production. With the expansion of home viewing, filmed images became so pervasive in American lives that the distinction between reality and fantasy grew blurred, endangering social stability as well as critical thought. Although motion pictures and television programming have broadened audiences' views of the world, the impact of their creations pose dangers when mistaken for authentic happenings.

Hollywood has long thrived on enchanting, easily reducible narratives that lend themselves to ready marketability. But through prolonged exposure the public has grown increasingly comfortable with images over reality. Families take vacations more for snapshots to impress friends and neighbors than for the experience and enjoyment of travel. Voting decisions are made on appearances rather than after an analysis of issues; and excitement and fast-paced fulfillment are demanded from relationships, employment, and daily living. More than a font of entertainment, Hollywood has forged images that have become an expected norm, giving credence to the synthetic and at times obscuring the authentic.

Although Hollywood has produced fine examples of popular culture, its orientation is first and foremost commerce. "It's not a town founded on ideals," character actress Marjorie Main once said, "it's built on making money." During the late 1970s market research became an integral part of the film industry. Within five years every important studio devoted a major portion of its marketing budget to audience analysis, the results of which change constantly, encouraging fads over substance. Television commercials, music soundtracks, and the merchandising of product tie-ins have all come to play an increased role in the marketing of feature films.

Perhaps more than other media, film and television respond to the shifting needs of their audiences. Both mirror and influence contemporary society. Yet despite constant changes, including recessions and foreign and domestic competition, Hollywood has maintained its monopoly on the production of motion pictures, television programming, and filmed commercials.

In the public's mind Hollywood is still the glamour capital, the home of the great dream factories. Hollywood's stars, if not as enduring as they once were, nonetheless hold tremendous power—politically, as well as socially and commercially. Hollywood's product can—and does—affect the tastes, attitudes, and mores of millions of people around the world—in dress, decor, even dating practices. Ultimately Hollywood's greatest creation may be itself. For nearly a century Hollywood has projected fables about the good life, images of what it means to be famous, and myths that dazzle, electrify, and shape the thinking of successive generations. Although the reality of Tinseltown may be tarnished and troubled, its mystique continues, modernized with the passage of time.

BIBLIOGRAPHY

BOOKS

Agan, Patrick. *Robert DeNiro: The Man, the Myth, and the Movies.* London: Robert Hale, 1989.

Anderson, Christopher. *Hollywood TV: The Studio System in the Fifties.* Austin: University of Texas Press, 1994.

Bach, Steven. *Final Cut: Dreams and Disaster in the Making of "Heaven's Gate."* New York: Morrow, 1985.

Balio, Tino, ed. *Hollywood in the Age of Television.* Boston: Unwin Hyman, 1990.

Barnouw, Erik. *Tube of Plenty: The Evolution of American Television.* New York: Oxford, 1982.

Bart, Peter. *Fade Out: The Calamitous Final Days of MGM.* New York: Morrow, 1990.

Baxter, John. *Hollywood in the Sixties.* New York: A. S. Barnes, 1972.

Belton, John. *American Cinema / American Culture.* New York: McGraw-Hill, 1994.

Bliss, Michael. *Brian DePalma.* Metuchen: Scarecrow, 1983.

———. *Martin Scorsese and Michael Cimino.* Metuchen: Scarecrow, 1985.

Bookbinder, Robert. *The Films of the Seventies.* Secaucus: Citadel, 1982.

Britton, Andrew, ed. *Talking Films.* London: Fourth Estate, 1991.

Brode, Douglas. *The Films of the Eighties.* Secaucus: Citadel, 1990.

———. *The Films of the Fifties.* Secaucus: Citadel, 1976.

Brosnan, John. *Future Tense: The Cinema of Science Fiction.* New York: St. Martin's, 1978.

Brownstein, Ronald. *The Power and the Glitter: The Hollywood-Washington Connection.* New York: Pantheon, 1990.

Cagin, Seth, and Philip Dray. *Hollywood Films of the Seventies.* New York: Harper & Row, 1984.

Ceplair, Larry, and Steven Englund. *The Inquisition in Hollywood: Politics in the Film Community, 1930-1960.* Berkeley: University of California Press, 1983.

Cerasini, Marc. *O. J. Simpson: American Hero, American Tragedy.* New York: Pinnacle, 1994.

Champlin, Charles. *George Lucas: The Creative Impulse.* New York: Abrams, 1992.

———. *The Movies Grow Up, 1940-1980.* Athens: Swall, 1981.

Clover, Carol J. *Men, Women, and Chain Saws: Gender in the Modern Horror Film.* Princeton: Princeton University Press, 1992.

Corman, Roger, with Jim Jerome. *How I Made a Hundred Movies in Hollywood and Never Lost a Dime.* New York: Random House, 1990.

Corrigan, Timothy. *A Cinema Without*

Walls: Movies and Culture after Vietnam. New Brunswick: Rutgers University Press, 1991.

Cowie, Peter. *Coppola.* New York: Scribner's, 1990.

Cripps, Thomas. *Making Movies Black: The Hollywood Message Movie from World War II to the Civil Rights Era.* New York: Oxford, 1993.

Crowther, Bruce. *Film Noir: Reflections in a Dark Mirror.* London: Columbus, 1988.

Curtis, Tony, and Barry Paris. *Tony Curtis: The Autobiography.* New York: Morrow, 1993.

Dalton, David. *James Dean, the Mutant King.* New York: St. Martin's, 1974.

Daly, Marsha. *Michael Landon: A Biography.* New York: St. Martin's, 1987.

David, Saul. *The Industry: Life in the Hollywood Fast Lane.* New York: Times Books, 1981.

Davis, Don. *Fallen Hero.* New York: St. Martin's, 1994.

Davis, Ronald L. *The Glamour Factory: Inside Hollywood's Big Studio System.* Dallas: Southern Methodist University Press, 1993.

———. *John Ford: Hollywood's Old Master.* Norman: University of Oklahoma Press, 1995.

Dick, Bernard F. *Billy Wilder.* Boston: Twayne, 1980.

———. *Radical Innocence: A Critical Study of the Hollywood Ten.* Lexington: University Press of Kentucky, 1989.

Doherty, Thomas. *Teenagers and Teenpics: The Juvenilization of American Movies in the 1950s.* Boston: Unwin Hyman, 1988.

Douglas, Kirk. *The Ragman's Son: An Autobiography.* New York: Simon & Schuster, 1988.

Dowdy, Andrew. *"Movies Are Better Than Ever": Wide-Screen Memories of the Fifties.* New York: Morrow, 1973.

Edgerton, Gary R. *American Film Exhibitors and an Analysis of the Motion Picture Industry's Market Structure, 1963-1980.* New York: Garland, 1983.

Elley, Derek. *The Epic Film.* London: Routledge and Kegan Paul, 1984.

Farber, Stephen, and Marc Green. *Hollywood Dynasties.* New York: Delilah, 1984.

Freeman, David. *The Last Days of Alfred Hitchcock.* Woodstock: Overlook, 1984.

Goldstein, Toby. *William Hurt: The Man, the Actor.* New York: St. Martin's, 1987.

Gomery, Douglas. *The Hollywood Studio System.* New York: St. Martin's, 1986.

———. *Shared Pleasures: A History of Movie Presentation in the United States.* Madison: University of Wisconsin Press, 1992.

Goodwin, Michael, and Naomi Wise. *On the Edge: The Life and Times of Francis Coppola.* New York: Morrow, 1989.

Hall, Ben M. *The Best Remaining Seats: The Story of the Golden Age of the Movie Palace.* New York: Potter, 1961.

Hamilton, Ian. *Writers in Hollywood, 1915-1951.* New York: Harper & Row, 1990.

Harmetz, Aljean. *Rolling Breaks and Other Movie Business.* New York: Knopf, 1983.

Harris, Marlys J. *The Zanucks of Hollywood: The Dark Legacy of an American Dynasty.* New York: Crown, 1989.

Harris, Thomas J. *Bogdanovich's Picture Shows.* Metuchen: Scarecrow, 1990.

Haskell, Molly. *From Reverence to Rape: The Treatment of Women in the Movies.* New York: Holt, Rinehart and Winston, 1974.

Haynes, Johnson. *Sleepwalking*

Through History: America in the Reagan Years. New York: Norton, 1991.

Higham, Charles. *Hollywood at Sunset*. New York: Saturday Review, 1972.

Hillier, Jim. *The New Hollywood*. New York: Continuum, 1992.

Horton, Andrew. *The Films of George Roy Hill*. New York: Columbia University Press, 1984.

Hunter, Allan. *Faye Dunaway*. New York: St. Martin's, 1986.

———. *Gene Hackman*. New York: St. Martin's, 1987.

Izod, John. *Hollywood and the Box Office, 1895-1986*. New York: Columbia University Press, 1988.

Jacobs, Diane. *Hollywood Renaissance*. New York: Delta, 1980.

Jones, G. William. *Black Cinema Treasures*. Denton: University of North Texas Press, 1991.

Jones, Gerard. *Honey, I'm Home! Sitcoms: Selling the American Dream*. New York: Grove Weidenfeld, 1992.

Kagan, Norman. *The Cinema of Stanley Kubrick*. New York: Holt, Rinehart and Winston, 1972.

Karp, Alan. *The Films of Robert Altman*. Metuchen: Scarecrow, 1981.

Karyn, Kay, and Gerald Peary, eds. *Women and the Cinema*. New York: Dutton, 1977.

Keller, Gary D., ed. *Chicano Cimema*. Binghamton: Bilingual, 1985.

Kelly, Mary Pat. *Martin Scorsese, The First Decade*. Pleasantville: Redgrave, 1980.

Kent, Nicolas. *Naked Hollywood: Money and Power in the Movies Today*. New York: St. Martin's, 1991.

Keyser, Les. *Martin Scorsese*. New York: Twayne, 1992.

Keyssar, Helene. *Robert Altman's America*. New York: Oxford, 1991.

Kim, Erwin. *Franklin J. Schaffner*. Metuchen: Scarecrow, 1985.

Kindem, Gorham, ed. *The American Movie Industry: The Business of Motion Pictures*. Carbondale: Southern Illinois University Press, 1982.

Knight, Arthur. *The Liveliest Art: A Panoramic History of the Movies*. New York: Macmillan, 1978.

Kolker, Robert Phillip. *A Cinema of Loneliness*. New York: Oxford, 1980.

Leab, Daniel J. *From Sambo to Superspade: The Black Experience in Motion Pictures*. Boston: Houghton Mifflin, 1975.

Leaming, Barbara. *Polanski: The Filmmaker as Voyeur*. New York: Simon & Schuster, 1981.

Lees, David, and Stan Berkowitz. *The Movie Business*. New York: Vintage, 1981.

Lenburg, Jeff. *Dustin Hoffman: Hollywood's Anti-Hero*. New York: St. Martin's, 1983.

Lenihan, John H. *Showdown: Confronting Modern America in the Western Film*. Urbana: University of Illinois Press, 1980.

Levy, Emanuel. *Small-Town America in Film*. New York: Continuum, 1991.

Litwak, Mark. *Reel Power: The Struggle for Influence and Success in the New Hollywood*. New York: Morrow, 1986.

Lloyd, Ann, and David Robinson, eds. *Movies of the Seventies*. London: Orbis, 1984.

MacCann, Richard Dyer. *Hollywood in Transition*. Westport: Greenwood, 1977.

MacKinnon, Kenneth. *Misogyny in the Movies: The DePalma Question*. Newark: University of Delaware Press, 1990.

McCarthy, Todd, and Charles Flynn, eds. *King of the Bs*. New York: Dutton, 1975.

McCarty, John. *Splatter Movies: Breaking the Last Taboo of the Screen*. New York: St. Martin's, 1984.

McGilligan, Patrick. *Jack's Life: A*

Biography of Jack Nicholson. New York: Norton, 1994.

———. *Robert Altman.* New York: St. Martin's, 1989.

McKinney, Doug. *Sam Peckinpah.* Boston: Twayne, 1979.

McMurtry, Larry. *Film Flam: Essays on Hollywood.* New York: Simon & Schuster, 1987.

Madsen, Axel. *The New Hollywood: American Movies in the '70s.* New York: Crowell, 1975.

Marc, David, and Robert J. Thompson. *Prime Time, Prime Movers.* Boston: Little, Brown, 1992.

Medred, Michael. *Hollywood vs. America: Popular Culture and the War on Traditional Values.* New York: Harper Collins, 1992.

Miller, Mark Crispin, ed. *Seeing Through Movies.* New York: Pantheon, 1990.

Mintz, Marilyn D. *The Martial Arts Films.* Rutland: Charles E. Tuttle, 1983.

Mintz, Steven, and Randy Roberts, eds. *Hollywood's America: United States History Through Its Films.* St. James: Brandywine, 1993.

Mitroff, Ian I., and Warren Bennis. *The Unreality Industry.* New York: Oxford, 1989.

Moldea, Dan E. *Dark Victory: Ronald Reagan, MCA, and the Mob.* New York: Viking, 1986.

Monaco, James. *American Films Now.* New York: New American Library, 1979.

Mordden, Ethan. *Medium Cool: The Movies of the 1960s.* New York: Knopf, 1990.

Morris, Gary. *Roger Corman.* Boston: Twayne, 1985.

Mott, Donald R., and Cheryl McAllister Saunders. *Steven Spielberg.* Boston: Twayne, 1986.

Musun, Chris. *The Marketing of Motion Pictures.* Los Angeles: Musun, 1969.

Navasky, Victor S. *Naming Names.* New York: Viking, 1980.

Nowlan, Robert A., and Gwendolyn Wright Nowlan. *The Films of the Eighties.* Jefferson: McFarland, 1991.

O'Connor, John E., and Martin A. Jackson, eds. *American History / American Film: Interpreting the Hollywood Image.* New York: Ungar, 1979.

Palmer, William J. *The Films of the Eighties: A Social History.* Carbondale: Southern Illinois University Press, 1993.

———. *The Films of the Seventies: A Social History.* Metuchen: Scarecrow, 1987.

Parker, John. *Warren Beatty: The Last Great Lover of Hollywood.* New York: Carroll and Graf, 1994.

Phelps, Guy. *Film Censorship.* London: Victor Gollancz, 1975.

Phillips, Gene D. *Alfred Hitchcock.* Boston: Twayne, 1984.

———. *John Schlesinger.* Boston: Twayne, 1981.

Plecki, Gerard. *Robert Altman.* Boston: Twayne, 1985.

Pogel, Nancy. *Woody Allen.* Boston: Twayne, 1987.

Poitier, Sidney. *This Life.* New York: Knopf, 1980.

Polan, Dana. *Power and Paranoia: History, Narrative, and the American Cinema, 1940-1950.* New York: Columbia University Press, 1986.

Polanski, Roman. *Roman.* New York: Morrow, 1984.

Pollock, Dale. *Skywalking: The Life and Films of George Lucas.* New York: Harmony, 1983.

Pratley, Gerald. *The Cinema of John Frankenheimer.* New York: A. S. Barnes, 1969.

Prindle, David F. *The Politics of Glamour: Ideology and Democracy in the Screen Actors Guild.* Madison: University of Wisconsin Press, 1988.

Pye, Michael, and Lynda Myles. *The*

Movie Brats. New York: Holt, Rinehart and Winston, 1979.

Quart, Leonard, and Albert Auster. *American Film and Society since 1945.* New York: Praeger, 1991.

Rattigan, Neil. *Images of Australia.* Dallas: Southern Methodist University Press, 1991.

Ray, Robert B. *A Certain Tendency of the Hollywood Cinema, 1930-1980.* Princeton: Princeton University Press, 1985.

Resnick, Sylvia Safran. *Burt Reynolds: An Unauthorized Biography.* New York: St. Martin's, 1983.

Rodriguez, Elena. *Dennis Hopper: A Madness to His Method.* New York: St. Martin's, 1988.

Roffman, Peter, and Jim Purdy. *The Hollywood Social Problem Film.* Bloomington: Indiana University Press, 1981.

Russell, Ken. *Altered States: The Autobiography of Ken Russell.* New York: Bantam, 1991.

Russo, John. *Making Movies.* New York: Delacorte, 1989.

Russo, Vito. *The Celluloid Closet: Homosexuality in the Movies.* New York: Harper & Row, 1987.

Sayre, Nora. *Running Time: Films of the Cold War.* New York: Dial, 1982.

Schatz, Thomas. *Old Hollywood / New Hollywood: Ritual, Art, and Industry.* Ann Arbor: UMI Research, 1983.

Segaloff, Nat. *Hurricane Billy: The Stormy Life and Films of William Friedkin.* New York: Morrow, 1990.

Selby, Spencer. *Dark City: The Film Noir.* Jefferson: McFarland, 1984.

Seydor, Paul. *Peckinpah: The Western Films.* Urbana: University of Illinois Press, 1980.

Shindler, Colin. *Hollywood Goes to War: Films and American Society, 1939-1952.* London: Routledge and Kegan Paul, 1979.

Shores, Edward. *George Roy Hill.* Boston: Twayne, 1983.

Simmons, Garner. *Peckinpah: A Portrait in Montage.* Austin: University of Texas Press, 1976.

Sklar, Robert. *Movie-Made America.* New York: Random House, 1975.

———. *Prime-Time America: Life On and Behind the Television Screen.* New York: Oxford, 1980.

Solomon, Aubrey. *Twentieth Century-Fox: A Corporate and Financial History.* Metuchen: Scarecrow, 1988.

Spiegel, Penina. *McQueen.* Garden City: Doubleday, 1986.

Spoto, Donald. *Marilyn Monroe: The Biography.* New York: HarperCollins, 1993.

Stanley, Robert H. *The Celluloid Empire.* New York: Hastings House, 1978.

Steven, Peter, ed. *Jump Cut: Hollywood, Politics, and Counter Cinema.* New York: Praeger, 1985.

Taylor, John. *Storming the Magic Kingdom: Wall Street, the Raiders, and the Battle for Disney.* New York: Knopf, 1987.

Taylor, Philip M. *Steven Spielberg: The Man, His Movies, and Their Meaning.* New York: Continuum, 1992.

Taylor, William R. *Sydney Pollack.* Boston: Twayne, 1981.

Telotte, J. P. *Voices in the Dark: The Narrative Patterns of Film Noir.* Urbana: University of Illinois Press, 1989.

Toeplitz, Jerzy. *Hollywood and After: The Changing Face of Movies in America.* Chicago: Henry Regnery, 1974.

Tuska, Jon. *Dark Cinema: American Film Noir in Cultural Perspective.* Westport: Greenwood, 1984.

Valentine, Maggie. *The Show Starts on the Sidewalk.* New Haven: Yale University Press, 1994.

Vineberg, Steve. *Method Actors: Three Generations of an American Acting*

Style. New York: Schirmer, 1991.

———. *No Surprises, Please: Movies in the Reagan Decade.* New York: Schirmer, 1993.

Vizzard, Jack. *See No Evil: Life Inside a Hollywood Censor.* New York: Simon & Schuster, 1970.

Walker, Mark. *Vietnam Veteran Films.* Metuchen: Scarecrow, 1991.

Walsh, Andrea S. *Women's Film and Female Experience, 1940-1950.* New York: Praeger, 1984.

Wasko, Janet. *Movies and Money: Financing the American Film Industry.* Norwood: Ablex, 1982.

Wexman, Virginia Wright. *Roman Polanski.* Boston: Twayne, 1985.

Wilkerson, Tichi, and Marcia Borie. *"The Hollywood Reporter": The Golden Years.* New York: Coward-McCann, 1984.

Wolfenstein, Martha, and Nathan Leites. *Movies: A Psychological Study.* New York: Atheneum, 1970.

Wood, Robin. *Arthur Penn.* New York: Praeger, 1970.

———. *Hollywood from Vietnam to Reagan.* New York: Columbia University Press, 1986.

Woodward, Bob. *Wired: The Short Life and Fast Times of John Belushi.* New York: Simon & Schuster, 1984.

Wyatt, Justin. *High Concept: Movies and Marketing in Hollywood.* Austin: University of Texas Press, 1994.

Yule, Andrew. *Fast Fade: David Puttnam, Columbia Pictures, and the Battle for Hollywood.* New York: Delacorte, 1989.

Zolotow, Maurice. *Billy Wilder in Hollywood.* New York: Putnam's, 1977.

PERIODICALS

Andrews, Nigel. "Sam Peckinpah, the Survivor and the Individual." *Sight and Sound* 42 (Spring 1973): 69-74.

Baughn, David. "Distributing Independent Feature Films." *Filmmakers* 12 (Sep. 1979): 18-21.

Boddy, William. "The Studios Move into Prime Time: Hollywood and the Television Industry in the 1950s." *Cinema Journal* 24 (Summer 1985): 23-37.

Boyer, Peter J. "Risky Business." *American Film* 9 (Jan.-Feb. 1984): 14, 76-77.

Brandes, David. "An Interview with Dino DeLaurentiis." *Filmmakers Newsletter* 10 (Apr. 1977): 30-34.

Burns, Gary. "Dreams and Mediation in Music Video." *Wide Angle* 10. 2 (1987-1988) : 41-61.

Bygrave, Mike. "Hollywood 1985." *Sight and Sound* 54 (Spring 1985): 84-88.

——— and Joan Goodman. "First-Time Directors: A New Breed." *American Film* 6 (Jan.-Feb. 1981): 22-26.

Chambers, N. C. "The 36th Academy Awards." *Films in Review* 15 (May 1964): 280-86.

Chute, David. "The New World of Roger Corman." *Film Comment* 18 (Mar.-Apr. 1982): 27-32.

Collins, Richard. "The Screen Writer and Censorship." *The Screen Writer* 3 (Oct. 1947): 15-17.

Corliss, Richard. "A Studio Is Born." *Time* (24 Oct. 1994): 68-70.

Corrao, Christopher. "The American Film Industry: Reality and Myth." *Filmmakers Newsletter* 5 (Nov. 1971): 32-40.

Daily Variety, 1946-1995.

"Dialogue on Film: Steven Spielberg." *American Film* 13 (June 1988): 12-16.

Dempsey, Michael. "After the Fall: Post-Cimino Hollywood." *American Film* 6 (Sep. 1981): 51-54.

——— and Udayan Gupta. "Hollywood's Color Problem." *American Film* 7 (Apr. 1982): 67-70.

Diehl, Digby. "Roger Corman: A Double Life." *Action* 4 (July-Aug. 1969): 10-13.

Edgerton, Gary, and Cathy Pratt. "The Influence of the Paramount Decision on Network Television in America." *Quarterly Review of Film Studies* 8 (Summer 1983): 9-23.

Farber, Stephen. "End of the Road?" *Film Quarterly* 23 (Winter 1969-70): 3-16.

———. "George Lucas: The Stinky Kid Hits the Big Time." *Film Quarterly* 27 (Spring 1974): 2-9.

———. "The Monster Marathon." *Cinema* 6 (Summer 1970): 10-15.

———. "The Return of the Grown-Up Movie." *American Film* 7 (Dec. 1981): 47-53, 76.

Film Daily Year Book of Motion Pictures, 1946-1994.

"Freedom vs. Fear: The Fight for the American Mind," *The Screen Writer* 3 (Dec. 1947): 1-4.

Goldman, Debra. "Business for Art's Sake." *American Film* 12 (Apr. 1987): 44-48.

Goldstein, Patrick. "Roger to Rookies: Make It Cheap." *American Film* 10 (Jan.-Feb. 1985): 36-43.

Goldwyn, Samuel. "Hollywood in the Television Age." *Hollywood Quarterly* 4 (1949-50): 145-51.

Gomery, Douglas. "The American Film Industry of the 1970s." *Wide Angle* 5.4 (1982-1983): 52-59.

———. "Failed Opportunities: The Integration of the U. S. Motion Picture and Television Industries." *Quarterly Review of Film Studies* 9 (Summer 1984): 219-28.

Hart, Henry. "1959's Ten Best." *Films in Review* 11 (Jan. 1960): 1-6.

Hentzi, Gary. "Peter Weir and the Cinema of New Age Humanism." *Film Quarterly* 44 (Winter 1990-91): 2-12.

Higham, Charles. "Hollywood Boulevard 1965." *Sight and Sound* 34 (Autumn 1965): 177-79.

Hoberman, J. "Ten Years That Shook the World." *American Film* 10 (June 1985): 34-59.

Hochberg, Joel. "The Vanishing Newsreel." *Films in Review* 10 (June-July 1959): 344-45, 362.

Huggins, Roy. "What's Wrong with the Television Series." *Action* 4 (Sep.-Oct. 1969): 28-31.

Jameson, Richard T. "Something to Do with Death: A Fistful of Sergio Leone." *Film Comment* 9 (Mar. 1973): 8-16.

Jensen, Paul. "The Return of Dr. Caligari: Paranoia in Hollywood." *Film Comment* 7 (Winter 1971-72): 36-45.

Johnson, Albert. "The Negro in American Films." *Film Quarterly* 18 (Summer 1965): 14-30.

Johnson, William. "Hollywood 1965." *Film Quarterly* 19 (Fall 1965): 39-51.

Jones, Jacquie. "The New Ghetto Aesthetic." *Wide Angle* 13.3 (1990-1991): 32-43.

Kauffmann, Stanley. "Where Have All the Powers Gone?" *Film Comment* 7 (Winter 1971-72): 28-29.

Kearney, Jill. "All About Sneaks." *American Film* 10 (Mar. 1985): 45-49.

Kinder, Marsha. "Music Video and the Spectator." *Film Quarterly* 38 (Fall 1984): 2-15.

Koszarski, Richard. "The Films of Roger Corman." *Film Comment* 7 (Fall 1971): 43-48.

Kowinski, William Severini. "The Malling of the Movies." *American Film* 8 (Sep. 1983): 52-56.

Lehman, Ernest. "Hollywood Comes of Age." *American Film* 6 (Mar. 1981): 13-14.

Leibman, Nina C. "Leave Mother Out: The Fifties Family in American Film and Television." *Wide Angle* 10.4 (1988): 24-41.

Lovece, Frank. "The Greening of Television." *American Film* 12 (Apr. 1987): 50-54.

MacCabe, Colin. "Puttnam's New Mission." *American Film* 12 (Oct. 1986): 39-45.

McArthur, Colin. "Polanski." *Sight and Sound* 38 (Winter 1968-69): 14-19.

McInerney, Peter. "Apocalypse Then: Hollywood Looks Back at Vietnam." *Film Quarterly* 33 (Winter 1979-80): 21-32.

Mellen, Joan. "The Return of Women to Seventies Films." *Quarterly Review of Film Studies* 3 (Fall 1978): 525-43.

Milne, Tom. "How I Learned to Stop Worrying and Love Stanley Kubrick." *Sight and Sound* 33 (Spring 1964): 68-72.

Noriega, Chon. "Godzilla and the Japanese Nightmare: When *Them!* Is U. S." *Cinema Journal* 27 (Fall 1987): 63-77.

Oxenhandler, Neal. "The Dialectic of Emotion in New Wave Cinema." *Film Quarterly* 27 (Spring 1974): 10-19.

Pampel, Fred, Dan Fost, and Sharon O'Malley. "Marketing the Movies." *American Demographics* 16 (Mar. 1994): 48-54.

Paul, William. "Hollywood Harakiri." *Film Comment* 13 (Mar.-Apr. 1977): 40-43, 56-62.

Rickey, Carrie, and Artie West. "The Return of the WASP Hero." *American Film* 7 (Nov. 1981): 45-50.

Ross, Andrew. "Ballots, Bullets, or Batmen: Can Cultural Studies Do the Right Thing?" *Screen* 31 (Spring 1990): 26-44.

Sansweet, Stephen J. "Wall Street Goes to the Movies." *American Film* 8 (Oct. 1982): 45-48.

Sarris, Andrew. "About All These Women." *American Film* 4 (Oct. 1978): 62-65.

Scheuer, Kenneth K. "Hollywood—An Invalid?" *Films in Review* 11 (Oct. 1960): 449-51.

Schickel, Richard. "Hollywood's New Directions." *Time* (14 Oct. 1991): 75-78.

Scott, Adrian. "You Can't Do That!" *The Screen Writer* 3 (Aug. 1947): 4-7.

Stauth, Cameron. "Big Money, No Small Change." *American Film* 15 (May 1990): 42-43, 53.

———. "The Cineplex Complex." *American Film* 15 (Dec. 1990): 16-17.

Stewart, James B. "Sony's Bad Dream." *The New Yorker* (28 Feb. 1994): 43-51.

"Summing Up the Seventies." *American Film* 5 (Dec. 1979): 26-31, 50-63.

Taylor, John Russell. "Movies for a Small Screen." *Sight and Sound* 44 (Spring 1975): 113-15.

Turan, Kenneth. "Superman! Supersell!" *American Film* 4 (Dec. 1978-Jan. 1979): 49-52.

Wyatt, Justin, and R. L. Rutsky. "High Concept: Abstracting the Postmodern." *Wide Angle* 10.4 (1987-1988): 42-49.

Yearwood, Gladstone L. "The Hero in Black Film." *Wide Angle* 5.2 (1982-1983): 42-50.

INTERVIEWS

Unless otherwise stated, these interviews were conducted and tape-recorded by the author as part of the Southern Methodist University Oral History Program on the Performing Arts.

Adams, Julie. Los Angeles. 19 July 1984.
Albright, Lola. Los Angeles. 31 May 1985.
Allen, Steve. Dallas. 18 Nov. 1975.
Autry, Gene. Los Angeles. 24 July 1984.
Ball, Lucille. Los Angeles. 21 Aug. 1980.
Berman, Pandro S. Los Angeles. 21 Aug. 1978.
Bogart, Paul. Los Angeles. 20 July 1984.
Chayefsky, Paddy. New York. 17 Oct. 1979.
Clayton, Jan. Los Angeles. 19 Aug. 1980.
Coca, Imogene. Dallas. 3 Dec. 1974.
Collins, Richard. Los Angeles. 25 July 1990.
Cristal, Linda. Los Angeles. 17 July 1991.
Cummings, Robert. Dallas. 22 July 1974.
Dailey, Dan. Interview conducted by

Sally Cullum. Dallas. 13 and 25 July 1974.

Davis, Ann B. Dallas. 2 Apr. 1975.

Davis, Madelyn and Bob Carroll. Los Angeles. 11 Aug. 1983.

Day, Doris. Carmel, California. 18 Oct. 1983.

DeCamp, Rosemary. Los Angeles. 13 July 1982.

DeCordova, Frederick. Los Angeles. 16 July 1982.

DeFore, Don. Los Angeles. 21 Aug. 1986.

Doran, Ann. Los Angeles. 10 and 15 Aug. 1983.

Dmytryk, Edward. Austin. 2 Dec. 1979.

Duff, Howard. Montecito, California. 18 Aug. 1988.

Essex, Harry. Los Angeles. 25 July 1989.

Ford, Glenn. Dallas. 2 June 1990.

Fowler, Gene, Jr. Los Angeles. 20 July 1985.

Garland, Beverly. Los Angeles. 10 Aug. 1988.

Garrett, Betty. Los Angeles. 23 Aug. 1978.

Gelbart, Larry. Los Angeles. 15 Aug. 1983.

Ghostley, Alice. Los Angeles. 19 July 1989.

Goodson, Mark. New York. 15 Mar. 1990.

Gordon, Gale. Dallas. 16 June 1975.

Gordon, Michael. Los Angeles. 7 and 12 Aug. 1981 and 26 July 1982.

Greaves, William. New York. 9 Oct. 1985.

Greenbaum, Everett. Los Angeles. 21 July 1990.

Hale, Barbara. Los Angeles. 19 July 1984.

Harris, Julie. Dallas. 10 Feb. 1989.

Henderson, Florence. Los Angeles. 18 Aug. 1983.

Henning, Paul. Los Angeles. 19 July 1975.

Hill, Arthur. Los Angeles. 5 Jan. 1977.

Holliman, Earl. Los Angeles. 24 July 1989.

Hudson, Rock. Los Angeles. 24 Aug. 1983.

Huggins, Roy. Los Angeles. 16 Aug. 1986.

Hunt, Marsha. Los Angeles. 12 Aug. 1983.

Hunter, Kim. New York. 2 Jan. 1979.

Hunter, Ross. Los Angeles. 17 July 1984.

Jeffreys, Anne. Los Angeles. 15 Aug. 1983.

Jones, Carolyn. Los Angeles. 3 Aug. 1976.

Jones, Shirley. Los Angeles. 27 July 1984.

Kanter, Hal. Los Angeles. 16 Aug. 1988.

Kroll, Lucy. Dallas. 15 Feb. and 1 Mar. 1990.

Lardner, Ring, Jr. New York. 11 Jan. 1985.

Laurie, Piper. Los Angeles. 21 July 1989.

Lee, Anna. Los Angeles. 13 Aug. 1981.

Lubin, Arthur. Los Angeles. 15 July 1985.

Maharis, George. Dallas. 3 Apr. 1975.

Mann, Delbert. Los Angeles. 21 July 1984.

Marie, Rose. Dallas. 14 Mar. 1979.

McLaglen, Andrew. Friday Harbor, San Juan Island, Washington. 13 Mar. 1992.

Milestone, Lewis. Los Angeles. 23 July 1979.

Mirisch, Walter. Los Angeles. 19 Aug. 1986.

Moore, Tom. Los Angeles. 18 July 1989.

Murray, Don. Santa Barbara, California. 20 July 1989.

Paige, Janis. Los Angeles. 6 and 11 Aug. 1981.

Parsons, Estelle. Dallas. 17 Dec. 1981.

Peck, Gregory. Los Angeles. 15 and 21 Aug. 1978 and 28 July 1979 and 22 Aug. 1980.

Pevney, Joseph. Carlsbad, California. 23 July 1989.

Reynolds, William. Los Angeles. 26 July 1989.

Robertson, Dale. Yukon, Oklahoma. 22 Apr. 1983.

Scott, Lizabeth. Los Angeles. 30 May 1985.

Stack, Robert. Los Angeles. 12 Aug. 1975.

Stinson, Bill. Los Angeles. 28 Aug. 1986.

Stone, Milburn. Rancho Santa Fe, California. 11 Aug. 1976.

Thompson, Marshall. Los Angeles. 22 Aug. 1980.

Uggams, Leslie. Dallas. 19 June 1991.

Van Schmus, Albert E. Interview conducted by Barbara Hall for the Academy of Motion Picture Arts and Sciences. Los Angeles. 1990-1992.

Walston, Ray. Los Angeles. 11 Aug. 1988.

Williams, Elmo. Brookings, Oregon. 7 and 8 Sep. 1989.

Wise, Robert. Los Angeles. 26 July 1979.

Wyatt, Jane. Los Angeles. 24 Aug. 1983.

Wynn, Keenan. Los Angeles. 18 July 1984.

Photo Credits

INDEX

CPSIA information can be obtained
at www.ICGtesting.com
Printed in the USA
FFOW030658231112
336FF

9 780155 015685